IN HIS OWN WORDS

Houston H. Holloway's Slavery, Emancipation, and Ministry in Georgia

Houston Hartsfield Holloway. Inscribed on the back, *"Rev. H. H. Holloway To His Daughter M. Dismuke Holloway Sept 2, 1894."*

Mary Louise Dismuke married John Wesley Holloway in his father's house at Turin on 6 August 1894, three weeks before her father-in-law inscribed this photo to her.

Photo by S. F. Jackson, Newnan, Georgia; courtesy of Nareda W. H. DeCleene.

IN HIS OWN WORDS

Houston H. Holloway's Slavery, Emancipation, and Ministry in Georgia

Houston Hartsfield Holloway

Edited and introduced by David E. Paterson

MERCER UNIVERSITY PRESS
MACON, GEORGIA

MERCER
UNIVERSITY PRESS

Endowed by
TOM WATSON BROWN
and
THE WATSON-BROWN FOUNDATION, INC.

MUP/ H909

Published by Mercer University Press
1501 Mercer University Drive
Macon, Georgia 31207

9 8 7 6 5 4 3 2 1

Books published by Mercer University Press are printed on acid-free paper that meets the requirements of the American National Standard for Information Sciences—Permanence of Paper for Printed Library Materials.

ISBN 978-0-88146-545-7

Cataloging-in-Publication Data is available from the Library of Congress

Contents

Illustrations

Maps

Abbreviations

AMEC	African Methodist Episcopal Church
CMEC	Colored Methodist Episcopal Church
GDAH	Georgia Department of Archives and History
GMD	Georgia Militia District
GPO	U. S. Government Printing Office
JWH	John Wesley Holloway, "Memoirs of John Wesley Holloway, Thebes, Ga., July 3, 1916"
MEC	Methodist Episcopal Church
MECS	Methodist Episcopal Church, South
NARA	National Archives and Records Administration
RG	Record Group
TUA	Thomaston-Upson Archives, Thomaston, Georgia

Citing Church Conference Minutes

African Methodist Episcopal Church

Conference minutes for AMEC conferences in Georgia were published as individual pamphlets. Wilberforce University Archives, Louis E. Stokes Library, Wilberforce, Ohio, holds the largest collection of these minutes. All citations are to copies held by Wilberforce, except for *Minutes of the Seventh Session of the North Georgia Annual Conference...* (1880) and *Minutes of the Fifteenth Session of the North Georgia Annual Conference...* (1888), copies of which are kept at the Robert W. Woodruff Library, Atlanta University Center, Atlanta, Georgia. Titles vary slightly by conference and year, but conference sessions are numbered consecutively; for example, *Minutes of the Fifth Session of the Georgia Annual Conference of the African Methodist Episcopal Church...* (1872). AMEC conferences cited in this book include the following:

GA	Georgia Conference
NGA	North Georgia Conference
MACON	Macon, Georgia, Conference
ATLANTA	Atlanta, Georgia, Conference

Because sessions might convene on dates ranging from November through February, the year in which a conference convened does not reliably correlate to session numbers; therefore, I cite AMEC conferences by [session number] [abbreviated conference title], [page]; thus, 5 GA, 23.

Methodist Episcopal Church

Many regional conferences printed their annual minutes as pamphlets; however, the MEC annually compiled and published volumes of these minutes, in abbreviated form, from all MEC conferences. These volumes are the most easily accessible form for MEC conference minutes because many libraries hold them (or some of them). A typical title is *Minutes of the Annual Conferences of the Methodist Episcopal Church for the Year 1868*. Page numbers run consecutively through consecutive years. I cite these minutes by MEC [year], [page]; thus, MEC 1868, 278. Minutes for the years 1878 and 1880 were divided into Spring and Fall Conferences, and I cite accordingly as MEC (Fall Conference) 1878, etc. Copies of these printed minutes are held at Pitts Theological Library, Emory University, Atlanta, Georgia. They are also available at Hathi Trust Digital Library (http://catalog.hathitrust.org/record/010309442).

Methodist Episcopal Church, South

The Georgia Conference of the MECS published, in pamphlet form, the minutes of their annual conferences, including committee reports and detailed statistics, but these are very difficult or impossible to locate outside of collections at Emory University. Fortunately, like the MEC, the MECS compiled volumes of annual conference minutes in abbreviated form (omitting committee reports and statistics) from its regional conferences. Published by the Southern Methodist Publishing House as *Minutes of the Annual Conferences of the Methodist Episcopal Church, South, for the Year 1867* (for example), these volumes are the most easily accessible form for MECS conference minutes. Bound volumes in library collections usually contain several years. Page numbers run consecutively through consecutive years. I cite these volumes by MECS [year], [page]; thus, MECS 1867, 121. Pitts Theological Library, Emory University, Atlanta, Georgia, holds a complete set of these printed minutes. Some years can be found online at various sites, including Google Books.

Citing Censuses

Citations to 1850 or 1860 Census, Manuscript Schedule 1 (Free Inhabitants) follow this form:

(year) Census, (state), (county), Free Pop., (page number), (dwelling number).

Citations to 1850 or 1860 Census, Manuscript Schedule 2 (Slave Inhabitants) follow this form:

(year) Census, (state), (county), Slave Pop., (page number), (column), (line or lines).

Citations to 1870 Census, Manuscript Schedule 1 (Inhabitants) follow this form:

1870 Census, (state), (county), Pop., (page number), (dwelling number)

Citations to 1880 through 1940 Censuses, Manuscript Schedule 1 (Inhabitants/Population) follow this form:

(year) Census, (state), (county), (if applicable: city or town, ward), Pop., (enumeration district [ED] number), (page number), (dwelling, household, or family number as indicated).

Acknowledgments

Descendants of Houston Hartsfield Holloway, Estelle H. King, Roy J. King, Jr., and Nareda W. H. DeCleene, generously shared information, unpublished documents, and photographs related to Holloway.

Susan Eva O'Donovan and Adam Rothman read early drafts of my introduction and offered valuable suggestions.

Among many who helped me, the ever-patient staff of Thomaston-Upson Archives, Thomaston, Georgia, under the direction of Penny Cliff, helped me connect with many local sources; Claude Burgess was especially persistent to gain access to the original Minutes of Bethesda Baptist Church and obtained a photo of the death notice of Louisa, Holloway's mother. This project could not have been successful without the help and cooperation of Jacqueline Y. Brown, associate librarian at the Louis E. Stokes Library, Wilberforce University. My research into Georgia Baptist and Methodist conference records was greatly facilitated by the genial help of Laura Botts, associate professor, head of Special Collections at Mercer University Library, and Debra Madera, Special Collections reference assistant, Pitts Theology Library, Emory University. Claire Bentley Foster kindly shared photos of the old Edward Holloway plantation house. Linda Hallman kindly looked up and copied deeds in the Upson County courthouse. Barbara Smallwood Stock conducted research for me at the Georgia State Archives, Morrow, Georgia. Tanya Briscoe helped transcribe Baptist and Methodist statistics. Sally Hoover, Bridwell Library, Perkins School of Theology, Southern Methodist University, pointed me to an online source for the *Christian Recorder*. Janice Oglesbee, pastor of Greenville United Methodist Church, scanned and sent me pages from the 1850s Greenville MECS membership lists. Laura Dodson at the interlibrary loan department, Norfolk (Virginia) Public Library, researched and borrowed countless rolls of microfilm for me. Shamele Jordan designed the genealogy diagram of Holloway's family.

I am grateful for public and commercial Internet sites that have digitized valuable historical sources. As the number of such resources grows, some documents that I traveled great distances to see when I began this project in 2007 are now accessible from my computer at home. Among the most valuable Internet resources for this project were Google Books, Ancestry Library Edition (Ancestry.com), Documenting the American South (DocSouth.unc.edu, sponsored by University of North Carolina at Chapel Hill), Accessible Archives (for the *Christian Recorder* newspaper), Georgia's Virtual Vault (provided by Georgia Department of State) and Footnote3 (for Southern Claims Commission reports). Ben McLaughlin posted useful extracts from the *Meriwether Vindicator* at the USGenWeb website for Meriwether County. I owe a debt of gratitude to the patient editorial staff at Mercer University Press, who helped me make this a much better book.

Above all, I thank my beloved wife, Judy L. Paterson, for unfailing encouragement and for allowing me to devote most of my home time the last five years to this project.

Houston Hartsfield Holloway family group. The photo does not identify the subjects, but from other photos we can readily identify the two seated men: Houston Hartsfield Holloway (left) and his eldest son, John Wesley Holloway (right). The most probable identities of the three people in the back row are: Cordelia Achsah Holloway (left), Edwin Stanton Holloway (center), Theodore H. Holloway (right).

The absence of Holloway's wife, Cordelia (d. 3 April 1894) and eldest daughter Mary Jane (d. 1893) suggests a date for this photo about 1894–1895. Holloway remarried in November 1895 to Polly Ann Slaughter, then about twenty years old. She is possibly the woman in the photo, but family facial resemblance persuades me she is Cordelia Achsah.

Photo by S. F. Jackson, Newnan, Georgia; courtesy of Nareda W. H. DeCleene.

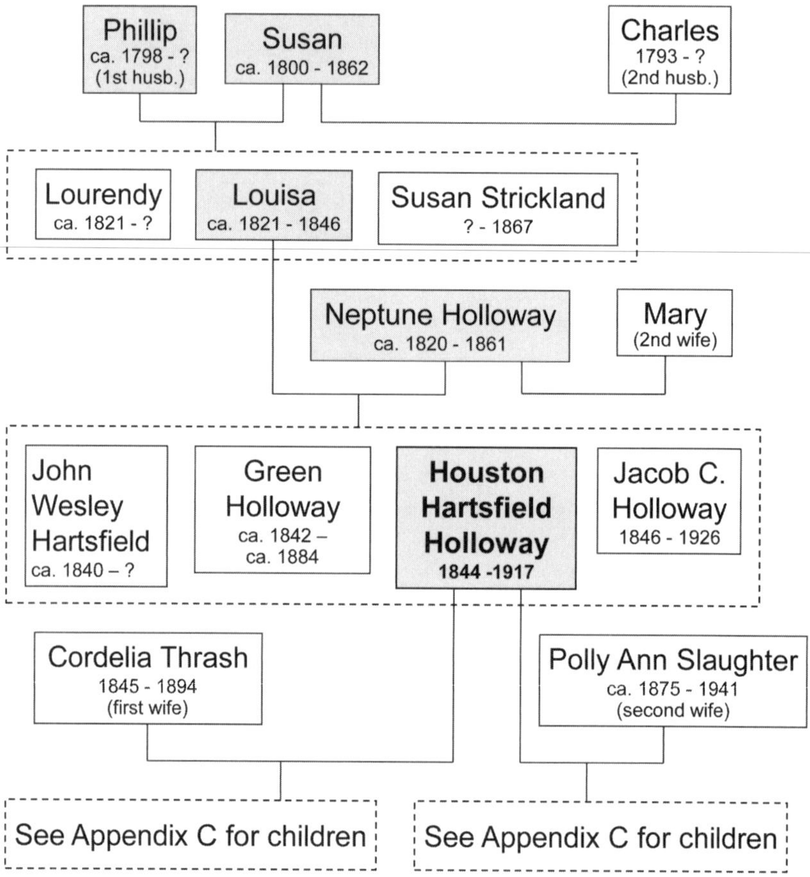

Holloway's genealogy. Houston H. Holloway and his direct ancestors are shaded in gray. Boxes with dotted lines enclose the known children of each couple. The editor could not discover Neptune Holloway's ancestors.

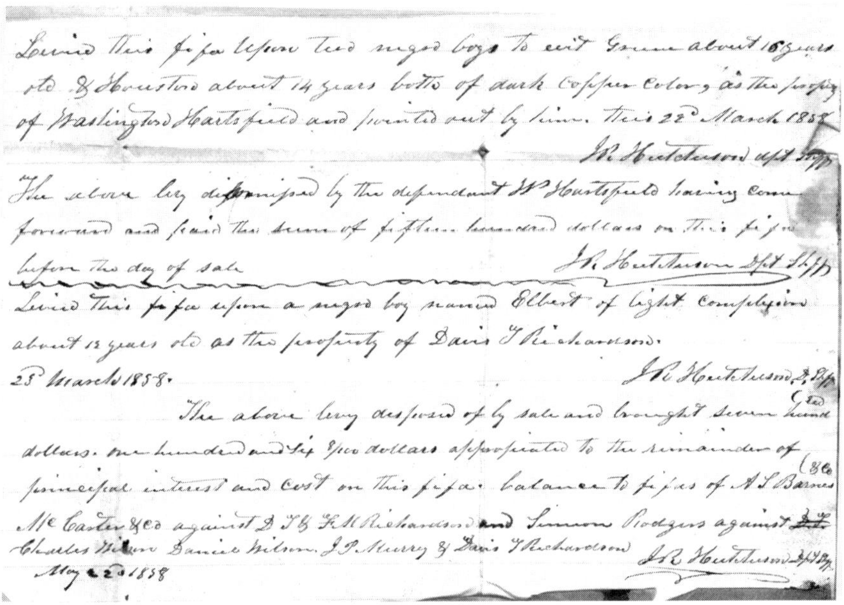
Levied this fifa upon two negro boys to wit Greene about 16 years
old & Houston about 14 years both of dark Copper color, as the property
of Washington Hartsfield and pointed out by him. this 22d March 1858
J R Hutcheson Dept Shff
The above levy dismissed by the defendant Wm Hartsfield having come
forward and paid the sum of fifteen hundred dollars on this fifa
before the day of sale J R Hutcheson Dept Shff
Levied this fifa upon a negro boy named Elbert of light complexion
about 13 years old as the property of Davis T Richardson.
23d March 1858. J R Hutcheson D Shff
The above levy disposed of by sale and brought seven hundred
dollars. one hundred and six 50/100 dollars appropriated to the remainder of
principal interest and cost on this fifa. balance to fifas of A S Barnes
McCarter & Co against D T & F M Richardson and Simeon Rodgers against
Charles Wilson Daniel Wilson J P Murry & Davis T Richardson J R Hutcheson D Shff
May 2d 1858

PART OF *FIERI FACIAS* LEVIED ON HOUSTON HOLLOWAY, 22 MARCH 1858. The *fieri facias* was a court order to the county sheriff to seize property from a defendant to pay an adjudged debt. The sheriff recorded his actions in the paperwork, including the sentence shown here: *"Levied this fifa upon two negro boys to wit Greene about 16 years old & Houston about 14 years both of dark copper color, as the property of Washington Hartsfield and pointed out by him this 22d March 1858."*

Original in Thomaston-Upson Archives, Thomaston, Georgia.

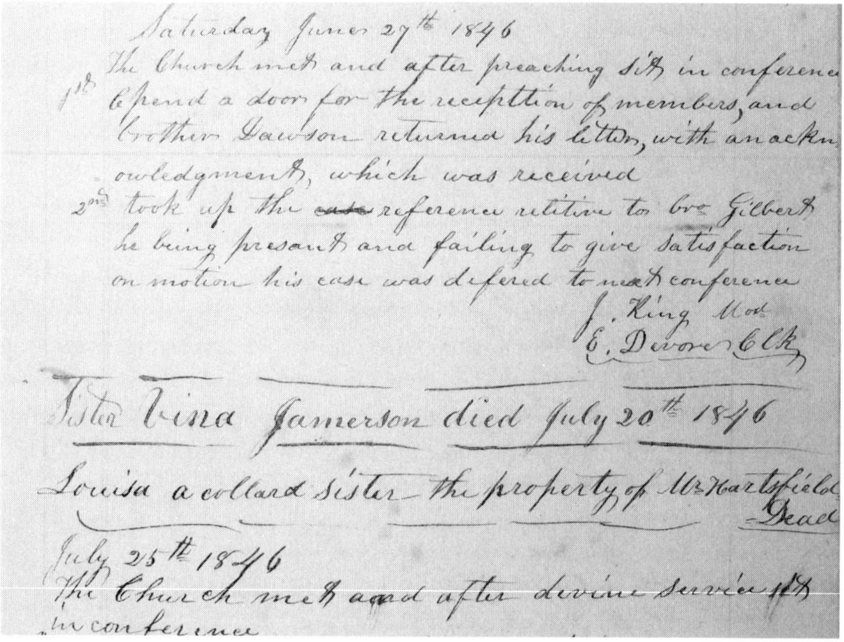

Saturday June 27th 1846
The Church met and after preaching sit in conference
1st Opend a door for the reception of members, and
brother Dawson returned his letter, with an ackn
owledgment, which was received
2nd took up the ~~case~~ reference relative to brc Gilbert
he being present and failing to give satisfaction
on motion his case was defered to next conference
J. King Mod
E. Devore Clk

Sister Vina Jamerson died July 20th 1846

Louisa a collard sister the property of Mr Hartsfield
Dead

July 25th 1846
The Church met and after divine service sit
in conference

Louisa's death notice in Bethesda Baptist Church minutes. Inserted between the minutes for 27 June 1846 and 25 July 1846, this record almost certainly dates Holloway's mother's death to sometime in July 1846. This document, correlated with the two-year age difference between Houston and his younger brother Jacob, is the strongest evidence that Houston H. Holloway was born about May 1844.

Bethesda Baptist Church Minutes Book 1, page 104; original in possession of First Baptist Church, Thomaston, Georgia; photo by Claude Burgess.

Edward Holloway plantation big house. This photo, taken in 1954, shows the house in decay. The front columned porch at the doors of the first and second floor had collapsed when this picture was taken. Holloway visited this house and its nearby slave quarter to see his kinfolk at lest three times, once before Christmas 1858 when he knew he was to be sold to Isaac Strickland, and when he returned to Upson County during Christmas holidays in 1859 and 1861.

Photo by Melvin Bentley; courtesy of Claire Bentley Foster.

James Crawford Freeman. Holloway's fourth and last slave owner and proprietor of the bridge, mill, neighborhood store, church, and other properties at Flat Shoals, Meriwether County.

Library of Congress Prints and Photographs Division, Brady-Handy Photograph Collection.

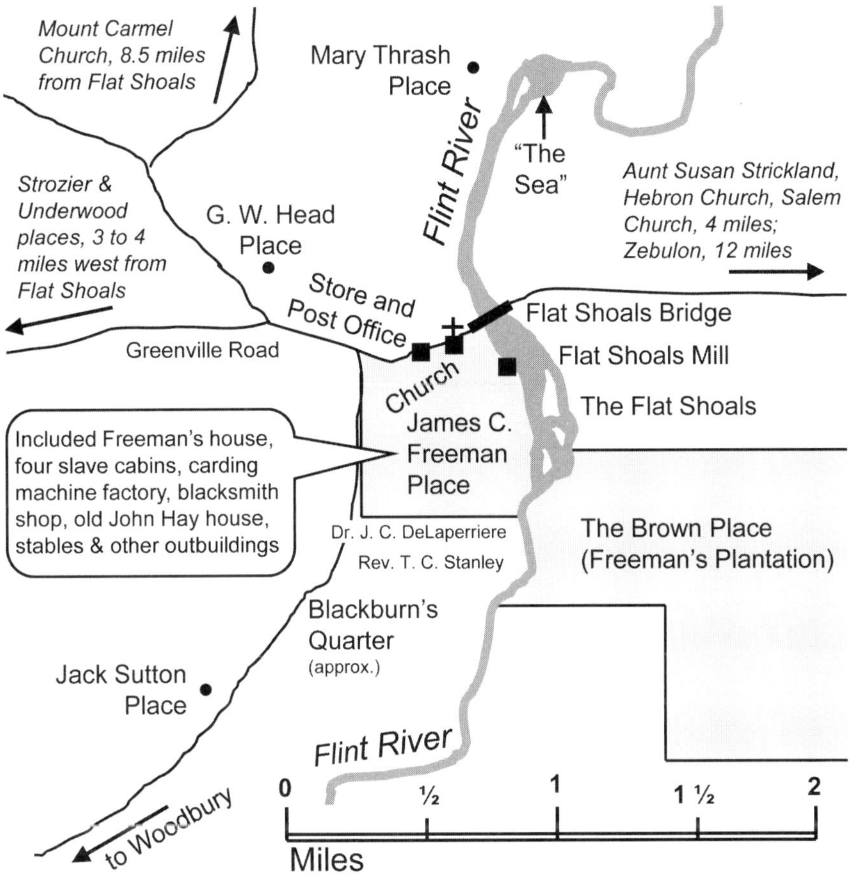

Holloway's Flat Shoals Neighborhood about 1860. The locations of Flat Shoals Church and Freeman's store are conjectural.

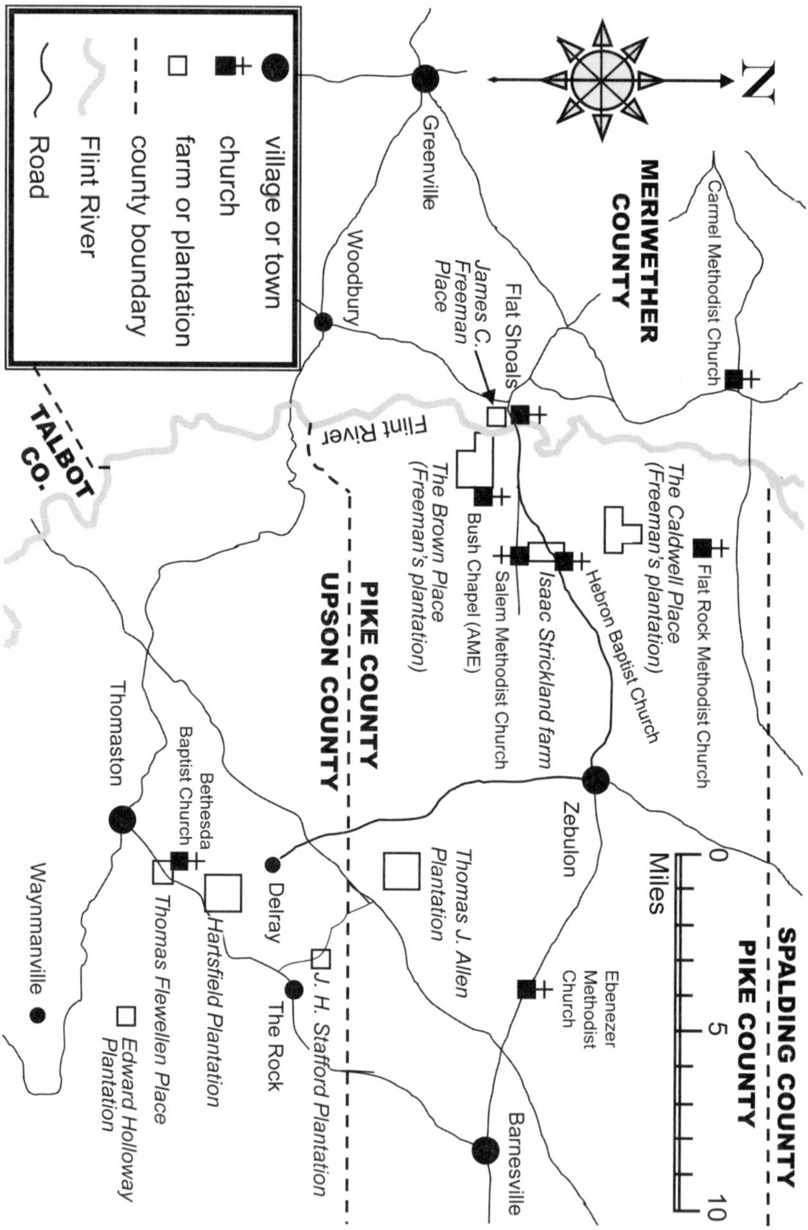

Holloway's Neighborhoods, 1844–1870

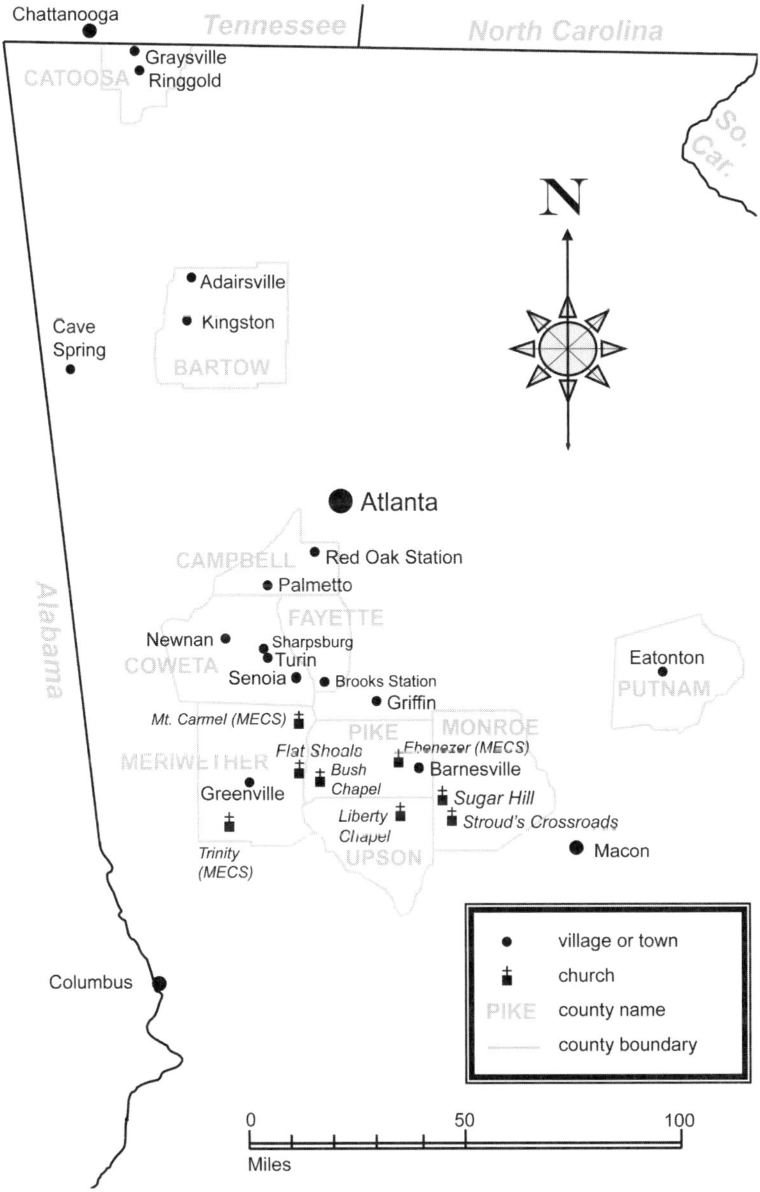

GEOGRAPHY OF H. H. HOLLOWAY'S MINISTRY, 1866–1883

Houston H. Holloway, ca. 1894. Taken at the same session as the frontispiece. The glasses may have been a photographer's prop.

Photo by S. F. Jackson, Newnan, Georgia, courtesy of Nareda W. H. DeCleene.

Introduction

Part 1: The Text

The Autobiography

Houston Hartsfield Holloway (1844–1917), born enslaved on an up-country plantation in Upson County, Georgia, emancipated in 1865 by Union victory in the Civil War, and converted to African Methodism in 1869, began to write his autobiography in about 1904. He probably finished the 24,000-word book late in 1913.[1] Holloway wrote for his family: "My Children To whom theas pages are addrest." Houston Hartsfield Holloway's autobiography is one of perhaps a handful of surviving autobiographies written by former American slaves, unmediated by an editor or amanuensis, with no mind to publication, and with no evident propaganda agenda.[2]

---

[1] On page four of the manuscript Holloway wrote, "This Brings me to the yeare 1858 this 47 years ago," suggesting that he wrote that page in 1904. On the page numbered 201, six pages before the end of the manuscript, he wrote, "at this day September the 16th 1913" (Houston Hartsfield Holloway papers, 1894–1932, MSS84205, MMC-3695, Library of Congress Manuscript Division Washington, DC).

[2] Two other examples are in David W. Blight, *A Slave No More: Two Men Who Escaped to Freedom including Their Own Narratives of Emancipation* (Orlando, FL: Harcourt, Inc., 2007). Blight discusses the significance of such unmediated narratives, comparing and contrasting them with the genre of ex-slave autobiographies written and edited consciously for publication (9–16).

In contrast with unmediated narratives, most published ex-slave autobiographies so closely followed a common structure and formulaic content that James Olney outlined a conventional ex-slave narrative with twelve typical elements. Holloway's narrative does not follow the formula and includes only one of Olney's twelve elements: "8. Account of a slave auction, of families being separated and destroyed…of slave coffles being driven south." Another event in Olney's list ("taking a new last name") occurs without notice or explanation in Holloway's narrative. See James Olney, "'I Was Born': Slave Narratives, Their Status as Autobiography and as Literature," in Charles Twitchell Davis, Henry Louis Gates, Jr., eds., *The Slave's Narrative* (Oxford: Oxford University Press, 1985) 153.

Holloway's autobiography is a rare look at nineteenth-century African Methodism in Georgia. For comparison, three bishops who built black Methodist denominations in Georgia after the Civil War published memoirs or autobiographies, and one college-educated AMEC churchman published an account of his itinerant service in Georgia during the crucial years 1866–1869.[3] By contrast, Houston Holloway always lived in the midst of working class black Georgians and their churches. Holloway's descriptions of his enslavement and religious influences are more detailed than any of the Georgia bishops' published accounts. Unlike their triumphal narratives of personal and ecclesiastical victory over all adversity, Holloway tells of hardships, disappointments, and occasional failures. Late in his narrative Holloway even admits despair that the Gospel message did not penetrate the hearts and minds of many to whom he preached.

Holloway set his own bounds of narrative decency or decorum; for example he censored his story of a visit to a conjuror: "I will not tell my reader what he did." Holloway also omitted events that may have embarrassed him. He was silent about an 1883 allegation of unaccounted "dollar money" that suddenly ended his itinerant preaching career. He refused to "say on paper what fell to my lot" in 1909 (even his eldest son, John Wesley Holloway, did not know what had

---

[3] See L[ucius] H. Holsey, *Autobiography, Sermons, Addresses, and Essays of Bishop L. H. Holsey, D. D.* (Atlanta: Franklin Printing and Publishing County, 1898), in which Holsey tells how he was born enslaved in GA and rose to be the first bishop of the Colored Methodist Episcopal Church; electronic edition at "Documenting the American South," http://docsouth.unc.edu/neh/holsey/holsey.html (accessed 30 December 2014); Wesley J. Gaines, *African Methodism in the South; or Twenty-Five Years of Freedom* (Atlanta: 1890), in which Gaines recounts the growth of the AMEC in GA through the late 1800s; William H. Heard, *From Slavery to the Bishopric in the A.M.E. Church: An Autobiography* (Philadelphia: A.M.E. Book Concern, 1928), electronic edition at "Documenting the American South," http://docsouth.unc.edu/neh/heard/heard.html #ill8, in which Heard tells of his humble birth to enslaved parents in GA and his rise to the church's highest rank; T[heophilus] G[ould] Steward, *Fifty Years in the Gospel Ministry from 1864 to 1914. Twenty-seven Years in the Pastorate; Sixteen Years' Active Service as Chaplain in the U. S. Army; Seven Years Professor in Wilberforce University; Two Trips to Europe; A Trip in Mexico* (Philadelphia: A.M.E. Book Concern, [1921]), electronic edition at "Documenting the American South," http://docsouth.unc.edu/church/steward/steward.html, 70–72 and 88–140. Born in New Jersey, Steward arrived in GA on the heels of the US Army in 1866 but left in 1870. He provides a particularly useful account of itinerant ministry in the AMEC in GA from 1866 through 1869.

happened that year).[4] Uncomfortable memories may also explain why Holloway omitted mentioned of his daughter Eunice Irene (born and died in the 1880s), especially since John Wesley Holloway blamed his parents for his favorite sister's death at the age of two: "She was allowed to eat green fruit and was not properly cared for."[5]

The Manuscript

Holloway's descendants donated his autobiography to the Library of Congress in 1978. In its current state the manuscript includes 182 unbound, ruled pages, each about 6 inches wide by 9.25 inches tall. Page numbering is inconsistent, and at least six pages are missing. Holloway noted that he rewrote the first sheet of his narrative when "the first one was lost while I was down with a hard spell of sicness in summer of 1908." When his son John Wesley Holloway paraphrased the narrative in 1932, five pages, perhaps 600 words describing events in 1879, were missing. Between 1932 and 1978 one more sheet disappeared, but John Wesley Holloway's paraphrase preserves the narrative substance, if not the text, of that page. The autobiography ends abruptly at the bottom of a page after sentences describing the year 1910.

Holloway's Language

Holloway's narrative is essentially an oral monologue penned to paper. His style presents a stark contrast to that of a contemporary autobiographer, AME Bishop William H. Heard, born enslaved in Elbert County, Georgia. Heard published his autobiography in 1928 to show how he had attained success from humble beginnings through hard work and self-improvement. He dedicated his book to "the self-made men in the ministry."[6] Like Holloway, another self-made man, Heard's parents lived on separate plantations in Georgia's cotton belt. Like Holloway, Heard was sold more than once. Likewise he received early religious instruction in the Methodist Episcopal Church, South. However, in contrast to Holloway (who was six years Heard's senior and whose literacy was almost entirely self-taught during a childhood in slavery), Heard learned to read and

---

[4] See p. 182, n. 47.

[5] John Wesley Holloway, "Memoirs of John Wesley Holloway, Thebes Ga., July 3, 1916," 235 (photocopy, in editor's possession, of unpublished manuscript [location of original is unknown], hereafter cited as JWH).

[6] Heard, *From Slavery to the Bishopric*, 7.

write after emancipation in 1865 via a mix of elementary public schooling and white tutors paid by his father. This formal tutelage, attained without legal proscription, resulted in a vast difference between the two men's levels of literacy. Heard wrote, "When I learned the parts of speech in Smith's Grammar and their relation to each other, it was a revelation to me."[7] No such revelation came to Houston Holloway as he labored alone at night in a plantation kitchen with McGuffey's *Eclectic Second Reader* and *The New York Reader, No. 2.* Untrained in the parts of speech, Holloway spells (for example) the article "an" and the conjunction "and" identically—almost certainly because they sounded the same to him, with the "d" silent.

Holloway's autobiography may provide an authentic approximation of his nineteenth-century regional speech. He uses phrases sometimes still heard in upcountry Georgia, such as the emphatic negative "no way" in the sentence "Mr Strickland…liking a negro that could read no way…[a]dvertised that he had a fine negro boy for Sale." Holloway says "listen at" for "listen to." In ways that are redundant in modern standard English, he uses the word "of" in phrases like "singing of a song" and "durin of the mounth of november." Once he places a verb's object immediately before the infinitive form of the verb in the sentence, "we had him to Expell from the church" (a rare usage that would nonetheless have been familiar to nineteenth-century Georgian ears).[8] He sometimes wrote the verb "took" as "to" and the feminine possessive "her" as "he." Houston Holloway's spelling occasionally finds parallels in other records; for example Thomas E. Rose, a white census enumerator in Upson County in 1880, consistently spelled "father" as "farther" just as Holloway does, and just as both men probably pronounced it.[9] Holloway repeatedly reminds us that his narrative is based on an oral culture, inviting us to "lisen at the little boy leaveing the old plantation"; "Lisen at them on the Big Corn pile"; and "I will Read you from memory one sentence of that speach." Houston Holloway's verbal idiosyncrasies speak to us, however imperfectly in script, from a world where oral fluency

---

[7] Ibid., 35–36.

[8] For example, Upson County Superior Court loose papers in the case of Cyrus Cotton *vs* Eleanor Blalock and James Blalock, Jr., alias James Grice (1831–1832), include testimony from John Jones of Jones County, GA, that "The old man then stated that if Cyrus Cotton ever got any…of his property he would have it to steal" (TUA).

[9] See examples in 1880 Census, GA, Upson County, Pop., ED 146, p. 3, line 23; p. 16 lines 41, 44; p.17, lines 7, 11 (column 8, family relationships).

trumped literacy. To hear his voice, readers may want to speak his narrative aloud.[10]

Editorial Method

Holloway appears to have corrected his narrative as he wrote, interlining some words, lining out others, and sometimes overwriting letters in a word. There is no sign that he ever rewrote, emended, or proofed his manuscript, except to replace the lost first page. I silently incorporate all of Holloway's manuscript corrections.

I use editorial interventions into Holloway's text to clarify difficult words and sentences or to format passages of blocked text for easier reading and comprehension. Holloway seldom used periods to end sentences and never used commas, colons, semi-colons, question marks, or quotation marks. To aid readability, I have inserted these kinds of punctuation marks in many places. Holloway did not use a hyphen when he broke words at the end of a line; I silently reconnect these words. Holloway seldom indented first lines of paragraphs, but I indent where the manuscript indicates paragraphs or change of subject. I silently start new paragraphs for some subject breaks not marked by Holloway.

I sometimes insert implied words or parts of words in [square brackets]. In most cases Holloway probably omitted words or letters by accident, but in other cases he may have written his narrative phonetically as he would have spoken it to friends and family. I footnote these idiosyncrasies at their first occurrence only. For example, he usually spells "there" as "thre" but to avoid confusion with "three" I sometimes insert clarification in square brackets ("th[e]re" or "thre[e]").

---

[10] Natalie Maynor ("Written Records of Spoken Language: How Reliable Are They?" in Alan R. Thomas, ed., *Methods in Dialectology* [Clevendon: Multilingual Matters Ltd, 1988] 111–15) discusses the challenges linguists face in finding reliable representations of regional speech before the days of the tape recorder. She exposes the unreliability of fake "dialect" that many WPA writers routinely injected into their interviews with ex-slaves in the 1930s, for example. In contrast, editors with the Freedmen and Southern Society Project found that manuscripts of barely literate authors "may appear impenetrable to the eye but are perfectly understandable when read phonetically…[and] offer intriguing evidence about the spoken language" (Steven Hahn, Steven F. Miller, et al., eds., *Freedom: A Documentary History of Emancipation, 1861–1867: Selected from the Holdings of the National Archives of the United States* [Chapel Hill: University of North Carolina Press, 2008] xix).

When a word is spelled so unusually that it defies easy comprehension, I place my reading in square brackets after the word and use "=" to indicate that the bracketed text explains the previous word, thus [=thus]. I clarify difficult phrases or sentences in footnotes.

I have transcribed Holloway's spelling and capitalization as I found them, but where his handwriting is ambiguous, I follow the advice of Fredson Bowers by choosing the reading that more closely conforms to standard modern English usage.[11] For example, whenever Holloway writes a word beginning with *s* or *c* he makes them tall like capital letters; however I could not believe that Holloway intended all words beginning with *s* and *c* (and *only* words beginning with *s* and *c*) to begin with a capital letter. I transcribe initial *s* and *c* as lowercase unless the word is a proper noun or begins a sentence. Holloway sometimes repeated a word at the end of a line and at the beginning of the next line, or at the bottom of a page and at the top of the next page; I silently omit the duplicate word.

Holloway wrote conversations and documents as blocks of text. In five places Holloway included extended dialogue as run-on sentences without breaks or punctuation. To make these dialogues more readable, I begin segments of the conversation on separate indented lines to distinguish each speaker's words.[12] I changed some of Holloway's line breaks (but nothing else) in his rendition of "The White Pilgrim" (p. 87) to conform to the original poem's structure. Where Holloway reproduced examples of passes, notes, and letters without any distinguishing format, I have retained Holloway's original words and word order

---

[11] Discussing "authorial orthographic idiosyncrasies" versus author's "actual intentions," Bowers wrote, "Some authors form a few miniscules [lower-case letters] very much like majuscules [capitals]. Ordinarily the context and syntactical position in the sentence prevent confusion." Bowers wrote that when author's intent for punctuation is ambiguous, "[a]rbitrary normalizing is the only answer"—a rule also eminently adaptable to Holloway's idiosyncratic cursive alphabet. Fredson Bowers, "Transcription of Manuscripts: The Record of Variants," *Studies in Bibliography* 29 (1976): 215.

[12] Four conversations treated in this way include the confrontation between the captain of patrollers and the slaveholders at the slaves' fancy ball (p.95), the exchange of news at the bridge between the citizen and the two soldiers (p.126), the exchange between Holloway and the boy on the mule (p.126-27), and the climactic conversation between Holloway and God (p.163-64). The fifth place is the song accompanying the game "I'm in My Lady's Garden" where I put each line of the song on its own text line, instead transcribing *en bloc* as written (p.97).

but have signaled headings and datelines, greetings, bodies, and closings (if applicable) with conventional right or left justification and indentation.

Holloway intended his book to have chapter breaks. Three times in the text he mentioned chapters, although he only explicitly titled one chapter ("Chapter Second"). Holloway planned to have a chapter describing how he arranged his marriage to Cordelia Thrash ("I will Tell you In the next chapter") and intended a chapter in which he would discuss conjurors ("I will tell you more about theas men in a Seperate Chapter"). Holloway never realized his chapter organization. In this edition, Chapter Second remains where Holloway put it. I begin Chapter Three immediately after Holloway's sentence, "I will Tell you In the next chapter." All other chapter breaks and chapter titles are entirely figments of my editorial judgment.

Footnotes identify enslaved or freedpeople by their most recent surnames found in the federal censuses, state voter registration lists of 1867, or tax digests. If the enslaved died before emancipation, or if I could not locate formerly enslaved people in post-slavery official records, I identify them by the surname Holloway gave them in his narrative. In cases where Holloway does not give someone's surname, and where I have been unable identify the person further, I use first name only. Footnotes use customary English spellings for common names in place of Holloway's idiosyncratic spellings. For names of Holloway's family members I follow the spellings used by Holloway's son, John Wesley Holloway.

Use of Surnames

Holloway never explains the origin of surnames he uses in his narrative, not even his own, and he shifts some surnames without notice. When talking about slavery Holloway calls people the names by which they probably were publicly recognized when slaves—and in his neighborhoods the practice seems to have been to use the surname of the slave owner. This is most clearly suggested in the story of the quilting where the peanut vendor calls him "Mr. Freeman." In the post-emancipation half of Holloway's book he calls people by the names they adopted in freedom. Holloway inadvertently confirms this convention by three times calling his enslaved neighborhood chum "Dallis Black Burn" (or "Blackburn"), but one time he calls him "Dallis Reding." Dallas had been enslaved to Martha Blackburn, but after emancipation he went by

Redding, his father's surname.[13] In freedom Holloway also adopted his own father's surname while his middle name, Hartsfield, presumably memorialized his mother, who had been enslaved in the Hartsfield family.

Identities of people in Holloway's narrative can be tenuous. For example, he named Anthony Alexander and Pauline Freeman as two of the "leading socitey colord people of the Flat Shoals." He tells us Pauline Freeman was a "principall house woman" in slave master Freeman's household, which probably explains why Holloway refers to her by Freeman's surname. After emancipation, the 1870 and 1880 censuses enumerate Pauline Alexander and Anthony Alexander as a couple with five children, the oldest born about 1860, but Holloway never mentions that they were married and only name coincidence connects them.[14]

Holloway's practice of shifting surnames without giving notice to his readers leaves a small doubt about the former enslaved identity of the preacher Claiborne Bush, who was Holloway's closest associate in the earliest days of his ministry. I believe from a preponderance of the evidence that Claiborne Neal in slavery and Claiborne Bush after emancipation were the same person. I discuss this evidence in Appendix A, pp. 200.[15]

---

[13] I confirmed the connection between Blackburn and Redding by comparing the names in Dallas's nuclear family, listed in John L. Blackburn's 1856 will, with the names of registered voters in Meriwether County precinct 1213 (Flat Shoals neighborhood) and names in Redding family groups in federal censuses. See p. 104, n. 1.

[14] See p.92 n.3 and n.5 for discussion of Anthony Alexander and Pauline Freeman.

[15] Surnaming practices of the enslaved varied by regional custom and individual choice. For example, see discussion in Michael Hait, "Myth of the 'Master's Name'" and readers' comments, including my rebuttal of Hait's conclusions, online at http://www.examiner.com/article/the-myth-of-the-master-s-name. Historiography on slaves' and freedpeople's surnames includes Herbert G. Gutman, *The Black Family in Slavery and Freedom, 1750–1925* (New York: Vintage Books, 1976) 230–56; Eugene D. Genovese, *Roll, Jordan, Roll: The World the Slaves Made* (New York: Vintage Books, 1976) 443–50; Leon F. Litwack, *Been in the Storm So Long: The Aftermath of Slavery* (New York: Vintage Books, 1980) 247–51; Elizabeth Regosin, *Freedom's Promise: Ex-Slave Families and Citizenship in the Age of Emancipation* (Charlottesville: University Press of Virginia, 2002) 54–78.

Part 2: Supplementary Information

During the course of researching and editing this book, I encountered much information about Houston H. Holloway that he had not included in his own autobiography. Some specific events in Holloway's narrative are discussed in this introduction, but only where significant additional documentation adds to Holloway's own content, or to explain Holloway's story in broader context. This introduction is, indeed, supplementary to Holloway's narrative and does not re-tell his autobiography.

Five principal sources provide most of my supplementary information. Houston and Cordelia Holloway's eldest son wrote "Memoirs of John Wesley Holloway," a rambling autobiography composed sporadically from 1916 through 1932. John Wesley Holloway recorded colorful anecdotes and commentary about life in his parents' home, his father's work, and the family's neighbors. Second, H. H. Holloway's letters to the AMEC newspaper, the *Christian Recorder*, from 1870 through 1883 express his thoughts about his church and ministry and give some details of his activities.[16] A third source is the printed AMEC annual conference minutes for the conferences in which Holloway served. Fourth are the manuscript returns of the decennial federal censuses. Fifth is James C. Freeman's disallowed claim to the Southern Claims Commission, containing detailed information about the geography of Holloway's Flat Shoals neighborhood, local events during the Civil War, and Freeman's account of implementing emancipation in 1865.[17] This supplementary information is

[16] Holloway's sixteen letters to the *Christian Recorder* include title (if any), issue date, and page: (partial abstract of letter) 5 November 1870, 4; "Two Years in Bartow County," 30 October 1873, 1; "Careless Fathers and Mothers," 18 November 1875, 1; "A Friend Shut Out," 24 February 1876, 2; "A Friend Shut Out," 20 April 1876, 7; "Note from Georgia," 10 August 1876, 1; "Our High School," 19 October 1876, 6; "Ignorance in the Ministry," 10 May 1877, 1; 2 August 1877, 4; "The Ministry," 25 October 1877, 1; "Campbell Normal School," 27 June 1878, 2; "Thirteen Years Ago," 4 July 1878, 2; "Our Membership," 12 December 1878, 1; 26 May 1881, 2; 29 June 1882, 2; "Work for the General Conference," 18 October 1883, 1.

[17] NARA, RG 233, Southern Claims Commission, Disallowed Claims, Office 244, Report #7, claim of James C. Freeman (hereafter cited as SCC Disallowed Claim of James C. Freeman) available in NARA Microfilm Publication M1407, fiche 2463–2365.

Although digitized text is an unparalleled tool to locate information quickly, even the most careful digitizing process can introduce errors. When I quote from a source, I

presented by topic and in roughly chronological order. Amplifying information for 200 of the 233 people named in Holloway's narrative are either in footnotes or in Appendix A.

Holloway's Birth and Birthplace

Houston Hartsfield Holloway was born in Upson County, Georgia (population in 1860 about 10,000, half enslaved), on the Henry Hartsfield plantation about three miles northeast of Thomaston (population in 1860 about 675). In 1824 (only twenty years before Holloway was born), Georgia's legislature had carved Upson from the former domain of the Lower Creek Nation. Georgia farmers and planters had quickly transformed the Creeks' most fertile oak-shaded meadows into cotton fields intermingled with wheat and corn plots and dotted with sheep pastures. As Upson transformed from mostly small farms to a mix of plantations and yeoman farms, the enslaved people increased from one-third of the inhabitants in 1830 to one-half by 1850. Upson County nestled at the center of the antebellum South in the middle land between eastern slave-exporting regions and western slave-importing regions, its population slowly churned by both activities. The nearest cities—Macon, Atlanta, and Columbus—lay a day's ride or more from Upson.

Holloway believed he was born "about the first day of May 1845" but he was almost certainly a year older. The monthly conference of Upson County's Bethesda Baptist Church on 25 July 1846 recorded the death of their sister in Christ, Louisa, Holloway's mother. This suggests Louisa had died in late June or sometime in July 1846. Holloway wrote that there were about two years between himself and his youngest brother, Jacob, who was about six weeks old when their mother died. This is consistent with a birthdate in May 1844 for Houston Holloway. Two slave holders' descriptions of Houston Holloway point

have viewed the original or a page image of the original to transcribe the text accurately. Because websites are by nature transitory, because content from some sources is available in more than one format and from more than one provider, and because I expect digital sources to proliferate, I usually cite the original source in my footnotes, not the place where I might have first found a derivative copy. For example, images of the original manuscript federal censuses are readily available on microfilm, and digitized images are visible three websites (one free and two commercial). Rather than cite any particular location or medium, I cite the manuscript census page depicted in the image. Likewise, many newspapers can be searched in digital form, but unless stated otherwise, I quote from page images and cite the original newspaper.

to a birth year no later than 1844. Washington Hartsfield told the sheriff on 22 March 1858 that Houston was "about fourteen years" of age. The 1860 manuscript census of Meriwether County enumerating slaves in James C. Freeman's household included only one young man who could match Houston Holloway, and that person was listed as sixteen years old.[18] There is no surprise that Holloway may have mistaken his birth date; as Frederick Douglass famously wrote, "I have no accurate knowledge of my age, never having seen any authentic record containing it. By far the larger part of the slaves know as little of their ages as horses know of theirs…I do not remember to have ever met a slave who could tell of his birthday."[19]

Holloway's Ancestors

On his maternal side Houston H. Holloway was a spiritual grandchild of the Great Georgia Revival (1827–1830), an extraordinary evangelical outpouring of the Holy Spirit with rapid growth of evangelical church membership and a Baptist resurgence of the Second Great Awakening of two decades earlier. Baptist historians traditionally date this revival from September 1827 when Adiel Sherwood preached to the Ocmulgee Baptist Association meeting and converted 4,000 people in one day.[20] The revival spread to other upcountry

---

[18] Bethesda Baptist Church, Upson County, Minute Book 1 (First Baptist Church, Thomaston, GA), 104. Holloway also wrote, "Now about the time of Broo Jacob was bornd Old Henry Hartsfield died Perhaps inside of 12 mounths after his Death all of the Slaves had to be Sould and inside of Same yeare my Good mother died." Henry Hartsfield died 5 October 1847. Holloway was too young to remember much of these events, and he confused the chronology by a year or two.

See p.23 for Deputy Sheriff Hutcherson's description of Houston "about fourteen years old" on 22 March 1858; and see 1860 Census, GA, Meriwether County, Slave Pop., p.97, second column, line 21 (data was to reflect as-of date 1 June 1860). Post-bellum censuses are wildly inconsistent as to his age: the 1870 census enumerated Houston as twenty-nine years old and wife Cordelia as twenty-six, while the 1880 census enumerated him as thirty-four and her as thirty-two.

[19] Frederick Douglass, *Narrative of the Life of Frederick Douglass, an American Slave. Written by Himself* (London: H. G. Collins, 1851) 9. Some former masters gave each slave his or her name, birthplace, approximate age, or birth date (information they had before closely withheld) at emancipation. See Litwack, *Been in the Storm So Long*, 188.

[20] Robert G. Gardner, Charles O. Walker, J. R. Huddlestun, and Waldo P. Harris III (*A History of the Georgia Baptist Association, Second Edition* [Atlanta: Georgia Baptist Historical Society, 1996] 109) call it "The Revival of 1827–1828," but Jarrett Burch

churches including the Baptist Church of Christ at Clouds Creek, Oglethorpe County, which from 1826 to 1830 almost doubled its black membership from forty-two to seventy-six. Five of those new converts were enslaved to members of the Hartsfield family, including Susan ("Sucky a woman of colour belonging to Henry Hartsfield"), who stepped forward after morning worship service on 11 April 1829, related her experience of God's grace, and received the right hand of fellowship.[21] Susan was Houston Hartsfield Holloway's grandmother. Born about 1800, Susan came into Henry Hartsfield's possession from the estate of his father Richard Hartsfield in Oglethorpe County, where she was inventoried in 1820 with her infant twin daughters "Luisa & Lurendy." The surviving twin, Louisa, would be Holloway's mother.[22]

Slave owner Henry Hartsfield was not a member of Clouds Creek Church, but his wife Elizabeth Olive Hartsfield was a member in good standing, so when Hartsfield moved his household southwest from Oglethorpe County to Upson County, Elizabeth and four Hartsfield slaves—Goyen, Sam, Gilbert, and Susan—took their letters of dismission from Clouds Creek simultaneously on 13 December 1834. Letters of dismission declared them to be members in full fellowship with Clouds Creek and recommended their reception into fellowship by any other church of the same faith and order. Two months later Elizabeth Hartsfield, Susan, and others enslaved to Henry Hartsfield presented their letters to Bethesda Baptist Church in Upson County. The church received them into membership on 21 February 1835.[23]

(*Adiel Sherwood: Baptist Antebellum Pioneer in Georgia* [Macon: Mercer University Press, 2003] 61) argues from evidence of baptism records that this Baptist revival lasted until 1830.

[21] Clarence L. Mohr, "Slaves and White Churches in Confederate Georgia," in John B. Boles, ed., *Masters and Slaves in the House of the Lord: Race and Religion in the American South, 1740–1870* (Lexington: University of Kentucky Press, 1988) 236, n. 13; Clouds Creek Baptist Church Minutes 1826–1856, Oglethorpe County, GA (microfilm RHS 1300, drawer 72, box 46) 20, 23, 59, 60, 66, 71.

[22] Inventory of trust property in Richard Hartsfield estate, unbound estate records, 1790–1962, Oglethorpe County (file 209-2-1, microfilm SLC 1893465, drawer 307, box 7, Georgia Archives, Morrow, GA (hereafter cited as Richard Hartsfield inventory).

[23] Clouds Creek Baptist Church Minutes 1826–1856, Oglethorpe County, GA, 126; Bethesda Baptist Church, Minute Book 1, 56. These letters of dismission are not known to survive, but Gardner, et al., *History of the Georgia Baptist Association*, 28, quote a typical letter of dismission.

Susan's husband, Philip, born about 1798, was "a professor of religion"—by which nineteenth-century white Americans meant a person professing some version of orthodox Christianity though we do not know his denominational affiliation, if any. After settling in Upson County, Henry Hartsfield forcibly divorced Susan from her husband by selling Philip several years before their grandson Houston was born. In accord with slave owners' belief that black families existed only by owners' indulgence, Philip's next master referred to Susan and her children as Philip's "former wife and children." In Barbour County, Alabama, home of his new master, Philip allegedly took a new wife on a neighboring plantation, but he ran away back to Upson County at least once, presumably to see his "former" family.[24]

Holloway's parents belonged to different evangelical denominations, but they worshipped together at Bethesda Baptist Church. His mother, Louisa, followed in her own mother's religious footsteps, joining Bethesda by professing her experience of grace in August 1840. Houston H. Holloway's father, Neptune Holloway, was a Methodist enslaved to Edward Holloway, who lived five miles from the Hartsfield place.

Louisa died about July 1846 when son Houston was two years old. On that melancholy summer day, in the somber log cabin where Louisa's white-draped body lay, Neptune Holloway's brother Edmund Lowe sang a Wesleyan hymn and other popular worship songs to comfort Neptune. Edmund Lowe was a licensed local preacher in the Methodist Episcopal Church, South (hereinafter abbreviated MECS).[25]

The following year Henry Hartsfield died and his estate was broken up.[26] Holloway's grandmother, Susan, after the forcible disruption of her marriage to Phillip, had married a man named Charles Holloway. Charles belonged to Edward (Ned) Holloway, who also owned Louisa's husband Neptune Holloway, and Charles Holloway persuaded Ned Holloway to buy Susan from the estate so that they could live together. Houston H. Holloway fell to the share of bachelor Washington Hartsfield, a merchant and farmer who lived on his stepmother's place. Although Holloway wrote that he felt like an orphan—"motherless and Fartherless"—Neptune Holloway would visit his children whenever he could,

[24] *Columbus Enquirer*, 11 September 1840, 3, see full text on pp. 185-86.

[25] For biography of Edmund Lowe see pp. 192-94.

[26] Bethesda Baptist Church, Minute Book 1, 104; "Culpepper Connections! The Culpepper Family History Site," "Henry Hartsfield" page at http://gen.culpepper.com/ss/p45961.htm (accessed 30 December 2014).

combing their hair, bathing them, and teaching them "how to gat along in the world."

Religious Influence in the Extended Community

Upson County churches in 1860 counted more than 12 percent of the county's enslaved people as members. Although almost 24 percent of Upson's white people were members, landowners and slaveholders were twice as likely to be church members as their property-less white neighbors. Many citizens joined churches for social reasons related to their wealth, which largely explains why twice as many white people as black people joined Upson County's churches.[27]

---

[27] Albert J. Raboteau (*Slave Religion: The "Invisible Institution" in the Antebellum South* [New York: Oxford University Press, 2004] 212) and John B. Boles ("Introduction" in Boles, ed., *Masters and Slaves in the House of the Lord*, 10–11) discuss the disparities between Christian beliefs, church attendance, and church membership among slaves and free people. Daniel L. Fountain argues that low enslaved membership in Christian churches can be explained if "Christianity never replaced African-based religious beliefs" (*Slavery, Civil War, and Salvation: African American Slaves and Christianity, 1830–1870* [Baton Rouge: Louisiana State University Press, 2010] 5). Fountain makes too much of church membership (or non-membership) as a measure of religious convictions and does not allow that a large part of the American population, black and white, was simply irreligious.

In 1860 the MECS, Georgia Conference, reported 323 black members in Thomaston and Upson Circuit (about 6.6 percent of the black population) and 579 white members, or 11.5 percent of the free population. I estimate black Baptist membership from printed minutes of the Towaliga, Echoconna, and Rehoboth associations for 1860, although only three of the eleven member churches in Upson reported membership by color. The percentage of reported colored members in these three churches varied widely (Shiloh, 18 percent; Antioch, 29 percent; Thomaston, 40 percent), but the total membership for the three that reported by color, 284, included 88 colored members, or 31 percent. This compares closely with black Baptist membership statewide (32 percent of all Baptists) shown in Gardner, et al., *Georgia Baptist Association*, 199. Assuming 32 percent to be roughly accurate for membership in the Upson churches that did not report by color, I estimate 280 black members out of 885 total Baptist membership, or about 5.7 percent of the black population and 12 percent of the free population. For comparison, Gardner, et al., *Georgia Baptist Association*, 199, found 10.8 percent of all white Georgians and 6.4 percent of all black Georgians were Baptists in 1860.

The census enumerated no other churches in Upson County and other evidence suggests the county had few if any adherents to other denominations. Department of the

Certainly church members were a minority in the whole enslaved population, just as they were a minority among white Southerners, but their profound moral example brought a civilizing influence to the whole community. Pioneer C. H. Raley who had lived in Upson County at its founding in 1825 recalled, "At first there was little or no civilization among the people. They would collect together, drink whisky and fight like dogs. But some preachers moved in and began to preach the gospel, and soon churches and schoolhouses went up, and in a short time a great change for the better was everywhere apparent."[28]

Houston Holloway lived his first fourteen years immersed in a community saturated with evangelical Christian religious influence. Co resident and enslaved on the Hartsfield plantation for many or all those years were Nancy, Goyen, Berryman and Amanda, all members of Bethesda Baptist Church. Hartsfield's slave, Gilbert, a licensed Baptist preacher, was sold to Burwell W. Jackson, also a member of Bethesda, when Holloway was young (between 1850 and 1853).[29] Other Bethesda members in the household included the widow "Miss Betsey" Hartsfield, her resident bachelor stepson Washington Hartsfield (Holloway's legal owner), and her stepdaughter Orra Hartsfield. Five miles southeast of the Hartsfield place lived Houston Holloway's father Neptune Holloway (Methodist), his grandmother Susan (Baptist), and Moses Holloway

---

Interior, *Statistics of the United States, (Including Mortality, Property, &c.,) in 1860; Compiled from the Original returns and Being the Final Exhibit of the Eighth Census, under the Direction of the Secretary of the Interior* (Washington: GPO, 1866) 368–69, reported 11 Baptist churches and 7 Methodist churches in Upson County in 1860. The Methodist total of 7 would have included the Thomaston church, the churches on the Upson Circuit, and perhaps two small Methodist groups for which I have found no statistics: Pleasant Hill Congregational Methodist Church (established 1855) and possibly a Methodist Protestant Church.

Upson County Baptist pastor and historian Edwin L. Cliburn cautions against uncritically using reported church statistics: "It is extremely difficult to keep books on people. They [church statistics] do, however, in spite of all that is lacking, give us a picture of the church through the years" (*In Unbroken Line: A History of the First Baptist Church of Thomaston, Georgia, from Its Beginnings at Bethesda to Its One Hundred Fiftieth Anniversary (1825–1975)* [Tallahassee, FL: Thomaston First Baptist Church, 1978] 868).

[28] Thomaston *Times*, 2 February 1900 (copied from Atlanta *Constitution*, 27 January 1900).

[29] Bethesda Baptist Church, Minute Book 1, 57, 62, 95, 104, Amanda's membership recorded on unnumbered page on 22 July 1855.

(Methodist preacher and Neptune's spiritual adviser). Neptune Holloway's brother Edmund Lowe, the licensed Methodist preacher, lived enslaved on William Lowe's plantation on the northern outskirts of Thomaston, only three miles from the Hartsfield place. Four miles from Hartsfield's farm Houston Holloway had another uncle who was a member of Bethesda, William White, born about 1824, employed in B. B. White's shoe factory at Thomaston.[30] These thirteen named people were Houston Holloway's kinfolk, friends, or co-residents at his childhood home explicitly known to be church members or practicing Christians. How many others Holloway may have known we cannot tell, because membership records are almost non-existent for Methodists in Upson County, and because we have only partial evidence for kinship among the enslaved.

Sold to James C. Freeman of Meriwether County in 1859, Holloway found himself adopted into a close-knit fifteen-person enslaved community with familiar religious convictions. Aunt Ellen the milkmaid and gardener adopted Holloway as her son, "was entencely religious," and influenced him to join the Methodist Church at Flat Shoals. "Jacob the preacher" was a fellow member with Holloway in a secret reading club during the Civil War. Richmond the blacksmith was a class leader in Flat Shoals Methodist Church and also a member of the reading club. The neighborhood included other religious leaders

---

[30] William, "property of bro. B. B. White," was received into Bethesda Baptist Church by experience on 2 September 1855. Houston H. Holloway never mentioned an uncle William White in his autobiography, but son John Wesley Holloway tells us, "My father had an uncle, William White of Thomaston" and his wife Aunt Ann, whom JWH visited in the 1880s. JWH kept up with the family while he taught in rural GA schools in the 1880s, but he wrote that he quit visiting after Uncle White's daughter Jeannie treated him unkindly.

William White may have been part of the diaspora of Henry Hartsfield's slaves after Hartsfield's death in 1847. There were often family connections among slaves belonging to related white families. Former Hartsfield slave Daniel Hartsfield explained that the white family of "Ben White who resided four miles from the Hartsfield plantation" were "kinfolks" of the Hartsfield family. Indeed, Benjamin B. White had married Mary Olive Richardson, who was daughter of Sarah (Olive) Richardson who was sister to both of Henry Hartsfield's wives, Mary (Olive) Hartsfield and Elizabeth (Olive) Hartsfield.

See Bethesda Baptist Church, Minute Book 1, entry for 2 Sep 1855; JWH, 35, 419; NARA, RG 15, Veterans Administration Pension files, pension claim of Cesar Davis (No. 1,194,816), Daniel Hartsfield's deposition taken 23 November 1899.

among the enslaved who would become well known to Holloway, including the powerful Methodist preacher Claiborne Neal, who preached Richmond's funeral in 1864, the Baptist Rev. David Harris, and Richmond's brother-in-law Rev. Mr. Owens. There were also personal connections interwoven with religious: Freeman assigned Holloway to Floyd Freeman's cabin, where Holloway discovered that Floyd had known his mother and father before they were married!

Holloway's narrative reveals a densely populated religious support network for enslaved Christians and their families. This network was four-dimensional, refreshed through time by each generation, and spatially distributed across neighborhoods peopled by family members, devout surrogate kin, friends, officially licensed preachers or exhorters, unlicensed preachers or teachers, and private counselors.

Conjurors, Spirits, Ghosts, and Divine Interventions

Holloway lived in a world where supernatural happenings were commonplace and some people wielded occult powers. "Two-headed men" or "conjurors" advertised that they could influence the minds of other people to suit themselves or their clients. When Holloway witnessed his master, James C. Freeman, deny a field hand permission to marry his chosen wife, he solicited the powers of two conjurors in the Flat Shoals neighborhood to influence Freeman's mind to let Holloway marry his sweetheart Cordelia Thrash. Holloway had been a member of the MECS for three years when he paid the conjurors to work their charms, but conjure and Christianity need not have been, as argued by one historian, different "belief systems" that "could not coexist." Likewise, it may be incautious to conclude, as asserted by two other historians, that belief in witchcraft made Christianity "merely a glaze over an essentially African culture"—especially as European-ancestored people held similar beliefs.[31]

The Biblical story of King Saul and the Witch of Endor (1 Samuel 28) is only the most obvious example of supernatural powers acknowledged by the Judeo-Christian priesthood but forbidden to God's people. The spiritual "Blow Your Trumpet, Gabriel" explicitly integrated conjure into Christianity: "O,

[31] Marie Jenkins Schwartz, *Birthing a Slave: Motherhood and Medicine in the Antebellum South* (Cambridge: Cambridge University Press, 2006) 60 (first quote); Sylvia R. Frey and Betty Wood, *Come Shouting to Zion: African American Protestantism in the American South and British Caribbean to 1830* (Chapel Hill: University of North Carolina Press, 1998) 210 (second quote).

Satan is a liar, and he conjure too, And if you don't mind, he'll conjure you."[32] Christian doctrine acknowledged the work of the devil, and church members believed in his powers, earthly agents and mediums. For example, Edward Oxford, a sturdy yeoman farmer in Middle Georgia, active in his Baptist Church, recorded that he "went to the Negro fortinteller." The pastor of East Macon Methodist Church in Bibb County, Georgia, met with a white church member in 1871 who "was sick, and imagined that he had been tricked by a negro, who put a charm on his well." The man would not believe otherwise. Theophilus G. Steward, an AMEC minister, encountered two white women in Charleston, South Carolina, in 1865 who believed their house was haunted by a dead man's spirits. They convinced Steward to exorcise the spirits; after Steward read the Bible and prayed in the house the women believed that the spirits were gone. Those Christians white or black in Holloway's world who accepted that humans could be the channel for supernatural knowledge, power, or influence—whether for good or for ill—accepted that the medium could be a fortune teller, conjuror, or mainstream Christian minister.[33]

From his early-twentieth-century retrospective viewpoint, Holloway wrote of two-headed men as if they were long gone, a tale "that will be quiet amuseing to my reader," but conjurors were not the only practitioners in an occult spirit world in which Holloway absolutely believed, a world that did not pass away with slavery. In 1894 when Holloway was at Turin, a white carpenter named Phil Thurman, who worked in Holloway's blacksmith shop, became involved in spiritualism. Thurman shared his books with Holloway's son, John Wesley Holloway, and tried to get the young man interested in the occult. The elder Holloway advised his son, "Don't have anything to do with Phil Thurman's spirits. It is the work of the devil. Once you get into it, you will never be able to

---

[32] "Blow Your Trumpet, Gabriel" in Thomas Wentworth Higginson, "Negro Spirituals," *Atlantic Monthly* (June 1867), http://www.theatlantic.com/past/docs/issues/1867jun/spirit.htm (accessed 30 December 2014).

[33] Reba Strickland Biehle, "Edward Oxford, Pioneer Farmer of Middle Georgia," *Georgia Historical Quarterly* 52/2 (June 1968): 197; [John W. Burke], *Autobiography: Chapters from the Life of a Preacher* (Macon, GA: J. W. Burke & County, 1884) 120; Steward, *Fifty Years in the Gospel Ministry*, 68–69. See also Genovese, *Roll, Jordon, Roll*, 217–18, for discussion and examples of belief in conjure among whites. Charles Joyner notes shared African and European inheritance of beliefs in "signs, charms, and exorcisms" (*Down by the Riverside: A South Carolina Slave Community* [Urbana: University of Illinois Press, 1984] 142–43).

get out of it." Not long afterwards, on two consecutive nights, a spirit in form of a marble visited John Wesley Holloway's parlor. The marble, of its own volition, rolled down the wall and across the floor. Remembering his father's counsel, John Wesley sat perfectly still in his chair, moving not a muscle, outwardly refusing to acknowledge the spirit-marble. The spirit departed, not to return, and a much-relieved John Wesley recalled many years later, "I have never again been approached in just that way."[34]

Spirits and ghosts of the dead dwelt in earthly places where, despite a non-corporeal nature, they could manifest themselves in very physical ways. While serving his Bartow County appointment in 1872–1873, Holloway and family "moved into a two room cabin down by the Rome R.R. The rent was cheap because the place was said to be haunted." John Wesley Holloway vividly recalled,

> We did not live long in that house. One evening somewhat after sunset while my mother was cooking supper in the shed room and my sister and I were in the front room playing before the fire, suddenly, two planks about 8 ft. long, stretching across at least three rafters, began to jump up and down like a see-saw. My mother came hastily to the door and asked what the trouble was. We innocently replied that the planks had been jumping around. "Who did it?" she inquired. ["]Nobody," we said. "O you are a story you did that!"[35] I just declare[d,] "we did n't mamma!" She was unconvinced but kept coming and going, watching the planks. At length, when the dust was settled and every thing was quiet, one of those planks rose up on end and slid down to the floor with a thud and fell back to the middle of the room with a report like a cannon. By this time my mother had come in screaming and just as she got the baby, Achsah, in her arms and my sister by the hand the other plank did the same thing. We never spent another night in that house.[36]

For Christians like Holloway, God's benign miracles and interventions in human affairs overpowered the devil's work in the lives of the faithful. Holloway related examples of miracles large and small that occurred in his own life and ministry. Holloway walked from Kingston to a preaching appointment at Drummond Hill, across the Etowah River. He took no money for the ferry fare,

---

[34] JWH, 215.

[35] This is an idiom still heard in the South. When my wife, a Memphis native, doubts my veracity she exclaims, "you are a lie."

[36] JWH, 19–25.

but found a fifteen-cent change bill lying in the road.[37] When the congregation returned an empty collection plate to the altar, Holloway rebuked them, saying, "The Good Lord knew how you was going to do o[v]er heare to night and caused some one to drop 15 cts in a Horse track for me to pick up and pay my fair cross the river and back again." While Holloway was walking home one day in Upson County, God's spirit spoke with him to reconsider his calling to preach, a conversation that eventually led to his withdrawal from the itinerant ministry. When Holloway ran out of money to pay for his son's Fisk education, he prayed two nights "and then left it all with the Lord. In about two weeks I received a letter from my son stating that some one had put two hundred and fifty dollars in the bank at Nashville to his account to aid him through college. I considered it the direct answer to my prayer."[38] Holloway's world included magic and miracles. Christians needed to discern from whom the power came.

Holloway's Self-education

Holloway revealed his deep interest in literacy and education in the first sentence of his autobiography, writing that "about the time that I bornd scarsley any colord people could read or write and very few whites in the Rurall sections of the cuntry." Some scholars estimate that literacy among antebellum slaves was about five percent.[39] Holloway's father Neptune could read and write, and his example no doubt determined young Houston to learn likewise. Holloway described his personal library as two elementary reading books, a piece of a New

---

[37] There were so few coins circulating in the South that some businesses issued their own "change bills," privately printed paper money in denominations of less than one dollar.

[38] George W. Moore, "Southern Field Notes," *The American Missionary* 48/10 (October 1894): 358.

[39] W. E. B. Dubois (*Black Reconstruction* [Philadelphia: Albert Saifer, (1935?)] 638) and Janet Duitsman Cornelius, (*When I Can read My Title Clear: Literacy, Slavery, and Religion in the Antebellum South* [Columbia: University of South Carolina Press, 1991] 7–9) both put literacy of antebellum slaves at 5 percent; Jaqueline Jones puts literacy of black Georgians in 1860 at 4 or 5 percent (*Soldiers of Light and Love: Northern Teachers and Georgia Blacks, 1865–1873* [Chapel Hill: University of North Carolina Press, 1980] 60). Holloway may have underestimated the literacy rate among whites in his rural neighborhood. The 1860 census of Upson County where Holloway was born, found 572 of 2057 (28 percent) of white people over age twenty could neither read nor write; the remaining 72 percent claimed to be able at least to read.

Testament, and a piece of a Baptist hymn book that he brought with him from Upson County and studied in the kitchen at James Freeman's homeplace. He read copies of James C. Freeman's newspaper, the *Savannah Republican*, and anything else that came to hand. Holloway received one letter during slavery, telling him his father was dead, but he did not say he ever wrote a letter in slavery. Holloway seems to have used his writing skills mostly to forge passes.

Holloway's reading and writing efforts were in accord with the findings of historian Heather Andrea Williams, who explains that usually slaves sought the power of literacy to facilitate forbidden freedom of movement. Although some literate slaves did write documents other than passes (e.g., letters) the most common use to which slaves put this skill was to write passes. It is no wonder then that Holloway told three times of forging passes for himself. Richard Wright, former slave and nineteenth-century black educator in Georgia, confirmed, "The height of slavery-time education was to read the commonest print and to be able to write a 'pass.'" Rev. Scipio H. Robertson, an AMEC preacher known to Holloway, learned to write so he could make his own passes. Robertson (writing in the third person) described his youthful self-education:

> His highest ambition at that time was to learn how to write his pass. He kept a copy of one and spent a whole year studying it; and, after wasting bottles of ink, he succeeded in learning to write; but it was bad and he was afraid to trust it. At last one night he left it lying upon the counter in a store and came back asking; "Has any one seen my pass?" After looking around some time the clerk said: "Here it is;" and the writer came out of the store saying to himself, "Thank God, somebody can read it."

Holloway likewise needed to be sure his lack of formal schooling did not betray his passes, but he tested them more directly: "I would go out and stand beside the Big rode and wate for some white man to pass and have him to see if my pass was right."[40]

---

[40] Heather Andrea Williams, *Self-Taught: African American Education in Slavery and Freedom* (Chapel Hill: University of North Carolina Press, 2005) 22–23; Richard R. Wright, *A Brief Historical Sketch of Negro Education in Georgia* (Savannah: 1894) 21; Gaines, *African Methodism*, 137.

Sheriff's Sale, 1858

Holloway tells us that in 1857 "my old master stood securrity for some one and had the debt to pay."[41] He describes how the sheriff auctioned him, his brother Green, and another boy, Cornelius, at the courthouse steps in Thomaston. Holloway would not have known the private manipulations, negotiations, compromises, and bargains behind this seemingly straightforward public sale. Although Holloway had been seized by the sheriff and advertised for sale by order of Upson Superior Court, he was actually sold privately. The difference would have been transparent to the teenagers on the auction block, but the well-documented chain of events demonstrates a complex slave market in this small town, with many citizens drawn into transactions by contract, collateral obligations, judicial oversight, and enforcement.[42]

In 1855 Washington Hartsfield and two business partners cosigned a note on behalf of another merchant, Levi D. Dickinson, for money that Dickinson owed to John Neal of Pike County.[43] In 1856 Neal sued in Upson Superior Court for payment, received a judgment in his favor, and obtained a *fieri facias* (a court order directing the sheriff to seize defendants' property, sometimes abbreviated *fi. fa.*) to pay the judgment of $2,370.75 principal, interest, and court costs.[44]

By May 1857 the sheriff had not seized enough property from Levi Dickinson to pay Neal in full, and Neal pressed the sheriff to seize property from the securities (cosigners). Washington Hartsfield (Holloway's master) and one of his partners begged the court to allow them to find a way to pay without having their property seized; meantime, they seem to have convinced all parties

[41] A "security" was a cosigner on a contract or promissory note.

[42] My study of *fieri facias* (commonly abbreviated as *fi. fa.*) preserved in Upson County shows that only 37 percent of bondpeople seized by the sheriff of Upson County from 1825 to 1865 were sold as advertised. Owners usually paid their debts in full before the day of sale. Most of the enslaved went home, but a few, like Holloway, may have been sold privately.

[43] By coincidence, John Neal was brother to James Neal, father-in-law of James C. Freeman, who would become Holloway's last owner as an indirect result of this sale.

[44] Loose papers of Upson Superior Court, *fi. fa.* no. 257, returnable to Upson Superior Court, TUA, May Term 1856, John Neal vs. Levi D. Dickinson, principal, and Washington Hartsfield, Davis T. Richardson, & Francis M. Richardson, securities. The *fi. fa.* authorized the sheriff to seize property to pay the court-awarded judgment of $2,201.47 principal, $162.66 interest up to 1 January 1856, and $6.62 costs.

to postpone collection actions. No debtor wanted his property seized and sold by the sheriff in summer or fall if he could prevent it because bids at such sales were likely to be far below prices attainable at other times of the year. Property seized by the sheriff always sold for cash; therefore, in Georgia's credit economy, many potential buyers could not bid or would bid less on cash terms. Slaves typically sold for best prices during "slave-trading season" from October to the end of March, when planters and farmers had sold their crops and had spare cash.[45]

After another year of delay, John Neal pressed for action and Deputy Sheriff J. R. Hutcherson "levied this fi fa upon two negro boys to wit Greene [Houston's brother] about 16 years old and Houston about 14 years old both of dark copper color, as the property of Washington Hartsfield and pointed out by him this 22d March 1858." In other words, when the deputy came to his plantation, Hartsfield nominated Green and Houston for seizure and sale. Deputy Hutcherson then lodged the boys in the county jail.[46]

On 31 March 1858 Deputy Hutcherson advertised the pending sale, scheduled for May 4, in the Macon *Georgia Journal and Messenger*: "UPSON MAY SALES—Will be sold before the Court House door in Thomaston, on the first Tuesday in May next, within the legal hours of sale the following property, to wit…two negro boys, Greene, about sixteen years of age, of copper color, and Houston, a boy of same complexion, about fourteen years of age, levied upon as the property of Washington Hartsfield, property pointed out by W. Hartsfield."[47]

Houston seems to have been sold on the day advertised, but *not* as part of the sheriff's legal sale because Washington Hartsfield redeemed his seized property by paying the sheriff $1500 the day before the advertised sale, and deputy Hutcherson paid the money to John Neal on sale day. Hartsfield probably paid Hutcherson to release Greene and Houston from the *fi. fa.* so he could sell them privately on more favorable credit terms, payable after farmers and planters had sold the year's harvest. Hartsfield probably left young Houston

[45] Michael Tadman describes the "slave-trading season" (*Speculators and Slaves, Masters, Traders, and Slaves in the Old South* [Madison: University of Wisconsin Press, 1989] 70–71).

[46] Loose papers of Upson Superior Court, *fi. fa.* no. 257, returnable to Upson Superior Court, May Term 1856, John Neal vs. Levi D. Dickinson, principal, and Washington Hartsfield, Davis T. Richardson, & Francis M. Richardson, securities (TUA).

[47] [Macon] *Georgia Journal and Messenger*, 31 March 1858, 4.

in the custody of the sheriff with instructions to auction the boy on Hartsfield's behalf as a private sale for *credit* with payment due Christmas Day. Sheriffs commonly earned commissions as auctioneers for private sales on the legal day of sale, after they had finished their court-ordered business.[48]

On May 4 the sheriff probably bid off Houston Holloway to Isaac Strickland with payment due 25 December 1858, and Hartsfield took the fourteen-year-old boy home to await payment. Holloway recalled, "On the 27th day of December 1858 About one oclock PM...Isaac Strictland who bought me in May came after me." When Strickland paid the purchase money it was time for Holloway "to leave the old plantation." As for Green and Cornelius, a bill of sale recorded in Upson Superior Court tells us that Washington Hartsfield sold them to Thomaston planter and merchant Travis A. D. Weaver for $2,400 on 11 December 1858.[49]

James Crawford Freeman

When Isaac Strickland found out Holloway could read, he immediately advertised the teenager for sale. Strickland sold him to a wealthy planter who lived four miles west on Flint River at a place called Flat Shoals. James C. Freeman, Holloway's master during his late teen years and early adulthood, undoubtedly had more influence on the youth than his previous three masters. Holloway's autobiography devoted almost 13,000 words—over half his book—to the years with Freeman, compared to about 660 words describing servitude under the Hartsfields and Strickland. Holloway described himself as Freeman's house boy whose duties included hostler (caring for the horses, buggies, and carriages), working as striker (blacksmith's assistant) with enslaved blacksmith Richmond, helping enslaved miller Floyd Freeman during busy grinding seasons, and collecting tolls from Freeman's bridge.

James Crawford Freeman (1820–1885) was born in Clinton, Jones County, Georgia, 1 April 1820. He attended the common schools and academies near his home, then spent one year at Forest Hill Academy, near Athens, Tennessee. On 9 May 1843 he married Amanda Neal, daughter of James Neal, a Pike County planter, slave trader, and waggoner. A year later the couple moved to Pike County. Soon after 1850 they moved across Flint River to a home on the Meriwether side of Flat Shoals. He farmed, eventually inheriting and acquiring

[48] December 25 was the most common due date for antebellum promissory notes.

[49] Upson County Deed Book H, 411.

about 137 slaves, enough to operate two plantations in Pike County, Georgia, and to staff his industrial businesses at Flat Shoals, Meriwether County. Politically Freeman was an old line Whig who voted the presidential ticket of Bell and Everett in 1860. To gain better education opportunities for his children, he moved to Griffin 1 April 1861, but when war broke out he moved back to Flat Shoals where he hoped to remain in quiet isolation and avoid political and military notice during the course of the war.[50]

Freeman's Reconstruction-era congressional biographer downplayed his slave-ownership, claiming, "He held over one hundred slaves by inheritance. He never cordially approved of the institution of slavery, and treated his slaves with great kindness—exacting of them much less labor than they voluntarily give to those who hire them since their emancipation." The implication that Freeman was wholly an accidental slaveholder—by inheritance—is belied by the fact that Freeman purchased Houston Holloway in 1859 and acquired at least one other man, Jones Harald, about the same time, besides several slaves he received by deed of gift from his father-in-law. Freeman could mix paternal indulgence with arbitrary despotism. He was happy for Holloway to learn to read, contrary to the intent of Georgia law, but he cruelly crushed the marital aspirations of Floyd, a youth employed on one of his plantations. Even a comparatively benign master like Freeman exercised a fundamental tyranny over the personal lives of his bondpeople.[51]

After the war, Freeman moved to Griffin in Spalding County, making his living as a farmer, merchant, and banker. Elected as a Republican to the House of Representatives in the Forty-third Congress (4 March 1873–3 March 1875), he is best remembered for appointing Henry Ossian Flipper to the U.S. Military Academy; Flipper became the first black cadet to graduate from West Point.

---

[50] William Horatio Barnes, *Biographies of Members of the House Representative of The Forty-Third Congress*, vol. 2 of The American Government (New York: Nelson & Phillips, 1874) 305–306; SCC Disallowed Claim of James C. Freeman, testimony of James Freeman at the re-examination of his claim before the commissioners in 1875, and affidavit of Jones Harald taken 13 March 1872; 1880 Census, GA, Fulton County, Atlanta, Pop., ED 92, p. 30, dwell. 218.

[51] Barnes, *Biographies*, 305; SCC Disallowed Claim of James C. Freeman, affidavit of Jones Harald taken 13 March 1872: "He is forty-one years old…has known [James C. Freeman] twelve years; belonged to him when a slave." This suggests that Freeman acquired Harald in 1859–1860. For another local example of post-war selective amnesia about trading in slaves see sketch of Elder Thomas Calvin Trice, pp. 198-200.

Sometime after the end of his single term in Congress, Freeman moved to Atlanta and traded as a merchant. He died on 3 September 1885 and was buried in Atlanta's Oakland Cemetery.[52]

Flat Shoals Neighborhood

The center of Holloway's neighborhood at Flat Shoals, Meriwether County, was James C. Freeman's 200-acre homeplace on the south side of the Greenville Road, including Freeman's two-story personal home, stables, four dwelling houses for the fifteen slaves who worked in Freeman's household and who operated his nearby industrial businesses, and the old John Hay house. One of the slave cabins probably doubled as kitchen for the big house. On the same acreage Freeman owned a carding-machine factory, a mercantile store that housed the Flat Shoals community post office (Freeman was postmaster), a blacksmith shop operated by Freeman's bondman Richmond, and a church. On the banks of Flint River stood a water-driven gristmill, built at a cost of over $10,000, for Freeman and James Neal by James L. Dunning ("one of our best workmen," said Freeman). Managed and operated by Freeman's bondman, Floyd, it had three sets of running stones and stood two or three stories high. Freeman's domain included a toll bridge across Flint River for which Floyd served as principal toll collector, watching for traffic from his vantage point in the gristmill. On the Pike County side of the river, Freeman owned a sawmill.[53]

About a mile north of Freeman's home was the Thrash Place, owned by widowed planter Mary Thrash. The Thrash Place overlooked a wide part of the river called The Sea where Holloway and his sweetheart, Cordelia Thrash, liked to sit and talk. West from Flat Shoals on the road to Greensboro were the plantations of Reuben C. Strozier and Gaston M. Underwood. Freeman's immediate neighbors to the south were the physician Dr. James C.

[52] Biographical Directory of the United States Congress 1774–Present, http://bioguide.congress.gov.

[53] 1860 Census, GA, Meriwether County, Slave Pop., p. 97, col. 2, lines 13–27 enumerated thirteen slaves living at Freeman's homeplace; Meriwether County Tax Digest, 1863, 1213 GMD; Meriwether County Deed Book X [1890–1892], 172–173; Pike County Deed Book G, 1843–1850, 464; SCC Disallowed Claim of James C. Freeman, James C. Freeman's testimony in the "re-examination of his claim, 1875 (quote)"; 1860 Census, GA, Meriwether County, Slave Pop., p. 97, second column, lines 13–27). The antebellum bridge across Flat Shoals may have been about the same length as the bridge at that location in 1910 (781.44 feet).

DeLaperriere and Rev. Thomas C. Stanley, a Methodist minister and former U.S. Navy chaplain, married to the daughter of Dr. John L. Blackburn (d. 1856) and Martha A. Blackburn. By 1860 widow Blackburn lived in Stanley's house. Her thirty-five slaves, well known to neighbor Houston Holloway, lived on a ridge known as Blackburn Quarter. Further south down the road to Woodbury lived John (Jack) Sutton and his bondpeople. On the Pike County side of Flint River, north of the Zebulon Road, near Hebron Baptist Church, were Isaac Strickland's farm (where Holloway's Aunt Susan lived) and Freeman's plantation, the Caldwell Place. South of Flat Shoals on the Pike County side of Flint River was Freeman's other plantation, the Brown Place.[54]

Today nothing remains of the hamlet at Flat Shoals except stone piers that once supported the mill. When I visited Flat Shoals in May 2012 someone was keeping the vegetation trimmed around the Thrash family cemetery atop a hillock overlooking The Sea, but scrubby pines, thick underbrush, and kudzu hid whatever else might remain of nineteenth-century human habitation.

Holloway's Flat Shoals Neighborhood in the Civil War

No combatants fired shots in anger in Flat Shoals, Meriwether County, Georgia, until Union cavalry discharged a few scattering volleys at scampering civilians as the soldiers rode through the neighborhood on their way to Macon in April 1865, but local residents, slave and free, closely followed news of secession and the war from the start. Holloway's narrative details how he joined a reading club of four enslaved men who read the newspapers and followed every development of the war. Perhaps these four men were among the best informed in their neighborhood, but as historians have found, political and military intelligence traveled a network that permeated the whole enslaved community.[55] As Holloway said of secession and the war, "we colord people was on to the whole of it."

---

[54] Freeman bought his plantation "The Brown Place" from Ezekiel Brown in 1853 and his plantation "The Caldwell Place" from James T. G. Caldwell in 1857. He added acreage to each by buying adjoining land. See Pike County Deed Book K, 373, 375, 395, and Deed Book L, 148, 272, 284 (both books at the Pike County Courthouse, Zebulon, GA; also available on microfilm at Georgia Archives, Morrow, GA).

[55] For discussion of political news networking among the enslaved see Susan Eva O'Donovan, "William Webb's World," New York *Times* (18 February 2011), http://opinionator.blogs.nytimes.com/2011/02/18/william-webbs-world/?_r=0 (accessed 9 January 2015).

James C. Freeman's wish to remain in quiet isolation from the war failed to come true. About the mid-point of the conflict, Confederate authorities escorted Freeman to Macon to conscript him into the army, but Freemen pleaded he belonged to an exempt category of men, millers, who provided a vital service to his local community. While the Confederates tried to force Freeman into military service, Jones Harald and Lewis Freeman, two of his enslaved men, dug a cave in Meriwether County in which they urged Freeman to hide "and they would feed him and take care of him." This would have been the same sort of cave that runaway slaves used as temporary homes when they "lay out" hiding from their masters—an irony Freeman doubtless recognized when he refused the men's kind offer. Nevertheless, Freeman told his most trusted and discreet older bondsmen that as a "result of the war on slavery, that they would all be free."[56]

In the latter days of the war, social order among poor white people began to break down, aggravated by inadequate food distribution for the civilian population. The Confederate government seized much of the food for the army by annual tithes on farm produce, but foraging parties from armies passing near Flat Shoals seized what they wanted from local farmers. They visited Freeman's plantation more than once, taking his corn and wheat, meal and flour, and leaving worthless paper vouchers (receipts) with Freeman or his overseer. The shelves of Freeman's store were empty of goods. Some poor women in Georgia towns rioted for bread in 1863 and 1864, and the same hunger and desperation seems to have reached poor rural women near Flat Shoals. Although the flimsy record of events does not say exactly when hungry women came after the contents of Freeman's gristmill, he recalled, "I gave a great deal away to the women. That was one thing that saved my property."[57]

---

[56] SCC Disallowed Claim of James C. Freeman, Interrogation of James C. Freeman, 13 March 1872, James C. Freeman re-examination in 1875, and affidavit of Jones Harald, 13 March 1872 (both quotes).

[57] SCC Disallowed Claim of James C. Freeman, Interrogation of James C. Freeman, 13 March 1872 (quote). For context and analysis of 1863 food riots in the urban South, including GA, see James M. McPherson, *Battle Cry of Freedom: The Civil War Era* (New York: Oxford University Press, 1988) 617–19; Stephanie McCurry, "Women Numerous and Armed: Gender and the Politics of Subsistence in the Civil War South," in Joan Waugh and Gary W. Gallagher, eds., *Wars Within a War: Controversy and Conflict over the American Civil War* (Chapel Hill: University of North Carolina Press, 2009) 1–26, list of GA riots on 24, n. 53 and n. 54.

In late April 1865 Brigadier General James H. Wilson's 15,000-strong cavalry corps swept through the western Georgia black belt—that rich cotton land crowded with the wives and families of planters and yeoman farmers, and their enslaved workforces—from Columbus and LaGrange to Macon. A brigade commanded by Colonel Oscar H. LaGrange in the left flank of Wilson's army crossed Flint River on Freeman's bridge at Flat Shoals, taking nearly two days for thousands of men to pass on their way to meet Wilson at Macon. The second night after LaGrange passed, his staff and division commander, General McCook, made Freeman's house their temporary headquarters for one night. Holloway dashed to the Thrash place to check on his wife and found "the yard was full of yankeys and the woman ware cooking and they wore Eating and a connell was siting on his horse Eating and duscussing the causses of the war with the wihite women"—a common scene repeated innumerable times along Wilson's route.[58] No mention of a Jubilee celebration at the Freeman place or the Thrash place; such talk was probably largely, expectantly, but discreetly discussed in the cabins.

Freeman's Flat Shoals mills, shops, and houses escaped destruction, but the troops stripped his Pike County plantations of work animals, cattle, corn, and wheat. In the weeks after Wilson's troops had passed, and as paroled Confederate soldiers returned home, desperate men repeatedly raided Freeman's gristmill in search of flour and meal. Soldiers' wives and widows had raided during the war, but now men home from the army took the lead. Freeman testified,

> [T]hey were foraging at my mill so that the miller [Floyd Freeman, Holloway's brother-in-law] got so afraid that when they would come down there & he would see a crowd coming (because when they would cross the bridge he could see them) he would lock the door and slip down out of the window and get away. And there was a crowd [of five or six men] went down there one day, and they saw him locking the door when they were in

[58] For example Harriet Rose and Minnie Rose, former slaves of Thomas E. Rose in Upson County, cooked for soldiers while the Union officers ate at the house with the white women. Minnie Rose testified that "about three hundred soldiers were fed at the house; helped cook the meals...there was two or three other women cooking for the soldiers; cooked corn bread for them" (NARA, RG233, Southern Claims Commission, Disallowed Claims, Office 187, Report 7, claim of Thomas E. Rose (available in NARA Microfilm Publication M1407, fiche 0070), statements of Minnie Rose and Harriet Rose.

> sight & they were bound to break open the mill, and I went to them and asked them not to do it. I told them there was nothing in there—that they had foraged it all out. They wanted to know why he ran, & I said "he was afraid of you, I suppose."

John Bell, an unsuccessful candidate for the U.S. presidency 1860, who had fled from Tennessee in 1864 and was staying at Freeman's house, came down to the mill, stood with Freeman, and persuaded the men not to break down the door.[59]

Holloway's Emancipation

Holloway's emancipation narrative shares much in common with the stories of thousands of bondpeople left in the wake of Wilson's Raid through rural Georgia who watched and waited to see what ol' massa or ol' missus would say and do. Most masters eventually summoned their workforce, even if grudgingly, usually read some official paper, and proclaimed the end of slavery, releasing their workforces to negotiate new employment relationships. Until offered a viable alternative to their previous livelihood, bondpeople were entirely rational to wait to hear terms from former masters rather than making unilateral decisions. Holloway referred to the slave-owning class as "the land lords" for good reason; in an agricultural economy, "the land lords" controlled the place of food production. They also controlled the only available housing.[60]

For a few young men without wives or children—or others among the enslaved who felt that they had little stake in their current home or employment—following the Yankee army was an adventure from which many returned in a few weeks or months. Holloway explicitly rejected this option ("I told my wife that I would not leave her and go with the yankeys"); but Holloway's cousin Daniel Hartsfield from nearby Upson County recalled, "I left the plantation and went to Macon when the yankees came through in April

---

[59] SCC Disallowed Claim of James C. Freeman, James C. Freeman re-examination of claim in 1875.

[60] See detailed discussion of this kind of emancipation in Litwack, *Been in the Storm So Long*, 187–93. Hahn, Miller, O'Donovan, Rodrigue, and Rowland, eds., *Freedom: A Documentary History of Emancipation, 1861–1867*, 76, found "many former slaves thought it best to bide their time...until they heard it directly from their former owners." Susan O'Donovan found similar behavior for the same reasons in southwest GA, where "former slaves remained in 'their old homes, quietly working'" (*Becoming Free in the Cotton South* [Cambridge: Harvard University Press, 2007] 119–20).

1865.... I enlisted in May."[61] Once in Macon some who passed the medical screening enlisted in one of three regiments of U.S. Colored Infantry raised by Wilson.[62] Others hired their time as hostlers, cooks, or personal servants to army officers. When the rest joined throngs of unemployed, homeless freedpeople, Wilson directed his officers and the civil authorities to round them up and compel them to work on municipal projects.[63] Landlords, overseers, and foremen who had crops to work sought to recover members of their workforce who had scattered at the arrival of the Union army. Herod Smith, one of James C. Freeman's leading hands on the Brown Place in Pike County, went to Macon "to get his boys back"—meaning those farmhands who had left with the soldiers.[64] Many enlistees returned to the old neighborhood after their units demobilized in January 1866. A small few did not wait to be discharged, as

---

[61] National Archives, RG 15, Veterans Administration Pension files, pension claim of Cesar Davis (No. 1,194,816), Daniel Hartsfield's deposition taken 23 November 1899.

[62] 136, 137, 138 Regiments, US Colored Infantry, established in June and July 1865 (with many enlistments dating to April), at full strength each mustered about 1,100 men. All three regiments mustered out in January 1866. Brief histories of these regiments are available through National Park Service Soldiers and Sailors database (http://www.nps.gov/civilwar/soldiers-and-sailors-database.htm), specific page for 136 USCI is http://www.nps.gov/civilwar/search-battle-units-detail.htm?battleUnitCode=uus0136ri00c (battle unit code for 137 USCI is UUS0137RI00C; battle unit code for 138 USCI is UUS0138RI00C).

[63] NARA, RG 393 Part 2, E 2460, Letters Sent, 2 of 2 (vol. 13/22, 24 CCMDM), 42 (J. H. Wilson to Col. J. G. Vail, 27 April 1865) wherein Wilson ordered Vail "to have all rubbish removed from the streets [of Macon].... The negroes of the city can be impressed for the purpose." See policy statement in NARA, RG 393 Part 2, E 2460, Letters Sent, 2 of 2 (vol. 13/22, 24 CCMDM), 130–31 (J. H. Wilson to F. G. Wilkins, mayor of Columbus, GA, 20 June 1865): "the civil and municipal authorities of the land everywhere within the limits of my command are authorized to arrest [vagrants]...and if labor cannot be found for them, to furnish it for the public welfare, by causing the vagrants to work upon public highways." For conditions experienced by thousands of freedpeople who followed Wilson's army to Macon, including murder, death, disease, hunger, forced labor, and expulsion into the countryside, see "The Negro's Hardships," *Southern Recorder*, 6 June 1865, 2, (quoting from Macon *Telegraph*).

[64] SCC Disallowed Claim of James C. Freeman, affidavit of Herod Smith, taken 13 March 1872.

Daniel Hartsfield admitted, "I deserted from the regiment…and got home before Christmas [1865]."[65]

James Freeman and his neighbors read the newspapers. By the end of May papers throughout the state had published the order issued on 15 May by Major General Quincy Adams Gilmore (commanding the Department of the South), which declared "the people of the black race are free citizens of the United States." Gilmore promised the U.S. government would "protect them in the enjoyment of their freedom and the fruits of their industry."[66] Freeman had probably seen a copy of President Johnson's "Proclamation 134—Granting Amnesty to Participants in the Rebellion, with Certain Exceptions," issued on 29 May 1865. Freeman, who professed himself a Union man, was ready to take the amnesty oath, including a promise to "faithfully support all laws and proclamations which have been made during the existing rebellion with reference to the emancipation of slaves."[67] When later asked by a federal commission, "Did you set your negroes free at any time, or how was it?" Freeman answered, "I set them free after the proclamation…. Just as soon as it came out." He could not have been referring to Lincoln's Emancipation Proclamation issued two and a half years earlier (1 January 1863). President Johnson's Amnesty Proclamation of 29 May 1865, incorporating support of Lincoln's earlier proclamation as a condition for amnesty, was the only presidential proclamation that could have prompted Freeman to act as he did "as soon as it came out."[68]

---

[65] National Archives, RG 15, Veterans Administration Pension files, pension claim of Cesar Davis (No. 1,194,816), Daniel Hartsfield's deposition taken 23 November 1899.

[66] "Important Order," [Milledgeville] *Southern Recorder*, 30 May 1865, 2.

[67] The full amnesty oath read, "I, ________, do solemnly swear (or affirm), in presence of Almighty God, that I will henceforth faithfully support, protect, and defend the Constitution of the United States and the Union of the States thereunder, and that I will in like manner abide by and faithfully support all laws and proclamations which have been made during the existing rebellion with reference to the emancipation of slaves. So help me God" (available at *The American Presidency Project*, www.presidency.ucsb.edu/ws/index.php?pid=72392 (accessed 20 February 2015).

[68] SCC Disallowed Claim of James C. Freeman, James C. Freeman's testimony before the Southern Claims Commission on 6 March 1875, 3. Freeman's testimony included the following exchange:

Q How many negroes did you own?

A I had 137 about.

Q Did you set your negroes free at any time, or how was it?

Besides James C. Freeman's account to the Southern Claims Commission, we have two accounts from Holloway describing his personal moment of emancipation: the autobiography written thirty years after the event and a letter from Holloway to the *Christian Recorder* in 1878. Early Monday morning on 5 June James C. Freeman freed the slaves in his two Pike County plantations, then summoned the slaves living at his home place to the porch of the big house. According to Holloway, "my old master called all his people or slaves together and read to them the proclamation of emancipation." Freeman concluded by saying, "As for you, you are now all free. I wish now to give you this advice: go to work, you will always have much to do if you do it."[69] Holloway's words (according to his autobiography) were inadequate to express the ecstasy he felt at that moment; he could only exclaim, "Amen Amen Amen."

Freeman himself later gave a more abbreviated account of that speech: "I just called them up and told them they were free by the laws of the country—the proclamation—and they could either stay there & finish the crop which was then Commenced, and I would give them an interest in it, or they could go where they concluded to." Holloway remembered that Freeman then told the assembled people that "he was Free to[o] he felt like a burd out of a cage." In sympathy with his former master's newfound liberty from slaveholding, Holloway repeated his previous sentiment, "Amen Amen Amen."[70] Then everyone on the Freeman home place went back to work as usual. Holloway recalled that "The week past off in a Blse of glory" but it was not until the Saturday evening that he "left off work for the first time in lief" and went to Pike County to visit Aunt Susan.

A I set them free after the proclamation.

Q How long after?

A Just as soon as it came out....

Q What did you do to set them free?

A I just called them up and told them they were free by the laws of the country—the proclamation—and they could either stay there & finish the crop which was then Commenced, and I would give them an interest in it, or they could go where they concluded to.

[69] "Thirteen Years Ago," *Christian Recorder*, 4 July 1878, 2 (see Appendix D, p.217-17).

[70] SCC Disallowed Claim of James C. Freeman, James C. Freeman's testimony before the Commission on 6 March 1875, 3.

A few days after Cordelia gave birth to the couple's first child (named John Wesley after Houston Holloway's eldest brother), Holloway received a letter dated 6 August 1865 from that brother, living in Talbot County, Georgia, announcing that "I writ this to let you know that I am free have you received your liberty yet." It was probably not coincidence that August 1865—the month the elder John Wesley "received" his liberty—was the month U.S. Army assistant provost marshals in Georgia toured their assigned counties to administer President Johnson's amnesty oath. Emancipation in upcountry Georgia came suddenly for some freedpeople and gradually for others, affected as much by the responses of former slave owners—who sometimes needed to be prodded by representatives of the federal government—as by the responses of the formerly enslaved.

Family Economy

Holloway recalled, "We knew nothing in thoes days about Buisness Hence the provost marshail had to see after and approve all of the contracts made betweean the colord people and there former owners the Incoming yeare." For a landlord, "It was very Humiliating to have to go to the then Hatefull yankey to aprove or disapprove his contract with his former slave." Negotiations could be fraught with fuss, heated disagreement, and injured pride. Although freedpeople were acutely aware that their labor had value, many struggled to gauge that value against the expenses of subsistence. When interviewed in 1936 Shade Richards, who grew up in of Pike County near Holloway's Flat Shoals neighborhood, described bargaining for wages during the first years of freedom as an argumentative and iterative process. Richards's parents worked for James Neal (James C. Freeman's father-in-law) during the first four years of freedom:

> His father and mother rented a patch, mule and plow from Mr. Neal and the family was together. At first they gave the niggers only a tenth of what they raised but they couldn't get along on it and after a "lot of mouthin' about it" they gave them a third. That wasn't enough to live on either so more "mouthin" about it until they gave them a half, "and that's what they still gits today."[71]

---

[71] George P. Rawick, ed., *Georgia Narratives*, vol. 13 in series 2 of *The American Slave: A Composite Autobiography* (Westport, CT: Greenwood Publishing Company, 1972) 204. Shade Richards's experience and Holloway's generalizations were seconded by contemporary ex-slave and GA educator, Richard R. Wright, who wrote in 1894, "It is

Holloway continued to labor at Freeman's blacksmith shop near the bridge. Georgia's post-war economy relied as much as before on credit. His blacksmith work provided an adequate income, but he could not collect what was due on all accounts—"I cleard something over 200 dollars but was never able to collect it all." After a brief stint (1867–1868) teaching school, which failed to provide a living, Holloway again "Took my hammer in hand and became a Travling Blacksmith." He employed a succession of strikers to help him, working in varying degrees of harmony. Child John Wesley Holloway remembered with pleasure that his father's striker Donas McGill "used to give me money and bring home a pocket full of ends from spokes for me to play with." When McGill migrated west to Muscogee County, he was replaced by another man, who demanded his pay when Holloway did not have it to give. The man tried to extract payment by entering Holloway's house and seizing "the big clock from the mantel." John Wesley Holloway wrote that, "My father walked up to him and fired a little pistol at him. The shot did not take effect, but the man put the clock back." The two men appeared before a justice of the peace the next day, but we do not know the court's decision.[72]

Home Life

The end of slavery meant the end of the former phenomenon of the "abroad wife," who, owned by a different master from her husband, and living on a different farm. Beginning in 1865 freedom to move meant that many married men would move their wives to co-habit in the husband's house. Relocations involved simultaneous negotiations of tenancy with the landlord who owned the house and renegotiations of employment among all parties; therefore, those who had a stake in the growing crop and had contracted with old masters or mistresses for the remainder of the year might not move until Christmastime (the same season that in former years slave hiring contracts had expired and the enslaved had taken a holiday before the new year). Holloway

---

difficult to comprehend the utter poverty and disheartening ignorance which enveloped the colored people at the beginning of [Reconstruction].... They did not know how to make contracts or agreements for wages. Consequently they worked the first year for a bare subsistence..." (*A Brief Historical Sketch*, 22).

[72] JWH, 12–13; 1870 Census, Muscogee County, GA, Pop., p. 119, dwell. 846 (Dormas McGill, age twenty-eight, male mulatto, "Blacksmith's Apprentice," born in MD). Few Justices Court records survive because Justices Court was not a legally designated "court of record" in GA.

wrote, "Some time in the mounth of December beganing about the first the colord people began to Brake up and leave There former owners."

Holloway moved his family to an isolated house in the piney woods about a mile north of widow Thrash's place. It was a one-room log cabin with bloodstains on the floor where a man had been killed (John Wesley Holloway later wrote, "My mother would scrape up the blood but it would re-appear."). The family did not live there long because one day Cordelia looked under the bed to find baby John Wesley sharing his tin plate of food with a monstrous rattlesnake. She snatched the child into her arms and ran "screaming at the top of her voice. She staid in the road till my father came home at night from the blacksmith shop, but she never entered that house again."[73]

The family moved back to Flat Shoals, into the house from which Holloway collected tolls for the long wooden bridge that he watched from the blacksmith shop nearby. Living in the family was elderly Cherry Thrash, Cordelia's mother, "a root doctor trained by the Indians" and a longtime member of the Baptist church.[74] On the hillside above the Holloway family lived Cordelia's sister Pherebe and her husband, Alexander Campbell. Opposite the Campbell house, on the south side of the Greenville road stood the big house where James C. Freeman lived with his wife and daughters. Relations between landlord and tenant were cordial enough that Holloway once took young John Wesley to Freeman's house to hear one of the Freeman daughters play the piano.[75]

Holloway and his Flat Shoals neighbors supplemented their meat and meal diet with fish from Flint River: "Often the men of the vicinity gathered on Saturdays to seine the river. We used to get a tub full for our portion."[76] Family and neighbors would sometimes meet for dinner. John Wesley Holloway remembered "being carried in my father's arms to a neighbor's house to dinner...[with] my aunt Jane and her husband uncle Simon Thrash.... At the neighbor's house the grown persons sat at the table and the children ate out of a wash-pot. There were a dozen or twenty of them. At a given signal they made for the pot like pigs for a trough. Some of them balanced themselves on the rim,

[73] JWH, 3, 5, 7.

[74] Ibid., 7, 9.

[75] Ibid., 9.

[76] Ibid., 13.

threw their feet up into the air and sucked the pot liquor exactly as pigs would have done. I wasn't on, and so I went hungry until I was fed from the table."[77]

Family life was not all work, recalled John Wesley Holloway: "We had a bateau and evenings my father would take us down the river, my mother and me."[78] Children had their place in Holloway's household, and that place was definitely subordinate to grown folks. John Wesley recalled "'seeing stars' one Saturday night when I worried my father to tie a bow-knot for me about my doll. He was bathing before the fire and talking at the same time over some affair with my mother. He suddenly lost his temper and struck me a 'back-handed lick' that almost finished me. I saw numerous stars and never played dolls again."[79]

In a pre-industrial society without organized childcare and where elders were often unavailable in the house to watch children while parents worked, adult supervision over children was necessarily inconstant. As Holloway's children reached their teens, Houston and Cordelia increasingly relied on the elder ones to care for the younger while their parents were away. Son John Wesley Holloway remembered that when he was about thirteen and the family lived in Senoia, "there was no over sight of the children. My own father and mother went off several times to Sharpsboro and left us children for two or three days at a time to shift for ourselves." Ironically, Holloway had written a letter to the *Christian Recorder* in 1875 titled "Careless Fathers and Mothers," lecturing parents on the possible fatal consequences of leaving their children unattended.[80]

Holloway's First School

In 1867 Holloway's neighbors persuaded him, as one of the few people in his neighborhood who could read and write, to teach in Pike County, at a school about a mile and a half east of Flat Shoals.[81] Holloway taught for only nine

---

[77] Ibid., 1, 3.

[78] Ibid., 13.

[79] Ibid., 3.

[80] Ibid., 34; *Christian Recorder*, 18 November 1875, 1.

[81] We do not know exactly where this school was. Holloway's son John Wesley Holloway, two years old in 1867, much later wrote (JWH, 12) that the school was at "Bush Chapel...the first church in the community," but his statement is questionable, not least because Bush Chapel was not the first church near the Flat Shoals community. Houston Holloway states the school was only 1.5 miles east of Flat Shoals, but Bush Chapel was (and still is) near the crossroads at Williamsville (now called Neal), over three

months, using just one book, a copy of Webster's *Elementary Spelling Book*, but his roll eventually grew to fifty pupils. Mark Twain's description of the corporal teaching style used by Tom Sawyer's fictional schoolmaster—"His rod and his ferule were seldom idle" and his "lashings were very vigorous ones, too"—closely matches the method used by Holloway, as described by his son, John Wesley Holloway: "Scholars studied out at the tops of their voices and a hickory pole, 8 or 10 ft. long was likely to decend with Herculean force upon you at any time. Great big girls—grown women, had to take it like the little ones and when they bawled out, there was a real racket." He added, "I suppose they were allowed to study so to drown the cry of the victim." Holloway quit teaching in 1868 because his school only paid him fifty cents per month. Reflecting on this first teaching job in a letter to the *Christian Recorder* in 1878, Houston H. Holloway admitted himself "incompetent" for the task but believed he had accomplished some "amount of good" as "three young boys who then learned their alphabet, are now holding important charges in the A. M. E. Church."[82]

Preaching for the MECS

In 1866 Holloway felt the Lord call him to preach, and his narrative details the two treks he and Claiborne Bush made to district quarterly conferences where each was authorized to exercise his spiritual gifts, Holloway to exhort and Bush to preach. Whereas an exhorter's license was limited to encouraging people to live a godly life and to repent from sin, a preacher could choose a text and expounded on it, teaching and interpreting Scripture.[83] All converts brought into

---

miles by road from Flat Shoals. Although the Methodist congregation that would constitute Bush Chapel may have existed earlier—and a stone plaque mounted on the current Bush Chapel building dates the church's founding to 1867—Holloway insists that Rev. Albert McGee organized Bush Chapel as an AME church in 1869, that the church building was erected in 1869 and dedicated in 1870. Chronology and geography preclude the current location of Bush Chapel from having hosted Holloway's school in 1867.

[82] Mark Twain, *The Adventures of Tom Sawyer* (Hartford, CT: The American Publishing Company, 1884) 167 (or any edition, Chapter 21, first paragraph); JWH, 12, 267, 25; *Christian Recorder*, 4 July 1878, 2. John Wesley Holloway's memory of his father's teaching method dates to the family's sojourn in Ringgold, GA, in 1871 when he was in his father's school.

[83] Alex[ander] W[alker] Wayman, *Manual, or Guide Book, for the Administration of the Discipline of the African M. E. Church* (Baltimore: Hoffman & County, n.d.) 18–20,

the church by Bush and Holloway were baptized by a white ordained minister who would visit every Second Sunday of the month because there were then no ordained black ministers in the MECS in Georgia.

Based on membership and population numbers alone, opportunities for black preachers in the post-emancipation MECS must have seemed plentiful. The 1863 Georgia Conference, MECS, had recorded that the Colored Mission associated with the Greenville Circuit had nine preaching places, "464 members, 100 probationers, and is reported to be in a prosperous condition." The U.S. Census in 1860 had counted 18 Methodist churches (meaning church buildings) in Meriwether County; therefore the Colored Mission's nine preaching places included half the county's Methodist churches, and Flat Shoals Church was surely one of the nine—indeed, Holloway tells us this church was served by a circuit rider.[84] Despite the large population of freedpeople in Meriwether and Pike counties, when Holloway and Bush returned to the district quarterly conference in July 1866, Holloway seemed surprised to find there were no other black men seeking admission to the conference. As he would learn, other Methodist denominations were competing for black members in upcountry Georgia.

Competition among Methodists

Leaders of the MECS were far from happy at ecclesiastical developments in the South after the Civil War. Georgia's black church membership grew fast because emancipation seemed to have fulfilled the promise of faithful Christian slaves' liberation theology, had broken slave-holders' stranglehold on churches and public worship, and had opened opportunities for independent, black led churches in which freedpeople could exercise their spiritual gifts without

---

describes and contrasts the functions of an exhorter and a licensed preacher. I could find no contemporary MECS document explaining the distinction between exhorter and preacher; however, church discipline varied little between any of the U.S. Methodist denominations.

[84] *Minutes of the Georgia Annual Conference of the Methodist Episcopal Church, South, Held in Columbus, Ga., Nov. 25–Dec. 3, 1863* (Macon, GA: Burke, Boykin & County, 1864) 24, http://american-south.org/export/html/geu/confederateimprints/amso_geu_confederateimprints_8hxs8.html (accessed 12 January 2015); Department of the Interior, *Statistics of the United States*, 369.

subordination to white ecclesiastical authority.[85] But most of this growth did not occur within the MECS because that church was associated with the old slavery regime. In contrast, missionaries from Methodist denominations headquartered in the North attracted huge numbers of black members even as black MECS membership hemorrhaged.

Missionaries from the northern Methodist Episcopal Church (MEC) penetrated the South with an air of triumph in the wake of federal armies and attracted many local freedpeople and many unionist whites. MEC missionaries, Northerners, and local Southern ministers who shifted allegiance from the MECS to the MEC attempted to gain Southern congregations and churches by emphasizing the MEC's priorities of education and equal racial participation in church leadership. While the MECS regarded these MEC missionaries as hostile trespassers on its ecclesiastical turf, the MEC regarded the MECS as an illegitimate, schismatic church inseparably linked to slavery and a defeated rebellion. Despite a bright start, MEC efforts in Georgia fizzled within a decade largely because white MEC churchmen compromised their promise of racial equality, but that failure was not obvious in 1866.[86]

Holloway witnessed the activities of the MEC missionaries aggressively challenging the legitimacy of the MECS and saw (as he would write) "Thousand of our people win into that church." The most visible MEC evangelist near Holloway's neighborhood was former MECS local preacher William Fincher in Zebulon, Pike County. Holloway characterized Fincher as "one of the most Eloquant colord ministers to be found any wheare.... he was a great politician also.... he was far be yond his day In knowlage."[87] Fincher's initial success expanded the MEC church in Pike County to 310 members by October 1869, but the local MEC congregation steadily declined thereafter, probably giving up its members to the local African Methodist Episcopal

---

[85] Christopher H. Owen, *The Sacred Flame of Love: Methodism and Society in Nineteenth-Century Georgia* (Athens: University of Georgia Press, 1998) 129–30.

[86] Ibid., 119–20.

[87] Fincher was an influential local figure whose has escaped scholarly attention, except for a discussion of his vagrancy conviction in 1866. See Robert J. Kaczorowski, in *The Politics of Judicial Interpretation: The Federal Courts, Department of Justice, and Civil Rights, 1866–1876* (Dobbs Ferry, NY: Oceana Publications, 1985) 34–35. A biographical sketch in Appendix A, pp. 202-204, offers a first step toward better understanding William Fincher's place in local GA politics and religion during Reconstruction.

churches.[88] Membership in the Barnesville circuit fell so low that the MEC conference merged it with the Pike and Upson circuit, and, by 1879, Fincher's last year as pastor, the Pike and Upson circuit had dwindled to ten members. Faced with vanishing membership, Fincher "located" (i.e., he quit the traveling ministry) in 1880 and returned to farming.[89] In 1869 Holloway, without benefit of foresight, saw the MEC's early success as evidence of grim ecclesiastical prospects for any ambitious local black preacher who remained in the MECS.

Holloway was not aware until 1868 that a black Methodist denomination, the African Methodist Episcopal Church (AMEC), had been aggressively proselytizing among black members of the MECS in many parts of Georgia since 1865. The AMEC emphasis on education for black people and black leadership for black churches offered strong competition to the MEC message. The MECS response to the AMEC was ambivalent. Because the AMEC originated as a breakaway church from the MEC (caused by the MEC's treatment of AMEC founder Richard Allen and other black members), the MECS and the AMEC shared a common history in opposition to an overbearing MEC. If MECS were to lose black members, they would rather lose them to the AMEC than to the despised Yankee MEC.[90]

With the MEC, AMEC, and to a smaller extent the African Methodist Episcopal Zion Church each evangelizing in parts of the South and successfully drawing away black MECS membership—sometimes entire congregations at a time—the MECS was anxious to stop the exodus. Their proposed solution was a racially segregated church leadership where black ordained preachers could lead racially segregated black churches without the appearance of social equality with white Methodists. At its General Conference in New Orleans in April 1866, the MECS laid out a plan for black churches and districts, and discussed the possibility of separate black conferences within the MECS General

[88] Clergy and their congregations would sometimes shift allegiance *en masse*. The *Southern Christian Advocate*, 10 April 1868, 2, reporting the first session of the GA Annual Conference AMEC, noted that Deacon Robert Strickland "with 250 of his followers" had transferred from the MEC to the AMEC.

[89] MEC 1869, 276, 278; MEC 1870, 286, 288; MEC 1871, 277, 279; MEC (Fall Conferences) 1878, 85; MEC (Fall Conferences) 1880, 302. (See pp. viii-ix for list of abbreviations used herein for church annual conference minutes.)

[90] Owen, *Sacred Flame of Love*, 121–22.

Conference.[91] Up to that time, district conferences had licensed Georgia's MECS black preachers and exhorters, who were not ordained and were not members of a regional annual conference.

As first steps in the new MECS plan the Georgia Annual Conference in November 1866 took the unprecedented action (for Georgia) of admitting black members to the conference. The assembly elected twenty-four "colored brethren," including Claiborne Bush, as local preachers and ordained eight as deacons. At the same conference, one black local preacher, Edward West, was elected and ordained elder. West, as the conference's only black ordained itinerant clergyman, was appointed to Trinity Church, an all-black congregation in Augusta.[92] At the same session the Georgia Conference split into the North Georgia and South Georgia Conferences, so that Holloway's and Bush's ministry at Flat Shoals in the LaGrange District became part of the North Georgia Conference, MECS.

The MECS North Georgia Conference meeting in November 1867 implemented a "Conference for the Colored People" composed of four districts reporting to same bishop as the rest of the North Georgia Conference. Holloway's neighbor Rev. Claiborne Bush was appointed to Pike and Flat Shoals in the Barnesville District of the new colored conference. Because the North Georgia Conference retained the old circuits with "colored charges" under white preachers near the same places served by the new black-led charges, white and black preachers shared the same field for black converts and members. For example, the Greenville and Colored Charge and the Pike and Colored Charge encroached on possible membership for Rev. Bush's Pike and Flat Shoals charge. Bishop Pierce acknowledged that the poverty of most black members would prevent them from providing a full-time support to their pastors; thus most black preachers would need to farm or work at trades during the week—just as Holloway and Claiborn Bush did.[93]

---

[91] Daniel W. Stowell, *Rebuilding Zion: The Religious Reconstruction of the South, 1863–1877* (New York: Oxford University Press, 1998) 87.

[92] MECS 1866, 24, 26, 28. As a licensed local preacher, Edward West had been *de facto* pastor of the 1,130-member Trinity. For more on Trinity see Glenn T. Eskew, "Paternalism among Augusta's Methodists: Black, White, and Colored," in Edward J. Cashin, Glenn T. Eskew, eds., *Paternalism in a Southern City: Race, Religion, and Gender in Augusta, Georgia* (Athens: University of Georgia Press, 2001) 96–101.

[93] MECS 1867, 120–22; Othal Hawthorne Lakey, *The History of the CME Church (Revised)* (Memphis: CME Publishing House, 1996) 151.

The hemorrhage of black leadership and membership continued. The 1867 session of the North Georgia Conference elected only three new black men to membership and promoted one preacher to the rank of deacon and one man to elder. The conference reported nine vacancies with the forlorn phrase "to be supplied."[94] Caste-based appointments that denied equal opportunity for black preachers unsurprisingly failed to attract willing or qualified black applicants.

In April 1868 the Quarterly Conference of Greenville Circuit licensed Holloway to preach and appointed him to Flat Shoals Circuit. He was a local preacher, not ordained, and had three designated preaching places: Mount Carmel and Flat Shoals in Meriwether County, and Ebenezer in eastern Pike County.[95]

In January 1869, the "Conference for the Colored People," formerly a unit within the MECS North Georgia Conference, became a separate Georgia Colored Conference with its own presiding elders and districts. The MECS North Georgia Conference minutes beginning in 1868 do not include the colored conference districts, and 1869 was the last year that a black itinerant received a pastoral appointment in the MECS North Georgia Conference. With one of the Colored Conference districts seated in Griffin, it is likely that Holloway as a licensed MECS preacher would have been aware of the new organization; nevertheless, from his retrospective view forty years later, he wrote that in 1869 he was ecclesiastically demoralized and believed his church "had Largely dropt us" (black people). Perhaps Holloway perceived the attitude of many whites as expressed by the editor of the Nashville *Western Christian Advocate*, who wrote that the MECS was "glad to get rid of the Negroes, not knowing what to do with them." Holloway committed himself to the AMEC church in November 1869, thirteen months before the December 1870 conference at which white and black leaders of the MECS met and formed the Colored Methodist Episcopal Church (CMEC). The new CME Church absorbed most of the MECS's remaining black members and its black-occupied church property, but Holloway's autobiography never mentions the new church.[96]

---

[94] MECS 1867, 117, 122.

[95] *Christian Recorder*, 4 July 1878, 2. The Carmel Church and Ebenezer Church buildings (both dating to the 1840s), in which Holloway preached, still stand and serve their congregations. Due to changes in county lines, Ebenezer is now in Lamar County.

[96] MECS 1868, 218, 222–23; MECS 1869, 319, 322–24; MECS 1870, 425, 429–31. Lakey, *History of the CME Church*, describes the transition from MECS Colored

Holloway Discovers the African Methodist Episcopal Church

In about 1868, while shopping in Griffin, Holloway intended to visit his old Flat Shoals neighbor, Anthony Alexander. He asked for directions but was sent to the wrong house, where he found Rev. Robert Alexander, pastor of the local AME church.[97] Born in North Carolina and able to read and write, Alexander had been one of the first men recruited by Henry M. Turner in 1866 to conquer Georgia for the AMEC. That same year, after preaching in Opelika, Alabama, he had barely escaped martyrdom at the hands of murderous white men who resented his school for black students and who could not accept a black preacher in their town. Holloway was astonished: "I had never seen such a man befour" and an "African Methodist Church" was "was quiet a novall Idea to me."

About six months later Holloway returned to Griffin and took another look at the novel African Methodist Church that had so intrigued him earlier. Robert Alexander was gone, but Albert McGhee was pastor of Griffin AME Church.[98] Holloway remembered, "I went out that night to one of his meetings

---

Conferences to the CMEC, 143–52, 159–224 (quote from *Western Christian Advocate* is on 187).

[97] Biographical sketch of Robert Alexander is on pp. 204-05.

[98] Albert McGhee (1822–1882) was born in Abbeville District, SC; converted to Christianity at a South Carolina camp meeting in 1847. At the AMEC South Carolina Conference, April 1867, he was admitted as a preacher on trial, then two days later was elected and ordained deacon. He was appointed to Griffin, GA, for three years (1867, 1868, 1869). A pioneer for the AMEC in GA, he traveled over most parts of the state. He was ordained elder at the second session of the AMEC Georgia Conference in 1868 and appointed to the church in Washigngton, Wilkes County (1870). He served as presiding elder of the Americus District (1871, 1872), then returned to the itinerant ministry as pastor at Cartersville (1874), Putnam County Circuit, No. 1 (1875), back to Washington, Wilkes County (1876, 1877). He was appointed to Greensboro (1878, 1879), to Rome (1880), and to Kingston Circuit (1881, 1882). The 1870 census stated that he could read but not write, but by 1880 he could do both; his wife Lucinda (b. c. 1832), also a native of SC, learned both reading and writing in the decade up to 1880. The couple adopted a girl named Mary. He died at his home in Cartersville, GA, on 7 August 1882.

See *Minutes of the South Carolina Conference of the African M. E. Church, 1865, 1866, 1867* (Charleston, 1867), 12, 14; 9 NGA, 49, 54; 10 NGA, 23, 37; 1870 Census, GA, Wilkes County, Washington, Pop., p. 17, dwell. 108; 1880 Census, GA, Bartow County, Cartersville, Pop., ED 1, p. 17, dwell. 171.

on Hill Street that his meeting Impresed me would be puting it very very mild." McGhee promised to visit Holloway's neighborhood to set up AME churches. In fall 1869 McGee arrived as promised, organized an AME church at Flat Shoals, and left Holloway in charge until the next annual conference. Rev. McGee then crossed into Pike County and organized Bush Chapel near a crossroads settlement then called Williamsville. Both churches became part of the AMEC's fledgling Marietta District.

Holloway formally withdrew from the MECS to join the AMEC in November 1869. Excited about the prospects of his new church, he wrote to the *Christian Recorder* a few months later, "Our Church is spreading very fast, and from present indications it will not be long before the doors of the M.E. Church, South, will be opened to us. All the white people of the neighborhood favor our Church."[99] Holloway seems to have felt the impact of the MECS leadership's postwar cooperation with the AMEC (including "a cordial welcome" and "hearty goodwill") against encroachement by the unwelcome MEC.[100]

AMEC's Education Challenge in Georgia

The AMEC ideal was a formally educated clergy teaching literate congregations, but in post-war Georgia this ideal was more aspiration than reality.[101] The AMEC church aggressively competed with other North-based Methodist denominations (MEC and African Methodist Episcopal Zion Church) to claim black members and churches from the MECS and needed more missionaries for this work than it could transfer from its Northern conferences. Men such as Elder Henry M. Turner vigorously recruited local preachers in the South. Turner would ask likely prospects, "Can you preach?" If the answer was "No," he would ask, "Can you sing and pray?" If he got an affirmative response, Turner would scrawl a license on the spot. [102]

Some of Turner's AMEC brethren were not happy with the impact of Turner's style of recruitment because they believed the limited education of these new preachers degraded the denomination's pastoral competence. The

---

[99] "A. M. Church News," *Christian Recorder*, 5 November 1870.

[100] Stowall, *Rebuilding Zion*, 12.

[101] Reginald F. Hildebrand, *The Times Were Strange and Stirring: Methodist Preachers and the Crisis of Emancipation* (Durham: Duke University Press, 1995) 62.

[102] Stephen Ward Angell, *Bishop Henry McNeal Turner and African-American Religion in the South* (Knoxville: University of Tennessee Press, 1992) 72–73.

Committee on Missions and Education at the March 1867 South Carolina Conference (which then included Georgia) proposed to improve literacy and leadership skills by recommending "in view of the small number of our Brethren in this Conference who can write intelligently, that the Conference require each Pastor to write out the minutes of some meeting, and send it quarterly to his Presiding Elder for criticism and correction, so as to advance his business knowledge, and hasten his fitness to do the business of the Church." The committee, mostly composed of preachers who had transferred from the Upper South or Northern states, spoke condescendingly of the newly ordained Georgians: "Your Committee also think the time has come when we should begin to lay the foundation of an educated ministry even among our Southern brethren."[103] A reporter covering the new AMEC Georgia Conference in May 1867 recorded some blunt debate: "Some of the members objected to ordaining members so fast. Rev. W. J. Gains made an able speech against the measure. He said they had enough of incompetent ordained ministers now, and he protested against so much liberality longer."[104]

Rev. Andrew Brown recalled of the early years of the AMEC in Georgia, "When I was Presiding Elder of the Marietta District there was but one colored man that could write his name and read the hymn book. We had to get little white boys and poor white men to act as secretaries of the Quarterly Conference.... At the Conference in Atlanta only one Secretary could be found, and he had to read his writing while it was hot, for if it ever got cold he could never have read it in the world."[105]

---

[103] *Minutes of the South Carolina Annual Conference of the African M. E. Church, 1865, 1866, 1867*, 25.

[104] *Christian Recorder*, 15 June 1867, 2. Janet Duitsman Cornelius (*Slave Missions and the Black Church in the Antebellum South* [Columbia: University of South Carolina Press, 1999] 199–200) discusses the shortage of qualified pastors in all southern black denominations in the first years after the Civil War, and quotes an Alabama Baptist: "[T]he brethren ordained me...not because of my fitness for the work, but in recognition of a necessity" (200).

[105] 7 NGA, 24. GA Annual Conference minutes show that Brown was appointed to Dalton in 1866 and 1867, then presided over the Atlanta District 1868–1871. The Marietta District first appears in minutes for the 1868 conference; perhaps due to rapid church growth around Atlanta, the Marietta District was established between conferences with Brown as *pro-tem* presiding elder until the full 1868 Conference.

Despite the limits of Holloway's education, he may have been more literate than many of his brother preachers. He certainly thought so and grumbled about Lacy Beck (his presiding elder) in 1874 that "He was not And Edgucated [man.]... Rev Lacy Beck knew that I was his superior in Lerning." Resentment at lesser men holding ecclesiastical appointments for which Holloway deemed himself better qualified is a recurring theme in his autobiography.

Holloway's Itinerant Ministry in North Georgia

In common with churches of other major nineteenth-century Methodist denominations, individual churches in the AMEC did not find and select their own pastors. Ordained AMEC preachers belonged to a regional conference that met annually. At an annual conference the presiding bishop appointed preachers for the coming year to each church or circuit (a group of small congregations who shared a pastor). Because these preachers usually moved to a new church or circuit each year they were "itinerant" and their work was "the traveling ministry." The main presumed benefit of itinerant clergy was that churches experienced the diverse spiritual "gifts and graces" of different preachers.

Bishop John M. Brown at the Fifth Session of the Georgia Conference (January 1871) appointed Holloway to his first itinerant charge, the mountainous region around Ringgold, Catoosa County, extending to the Tennessee state line.[106] By the fall of the year the weather was so cold that Holloway pleaded to be moved further south. For the next two years the bishop appointed him to the vicinity of Kingston and Adairsville in Bartow County, about halfway between Tennessee and Atlanta. Holloway found congregations in his churches to be very small because "there were not many colored people in this part of the State" and those few he characterized as "very ignorant" of their Methodist faith. There were three Methodist sects sharing the same tiny church house at Kingston—"built for any man that could preach, or wanted to preach"—but Holloway planned to secure the building for his own denomination. He had learned a strategy from Presiding Elder Albert McGee to first win over the people and the church property would follow. After many months Holloway enrolled 110 more members, and one by one the three owners of the church property donated or sold their shares until the AMEC owned the building. Holloway also embraced the AMEC emphasis on education, so that

[106] 5 GA, 18.

his congregation praised his zeal "in establishing schools on his circuit, and securing us a good teacher."[107]

Holloway Plants Roots in Coweta County

At the January 1874 annual conference, the bishop assigned Holloway southward into mid-west Georgia, to the Palmetto Circuit, Campbell County (next county to the north of Coweta). Holloway was glad to be out of the remote, chilly, mountainous, and sparsely populated north. In Palmetto Holloway met Taylor Slaughter, a local AMEC elder and prosperous farmer who owned eighty acres near the town. Twenty-two years later, after the death of Cordelia, Holloway would marry Slaughter's daughter. Holloway's youngest brother, Jacob C. Hartsfield, had settled in Palmetto where he taught in a popular school for a few years. It is not clear what drew Holloway to Coweta County, immediately south of Palmetto and Campbell County, but from 1875 he took every opportunity to make Coweta, and eventually the town of Turin, his permanent home. Five of eight of Holloway's last church appointments from 1875 to 1882 were in Coweta County.

Making Ends Meet as an Itinerant Minister

When Holloway became an itinerant Methodist preacher in 1870 he could not support his family on his minister's salary. The Georgia Conference of the African Methodist Episcopal Church required and expected its ministers to teach school, but the small tuition, even when parents paid, made little difference to Holloway's family income. Sometimes Holloway was too generous; his eldest son wrote that, in Kingston, Georgia, James Dungeon borrowed most of the money Holloway made teaching school and never paid it back. John Wesley Holloway tells us that his father at his first pastoral appointment in Kingston "worked in a shop for a man named Harris and also at Waring's Lime Kiln two miles above the town."[108] While living at Powell's Station, Coweta County, Holloway worked for George Powell, "known to the blacks as Marse George and his wife, as Miss Sallie."[109] In Senoia, Coweta County, Holloway and family took up residence in a one-room cabin on James B. Hunnicutt's lot

---

[107] *Christian Recorder*, 30 October 1873, 1; JWH, 19, 267. Holloway's teaching assistant was a Mrs. Herrington.

[108] JWH, 19.

[109] Ibid., 271.

where Holloway opened a blacksmith shop and put twelve-year-old John Wesley to work as his striker. John Wesley Holloway tells us his father "ran the shop in his own name, but Hunnicutt did the collecting."[110] The shop's profitability was mixed: "My father 'booked' a great deal and collected but very little. The result was that we had plenty to eat and wear, but nothing else."[111] At Holloway's last appointment, Sugar Hill for 1882, he opened a small blacksmith shop on the road between Barnesville and Culloden at the house of W. B. Adams.

Like other nineteenth-century working-class Georgia parents, Houston Holloway routinely exploited the labor of his children to ensure an income for the family. Freedpeople recognized the value of children's labor, whether working under supervision of parents or hired out to others. Houston H. Holloway did not have his own farm, so he hired out eldest son John Wesley four times, beginning when he was about eleven years old.

The younger Holloway recalled that in about 1877 while the family lived at Powells (a tiny settlement four miles northeast of Newnan), "My father [hired me]...to an Englishman living two miles up the RR, married to a poor white woman. There were two children, a baby and a boy about my own age. They lived on fat meat and corn bread. A skillet full of gravy with the bacon floating on top. The man could draw pictures, a thing that drew all my interest. I staid here but two or three days and ran away. I slept in the kitchen on the hearth."[112] (In slavery days, children hired to poor white families typically slept on the hearth.) Probably hired to do any and all chores for the family, John Wesley Holloway did not record why he ran away—perhaps he was homesick.

Next Houston Holloway hired his son "to a farmer living adjoining a water mill a mile or two north. I slept on the floor in the kitchen, and hoed cotton in the days. I sang all day." Young John Wesley Holloway favored a Republican political song that mocked the 1876 Democratic presidential ticket. The song was particularly attractive to the youth because it was "particularly objectionable" to his employer, a Democrat: "Tilden's the dump-cart / Hendrick's the hoss, / Wheeler's the driver / And Hays is the boss."[113] When the Holloway family

[110] Ibid., 405.

[111] Ibid., 43.

[112] Ibid., 401.

[113] Ibid., 30, 271. Rutherford B. Hayes and William A. Wheeler were on the winning Republican ticket for president and vice president in the hotly contested 1876

moved to Senoia, "I was hired to a family consisting of two old people and a grown son. At dinner time I was given food in a tin plate and told to eat in the shed outside. I set the plate as high as I could and ran home."[114]

Holloway next hired John Wesley to Senoia's town marshal, Joseph J. May, who placed him on his farm a mile from town under the supervision of his grown son, Tom. The young Holloway recalled, "I was the plough-boy. I remained here three months. I liked to plow and sing.... We moved to Turin is why I left him. Later I went back and asked for my money $1.50 per month. He said, 'Why, John, you owe me!'"[115] John Wesley Holloway did not record the outcome of this encounter but implied that he left without his money.

By hiring out his son to work, Holloway demonstrated how hiring practices changed after emancipation. Freed adults were entitled to the earnings of their children. Instead of slaveowners forcibly separating families by hire, parents negotiated their own families' hire and selected the hirer. Living and working conditions for hired freedchildren were hard to distinguish from the conditions of slavery—except that whippings by white employers were probably less common, and the consequences of running away (at least from J. W. Holloway's account) were less dire. Indeed, Holloway mentions no consequences in his own case.

Preaching Funerals

In Holloway's part of Georgia, funeral sermons were commonly delivered weeks (and sometimes months) after the deceased had been buried. Funeral services were attended by large crowds and were occasions for religious conversion as people reflected on their own mortality. One prominent event in Holloway's autobiography is the funeral of Richmond the blacksmith at Flat Shoals. Holloway wrote that "a multitude was on hand" to hear Claiborne Neal preach the funeral on a Sunday twenty-nine days after Richmond's death. Preaching a funeral was an opportunity for a preacher to display his oratorical talents, perhaps to convert sinners, and to take a collection.

---

election; Samuel J. Tilden and Thomas A. Hendricks were the losing Democratic candidates.

[114] Ibid., 271.

[115] Ibid., 402; Joseph J. May, Town Marshal, age forty-five in 1880, was enumerated in 1880 Census, GA, Coweta County, Senoia, Pop., ED 39, p. 13, dwell. 114.

Holloway left no record of his own preaching performance at funerals, but we have a letter his friend and future father-in-law, Taylor Slaughter, sent to the *Christian Recorder* describing how Holloway officiated at the funeral of Rev. Johnson Parks in Palmetto on 16 May 1875:

> At the hour of eight in the morning, great bodies of people were seen making their way to Palmetto AME Church. By eleven o'clock there was a congregation of about 1500 people assembled.... The Congregation being so large...and still increasing the speaker agreed to stand in the door as the day was pleasant.... The speaker read the hymn, "And is our loving brother fled,/ And is he numbered with the dead," which was sung with spirit, followed with prayer, etc. His text was, "Let me die the death of the righteous, and let my last end be like his" Num.23 [:] 10.... I will just say that the subject was handled to the great satisfaction of all the friends. Mr. Holloway is a young man of whom no congregation need be ashamed. Not a thing could be heard but the shouts of the triumphant Christians. It is known that many of the most obdurate sinners in the community were moved.[116]

Holloway found when he was appointed to Sugar Hill Circuit that a popular local elder Henry O'Neal held a monopoly on preaching funerals of all the men and women who died in the community. O'Neal made a circuit of the preaching places and took a "good collection from The Big crowd that followrd him." As an itinerant, Holloway moved almost every year and therefore could not hope to build a popular following like that of O'Neal. Nevertheless, Holloway could surely occasionally supplement income from his blacksmith work with funeral sermons like the one he had preached for Johnson Parks.

Dollar Money

Collecting dollar money was one of the most onerous challenges for Georgia's AME pastors. In 1868 the AMEC General Conference mandated that ministers collect one dollar from each member annually to support the church's centrally funded programs, mostly to pay bishops and officers' salaries, and pensions for retired bishops, ministers, and their widows and orphans. Without a central agency to enforce disciplined giving, the first years' receipts were small and irregular, but in 1872 the church organized a financial board to manage receipts and disbursements and appointed a traveling financial secretary

---

[116] *Christian Recorder*, 15 July 1875, 2.

who attended annual conferences throughout the country to collect the dollar money. Pressure increased on ministers like Holloway to meet their collection quotas. At the 1874 session of the North Georgia Conference, for example, "The brethren who failed in the Dollar Money were called before the altar and lectured by the Bishop."[117]

Vigorous pursuit of dollar money gradually increased the take, but the program was never as fruitful as intended. For example, the 1875 session of Holloway's North Georgia Conference reported 11,878 members, but collected only $1,661.75—merely fourteen cents per member. The printed conference minutes devoted five pages of fine print to name each person who had contributed his or her share, to acknowledge donors—and perhaps to shame those not named. The AMEC's national newspaper the *Christian Recorder* in the mid-1870s routinely printed names of members who had paid dollar money.[118] The church's unrelenting pursuit of dollar money would eventually contribute to Holloway's decision to quit the itinerant ministry.

Holloway at Annual Conferences

Like many other Methodist churches, the AMEC connection included geographically proximate churches led by presiding elders and grouped into district conferences that met quarterly. The annual conference, led by a bishop, was the regional governing body for a district that typically included many districts. At the annual conference the presiding bishop heard reports of work accomplished the past year, organized work for the coming year, disciplined wayward members, appointed committees to draft formal reports on matters interesting to the church, and collected dollar money raised by the preachers during the past year. Depending on the amount of business, nineteenth-century

---

[117] Charles Spencer Smith, *A History of the African Methodist Episcopal Church, Being a Volume Supplemental to a History of the African Methodist Episcopal Church, by Daniel Alexander Payne, D.D., LL.D., Late One of Its Bishops, Chronicling the Principal Events in the Advance of the African Methodist Episcopal Church from 1856 to 1922* (Philadelphia: Book Concern of the A. M. E. Church, 1922) 344; 2 NGA, 7. From 1844–1868, before the "dollar money" tax, ministers were charged with collecting two cents per month from each member for the same purposes.

[118] 3 NGA, 22, 23–27; Smith, *History of the African Methodist Episcopal Church*, 344. Lists of GA dollar money donors include *Christian Recorder*, 6 January 1876, 3; 24 February 1876, 3; 24 May 1877, 4. After fifty years continuous effort, dollar money collections reached a record high in 1922, averaging 63 cents per member.

AMEC annual conferences in Georgia lasted from two to ten days, with five or six days being typical.

The local AME church in the town selected to host conference would usually hold the sessions in the church's own building and arrange for local members to take visiting preachers into their homes for lodging and meals. The host church would also arrange with friendly churches of other denominations to open their pulpits for weekday and evening preaching and worship services in which visiting pastors could display their oratorical talents. Pastors of other denominations might visit the conference and take seats as guests, and the host church might invite local municipal leaders, or if conference was in Atlanta, the governor, to hear the bishop preach or to listen to the most interesting reports.

AME annual conferences were a great public display of respectability, talent, and power that advanced the church's prestige in the broader local community and confirmed its dignity and influence in the minds of church members. Railroads usually sold tickets at half-fare to ordained clergy traveling to and from conference. Local newspapers invariably treated the conference as a newsworthy item and published preaching schedules so that interested readers could attend. Since most newspaper subscribers were white, an AMEC annual conference presented many readers a rare and socially acceptable opportunity to hear black men preach and lead a worship service.

Committee names suggest the topics of religious, social, political, and economic interest to the church conference: "On Finance," "On Temperance," "On Missions," "On the State of the Country and Immigration," "On Homesteads, Deeds and Church Property," and "On Railroads" (which examined racial segregation and civil rights violations in railroad passenger cars). Holloway served on committees for education and for complaints and charges against ministers. In 1874 he sat on a committee examining ministers' progress in their mandatory study programs (his committee found the candidates deficient and recommended they be continued on trial).[119] Holloway's proudest committee moment was at the 1881 North Georgia Conference when he read the report on "The State of the Country" to an audience that included visiting Georgia Governor Alfred H. Colquitt.[120]

---

[119] 1 NGA, 5 and 6; 4 NGA, 7.

[120] I could locate neither a copy of the minutes of the Eighth Session of the North Georgia Conference (1881), nor a newspaper account with details of Holloway's report. Colquitt was an active member of the MECS and interested in all things Methodist.

The last event of each conference, much anticipated and sometimes feared, was when the bishop read the pastoral appointments for the coming year. The secretary of the Third North Georgia Conference added a touch of humor to this moment, recording: "At 7 o'clock the Bishop read out the appointments, each brother seemed to meet his doom with courage bold; not a murmur was heard."[121]

Holloway Refuses the Bishop's Appointment

Holloway murmured at his appointment in January 1875 at the Second Session North Georgia Conference when he was assigned to Cave Spring, a new circuit within the Marietta District located in Floyd County between Rome, Georgia, and the Alabama border. Holloway wrote, "To that place I refused to go." Holloway does not explain why he rebelled against that appointment, but there were two likely reasons. A layman at the conference had told Holloway that Presiding Elder Lacy Beck was "going to send [Holloway] as far back up the State Rode as he could." Holloway believed that "Rev Lacy Beck knew that I was his superior in Lerning And He got the Idea into his head that I was trying to get His place as presiding Elder." Already resenting Beck, Holloway was predisposed to resist any appointment that appeared to carry out Beck's threat. Second, after three consecutive appointments to the remote mountains of Catoosa and Bartow counties, Holloway's 1874 appointment to Palmetto had finally placed him closer to family members and to familiar places he regarded as home. An appointment to Cave Spring perhaps seemed to banish him again to the wilderness. By refusing an appointment, Holloway risked expulsion from the conference, or at least punishment of not getting an appointment for the next year. Although no disciplinary action appeared in the conference minutes, Holloway would not go unpunished.

Holloway took up the blacksmith's hammer once again, but he reconsidered his disobedience. He decided to build new church congregations in Campbell County, which up to that time had been part of the Palmetto Circuit. Holloway must have moved fast to define the bounds of his own new ministry and to persuade the presiding elder of the Griffin District, Joseph A. Wood, to endorse and establish this appointment before the adjourned conference minutes were printed. When the appointments for 1875 were published, they showed

[121] 3 NGA, 9.

Cave Spring given to another preacher while Holloway was appointed to his own newly formed Fairburn Circuit in Campbell County.[122]

Six months later, the Griffin District Quarterly Conference met on 27 June 1875, Bishop T. M. D. Ward presiding. The "Committee on Charges and Complaints" inquired into what should be done with Holloway "for not going to [his] appointment" at Cave Spring. At the recommendation of the committee, Bishop Ward reprimanded Holloway—but that was not to be his only punishment.[123] Holloway worked hard to redeem his reputation in the eyes of his conference hierarchy. When he attended the next annual conference in December 1875, he delivered twelve dollars "dollar money" collected from eleven members and one friend of the church. This was quite a triumph because his collection exceeded the dollar money from eleven of the fifteen appointments in Presiding Elder Woods's Griffin District. The December 1875 conference recognized the vitality of Holloway's new churches by retroactively establishing Fairburn Circuit with four sites (Fairburn, Red Oak, Cook's Chapel, and Campbellton), but the bishop appointed someone else as pastor of the new circuit for the coming year. Holloway was left without appointment for 1876, surely because of his prior disobedience.[124]

Holloway finally worked his way back into the bishop's good graces by accepting appointment about May 1876 to Newnan, Coweta County—the previous minister having failed to complete the year. Holloway undoubtedly welcomed this appointment since he had chosen to make his home in Coweta County. His next four appointments (1877–1880) were in Coweta County, followed by a year near Eatonton, Putnam County, and finally to the Sugar Hill Circuit, Upson County, very near where he had been born.

Holloway Quits the Itinerant Ministry

All seemed well for Holloway's standing with his presiding elder when the Forsyth District Conference met in April 1882. Holloway was elected one of two secretaries and appointed to two committees. As the conference concluded the members voted to raise $900 for the salary of Presiding Elder Andrew W.

---

122 2 NGA, 16, 17.

123 *Christian Recorder*, 5 August 1875, 8.

124 3 NGA, 11, 15, 21, 27. Holloway seems to have taken every preaching opportunity to keep himself favorably noticed. For example, a writer to the *Christian Recorder* reported Holloway preaching at Newnan Circuit Camp Meeting on 29 July 1875 (*Christian Recorder*, 14 October 1875, 8).

Lowe and nominated Holloway for district steward—whose primary duty was to collect the presiding elder's salary from the various churches in the district.[125] Perhaps it was at this quarterly conference that Lowe persuaded Holloway to take 111 copies of the North Georgia Annual Conference Minutes and sell them to his people at ten cents a copy.

The last Forsyth District quarterly conference for 1882 convened at Liberty Chapel, Upson County, with Presiding Elder Andrew W. Lowe in the chair. Holloway reported his work. Although he had greatly expanded the membership of his churches, he had not collected much money. Presiding Elder Lowe called for his money from the sale of the conference minutes, but Holloway had been unable to sell even one copy. Lowe hinted that Holloway would get no appointment until the eleven dollars and ten cents were in his hands, regardless of whether Holloway could sell them or not. Holloway wrote, "From heare I began to gat on to it"—meaning he understood that his future in the ministry was in jeopardy. According to Holloway's account, this matter of the unsold conference minutes led him to leave the traveling ministry and settle finally in Turin, Coweta County. The un-sellable conference minutes were, indeed, one cause of a rift between Holloway and his church leaders, but he also failed to account for some dollar money, a problem he omitted from his autobiography.

At the January 1883 session of the Macon, Georgia, Conference (newly formed out of part of the North Georgia Conference), the judiciary committee read two letters containing separate charges against Holloway. The first letter undoubtedly concerned the unsold conference minutes, about which the committee reported, "we recommend that his appointment be withheld until said debts are paid." The second letter alleged there was "dollar money collected by him in his charge and not reported to the Conference." On recommendation of the committee, Holloway received no appointment.[126] Perhaps in fall 1883, as time approached for the next annual conference, Holloway sent $11.10 to Rev. Andrew W. Lowe with the letter of resignation he recited in his autobiography. However, the matter of the dollar money festered for almost seven years until Holloway sent another letter enclosing fifteen dollars to the Eighth Session of the Macon Conference in November 1889. The minutes recorded that "On

[125] *Christian Recorder*, 29 June 1882, 2.

[126] 1 MACON, 13, 23, 30.

motion, the money was received. Bro. Holloway was exonerated from the charge and his character 'passed.'"[127]

Letters to the Christian Recorder

When Holloway joined the AMEC he found a church for black people organized and run by black men, but he also discovered a newspaper, the *Christian Recorder*, edited and published by black men in Philadelphia. The *Recorder* discussed the religious, political, economic, and social interests of black Americans. For the self-taught Holloway, whose access to secular literature had been primarily through James C. Freeman's subscription to the *Savannah Republican* and whatever books and pamphlets Freeman may have had in his study, the *Recorder* must have opened a window on a whole new intellectual world. Within months of joining the AMEC, Holloway began to write for the *Recorder*. His first effort was not well received. Perhaps only half-legible and only half-intelligible to the overworked office staff, Holloway's piece was noticed in the 10 September 1870 issue: "Important items for Recorder from...[six correspondents including] Rev. H.H. Holloway...have been received at this office. These articles require to be re-written, which the publisher has not time to do, and the Editor being absent, they must necessarily be laid aside." Eight weeks later the editor was back at the office and wrote in the *Recorder*'s 5 November 1870, issue, "Some of the following 'News' has been in the office for several weeks: owing to our absence, and by overburden of the Publisher, it has never appeared. We print it now." Among this old news was a short extract from Holloway's letter: "Rev. H. H. Holloway writes from Flat Shoals; (will our brother always tell us the State?) 'Our Church is spreading very fast, and from present indications it will not be long before the doors of the M.E. Church, South, will be opened to us. All the white people of the neighborhood favor our Church.'" The same issue included an obituary for Holloway's mother-in-law, Cherry Thrash, signed by him, but written in a style that suggests someone else (perhaps a member of the Thrash family) composed it.[128]

From 1870 through 1883 Holloway wrote sixteen letters published by the *Christian Recorder* in whole or in part. Several of the letters are so unlike the

---

[127] 8 MACON, 15. Holloway served his last itinerant appointment at Sugar Hill (1882) as a member of the North Georgia Conference, out of which the Macon Conference was formed.

[128] *Christian Recorder*, 10 September 1870, 4; 5 November 1870, 2, 4.

language of his manuscript autobiography that Holloway perhaps wrote with a collaborator, or the letters were heavily edited at the *Recorder*.[129] One letter that shows neither sign of collaboration nor heavy editing, published 4 July 1878 (reprinted as Appendix D), is a fascinating rehearsal for Holloway's autobiography written two decades later, both in content and as evidence of his evolution as a writer. The letter gives a few details not told elsewhere of Holloway's emancipation in June 1865 and of his early work as a licensed exhorter and preacher for the MECS and AMEC in the late 1860s. Holloway recounts his career in the church, his great harvest of souls, and the shortage of preachers like himself in the field. The letter also shows Holloway glossing over a career hiccup—calling his refusal to go to Cave Springs a "respite of five months" and boasting that he had never been "marked" (formally charged with misconduct).[130]

In the same letter the *Recorder* staff corrected most of Holloway's idiosyncratic spelling and punctuation, but the letter includes some of Holloway's pet linguistic mannerisms and quirks that would appear in his autobiography, such as referring to himself as "your humble correspondent," and spelling the article "an" as "and" (one example in the letter's second sentence escaped the *Recorder*'s proofreader). Holloway could not decide whether to refer to himself in the first person singular, first person plural, or the third person, intermingling all three usages in this letter. By the time he would start his autobiography twenty years later, he had cultivated an effective first person narration.[131] The same letter gives us an earlier version of the story of Holloway's accidental exposure to the AMEC when he met Rev. Robert Alexander in Griffin in 1867. This was a tale he seems to have sanded and buffed with each retelling, especially one sentence, crafted with a deliberately ironic twist. The 1878 version reads, "On going out he found a man by that name, but not the

---

[129] List of all sixteen letters is on p.9 n.16. Letters in the *Christian Recorder* in which this editor finds most evidence of collaboration or editing are "Ignorance in the Ministry," 10 May 1877, 1; "The Ministry," 25 October 1877, 1; "Our Membership," 12 December 1878, 1; 5 November 1874, 4. Cherry Thrash's obituary (5 November 1870, 2), although published over Holloway's name, was probably entirely written by someone experienced in that genre.

[130] Appendix D includes the full text of this letter.

[131] After writing about 18,000 words of the autobiography in first-person singular, Holloway reverted to a mixture of first person singular and plural; for example, writing of himself, "We left the work in the fall of 1877 we think much Improved" (p.155).

man he wished to see." The polished autobiography version reads, "he was not the man that I was hunting for but he was the man I found."

Given Holloway's pride in his own literacy, he assumed any African Methodist committed to the welfare of his church and people would support the *Recorder*. In two 1876 letters titled "A Friend Shut Out," Holloway thundered his wholehearted advocacy of the *Recorder*. He explained that he had read the paper since 1869 and had tried to get the North Georgia Conference to make each itinerant minister report annually in conference the number of subscribers in his churches; however, Rev. Scipio H. Robinson and others would not support his resolution. Holloway doubted that there were even ten subscribers among all the preachers in the North Georgia Conference. He labeled non-subscribing preachers "haters of the *Recorder*" and urged the General Conference to count subscribers as part of the annual church statistics.[132]

Four months later Holloway ruefully admitted that he had failed to pay his own subscription. As self-imposed penance he pledged to send all the money he might have spent on tobacco (which he did not actually use "in any form") to the AMEC publishing house until he had paid all he owed, and then continue the same weekly payment to buy books "until I got as many as I needed."[133] When Holloway took charge of Wesley Chapel on the Newnan Circuit in 1877, he found the Sunday school bereft of books and a choir with no hymnals. True to his promise to support the AMEC Book Concern, he raised more than sixteen dollars and bought what the church needed.[134] In Holloway's churches, striving for literacy was mandatory.

Holloway put his discontent with church leadership before the church in the 19 October 1876 issue of the *Christian Recorder*. He wrote, "we have several men exalted to many high positions in Georgia that were inadequate to the task given them. In the first place they had too much self and not enough Christ. Thirdly I have heard a great deal of pets in the Conference who have proved themselves unworthy." Then Holloway complained about the hardship imposed on itinerant ministers by annual moves: "[M]en ought to be allowed to stay on circuits and stations from 3 to 4 years when they are liked by the people and are doing good work."[135]

---

[132] *Christian Recorder*, 24 February 1876, 2; 20 April 1876, 7.

[133] Ibid., 10 August 1876, 1.

[134] Ibid., 24 May 1877, 4.

[135] Ibid., 19 October 1876, 6.

In letters to the *Christian Recorder*, Holloway boldly complained about ignorant clergy. In one 1877 letter, titled "Ignorance in the Ministry," he indicted Southern churches for lax standards in licensing preachers. Holloway pointed to an urban Baptist church with 300 members of whom twenty-three were preachers. He knew of an AMEC circuit where sixteen out of forty male members were preachers or exhorters; "Not one of them can write a letter" or "read a chapter in the New Testament, so it could be understood," added Holloway.[136] In his next letter, titled "The Ministry," Holloway urged that a candidate for the ministry "should be inwardly moved by the Holy Spirit to preach" (although he did not explain how church leaders could discern a candidate's inward spiritual motivation). Ministers should be able to preach Christ's message and understand the articles of faith of their church well enough to defend them in debate against theological "assault" from non-members.[137]

Holloway's last letter to the *Christian Recorder*, published 18 October 1883, complained that senior church leaders exploited and impoverished itinerant ministers. Although this letter never revealed that Holloway had recently left the itinerant ministry, this public airing of financial grievances with his church largely explains why he quit. Holloway claimed that the AMEC General Conference had set presiding elders' salaries at $400 per year, but at local quarterly conferences presiding elders might assess each of their circuits and stations between $10 and $25, then extract that money from the pastors in charge if the membership did not contribute enough to cover the assessments. When gifts of "boots, or pants, or a hat" and travel expenses were included, Holloway claimed a presiding elder's support could total $1500. Burdened with collecting these assessments, on top of raising dollar money for the bishops, "a preacher in charge, having a wife and children, with wants too numerous to mention, must suffer. And if the pastor does not collect the assessments, he is sent, as I have heard them say, at the next annual conference, to a place where the dogs will not bark at him." Holloway claimed that the AMEC did not reward ability, leaving "many able men at the rear of the itinerant host" but advancing "many a weak yet ambitious aspirant" to the front. Holloway told the *Recorder*'s readers they should not be surprised that 40,000 members of the AMEC in the previous fourteen years had joined the Baptists, the MEC, and the CMEC "all on account of bad management."

---

[136] Ibid., 10 May 1877, 1.

[137] Ibid., 25 October 1877, 1.

Holloway's letter shows that he could be both highly critical of and loyal to his church at the same time. He urged internal reform but never threatened to leave the church. Two of Holloway's old adversaries took more drastic action. Presiding Elder Lacy Beck (whom Holloway had characterized as inferior in learning to himself) failed to deliver his dollar money in 1875, so the bishop stripped him of his appointment. Beck led three other disgruntled former AMEC members in 1878 to found their own short-lived Methodist denomination, the Independent Southern Methodist Church, in protest against the burdensome dollar money tax levied to support the bishops.[138] Twenty years later, in 1898, William H. Harris (who as Holloway's presiding elder many years before had tried to extort a suit of clothes from him), was expelled from the Georgia Conference for rebellion against the church. Although the conference minutes do not give details, Harris had probably joined the breakaway Independent African Methodist Episcopal Church, founded in 1897 by ministers who disputed with their AMEC district superintendents over church administration. Unlike these rebellious AME preachers, Holloway was no schismatic.[139]

Holloway's Sabbath School Picnic Critiqued by the Recorder

Newspapers occasionally noted Holloway's public appearances outside the pulpit. When Presiding Elder J. A. Wood of Griffin District convened a special church meeting 10 May 1878 to accept a generous gift of land and a schoolhouse from a wealthy local black man, Holloway gave a fifteen-minute lecture on "Reformation of Manners"—one of three speakers to address "a large crowd."[140] On another occasion, Holloway reported the success of his Sunday school picnic in Newnan Circuit, 30 June 1877, attended by more than 100 children, where Presiding Elder J. A. Wood presented a fine dress as a prize to the girl who could recite the most memorized verses, and a Bible to the boy who could do the same.[141]

---

[138] Ibid., 9 May 1878, 30 May 1878.

[139] Ibid., 27 January 1898. About the same time that the AMEC expelled Harris, the church expelled several other preachers in his geographic area—FL and south GA—for rebellion, specifically for having joined the Independent African Methodist Episcopal Church.

[140] *Christian Recorder*, 27 June 1878, 2.

[141] Ibid., 2 August 1877, 4.

In summer 1878 Holloway forwarded to the *Christian Recorder* a clipping from the Coweta County newspaper *Farm and Home*, in which a white correspondent described "the Sabbath School pic-nic by the colored people" attended by between 500 and 1,000 people, including a hundred white picnickers. Rev. Holloway was in charge of the exercises; according to the reporter, Holloway opened the singing and prayer, introduced the seven speakers, introduced Miss Julia Lockett ("colored") of Griffin (who read an essay), and delivered the closing remarks "in a humorously pleasant way." The speakers and their topics provided a notable contrast. The first three were local white men who spoke of the value of "Early religious training, education, economy, the appreciation and not abuse of freedom and the necessity of industry and perseverance in all the transactions of life." Such speeches by white men lecturing freedpeople on the awesome responsibilities of liberty and the necessity of work had been standard fare since 1865 and may have been politely if not enthusiastically received. The next four speakers were black men (including Presiding Elder J. A. Wood), whose addresses "were of a literary character, interspersed with various matters of a general interest." The black speakers aimed to elevate, educate, or entertain the people—not to lecture them. After the men spoke, Miss Julia Lockett read her essay, unfortunately not described by the reporter. Finally, barbecue, "cakes, jellies pies and all other good things" were served, with a separate table provided for white attendees.[142]

The white reporter was sure that such splendid gatherings would show "the colored people who are their true friends" and better prepare them to "fill the [subordinate] place that fortune has placed them [in]." The Philadelphia-based editor of the *Christian Recorder* was not so sure, and in comments almost as condescending as the white speakers at the picnic, disapproved the segregated eating arrangements: "It is not, of course, what we would like." He also criticized "the complete absence of politics in the speeches" and insisted that "whenever two or three meet together…they ought to talk politics." Reminding readers that segregation used to be practiced in the North, he insisted that Southern black people must declare a twenty-year war on caste just as their Northern brethren had done to rid the North of "separate tables, carriages, cars &c."[143] With local white landowners lecturing Coweta County black folk on what was best for them, it might have been understandable if lectures from a Northern black

---

[142] Ibid., 22 August 1878, 2.

[143] Ibid.

editor safely above the Mason Dixon line had hit a Southern nerve, but Holloway seemed to share the editor's optimism. He praised his beloved *Recorder* for "combating with the four last giants or enemies of the human race—Ignorance, oppression, Negro hatred, and caste" which he wrote "are on the retreat towards hell from whence they came."[144] Observing the fledgling Jim Crow South of 1878, the *Recorder*'s editor and Holloway both underestimated the depth of white population's personal investment in racial hierarchy. A quarter-century after this segregated picnic, no lesser celebrity than AME Bishop Henry M. Turner, longtime fighter for black civil rights, lectured to packed houses in Georgia—with separate seating for white visitors—and admitted defeat, advocating black people's return to Africa, declaring, "this is the white man's country and always will be."[145]

Death of Cordelia

About 1887 Holloway's wife, Cordelia, fell at her washtub with a stroke from which she never recovered. She lingered, increasingly bedridden, for seven years. [146] Cordelia Holloway died 3 April 1894. Houston Holloway was devastated, writing, "of all the pangs of sorror that I was ever cald upon to endure this was the most severe. I realey wanted to Die in her place." At Holloway's request, Rev. A. L. Shaw, Cordelia's pastor for four years, preached her funeral within two days of her death. All witnesses (neighbors, eldest son, and Holloway himself) agreed that husband and wife had not exchanged a harsh word in their thirty years of marriage. [147]

---

[144] *Christian Recorder*, 12 December 1878, 1.

[145] Thomaston *Times*, 24 March 1899 (reports Bishop Turner's lecture to racially segregated audience in Thomaston); Thomaston *Times*, 8 June 1900 (quote).

[146] JWH, 405.

[147] *Christian Recorder*, 24 May 1894, 5.

Holloway Speaks at Fisk in 1894

Only weeks after Cordelia's death, Holloway turned from what he had called the "sadest day of my lief" to the "proudest day of my life," attending commencement exercises at Fisk University in Nashville to see his son John Wesley Holloway graduate with a Bachelor of Arts degree. At the alumni dinner, Holloway was asked to speak. As reported to the *American Missionary* magazine,

> Mr. Holloway told of a letter he received from [Fisk] President Cravath when he felt compelled, owing to the hard times, to have his son John, who had been in the University only four months, return home. Mr. Holloway, being unable to decipher the president's [notoriously illegible] writing…asked a Southern minister of his village to read it. The minister read the letter, and advised him not to waste his son's time with a college course; this did not prove good logic to Mr. Holloway, as he observed that this minister's son was taking a college course of study without wasting his time.

(John Wesley Holloway identified the "Southern minister" to whom Holloway showed Cravath's letter as Holloway's neighbor and employer, Rev. James B. Hunnicutt; "Hunnicutt had been after pa to get me home from the first, [saying] 'There is no use in going to school studying the dead languages. I spent 20 yrs. at it, and it didn't do me any good.'"[148]) Holloway continued,

> Not being satisfied with the minister's advice I went that night down into the woods and knelt beside a hickory-tree, with the letter spread out, and prayed as follows: "Lord here is a letter from Dr. Cravath; I suppose you know him. Here is his letter which I cannot read, but I am told that you can read as well in the dark as you can in the light. Dr. Cravath says for me to do all I can for my son, and look to you for the balance. Now I cannot do anything for my son; if he is to be aided you must do all, for one thing is certain I have no money; you have left none with me, and I do not know with whom you have left it. Now, dear Lord, I leave this whole matter with you. In your own way and time do for my son what seems best. I cannot do anything. I ask it all for Jesus' sake. Amen." I repeated about the same

[148] Both of Hunnicutt's sons, Fred and Tom, attended University of Georgia, but J. W. Holloway alleged that they "came home from college, at Athens, Ga., avowed infidels, the occasion of great distress to the community, the church, and his [Hunnicutt's] parents, especially to the mother, who was very devout" (JWH, 67, 211).

> prayer the following night, and then left it all with the Lord. In about two weeks I received a letter from my son stating that some one had put two hundred and fifty dollars in the bank at Nashville to his account to aid him through college. I considered it the direct answer to my prayer. This is the proudest day of my life to see my son John graduate from Fisk University. May the blessing of God rest upon it and upon the Association which founded and fosters it.[149]

That snippet from Holloway's dinner speech at Fisk is the longest reported example of his extemporaneous speaking style. His ironic and humorous exposition of the earthly foibles of men contrasts effectively with his reverent but intimate approach to God.

The Sam Hose Lynching, a New Brick Church, and Holloway Buys a House

Sam Hose died on 23 April 1899 near Newnan, Coweta County, Georgia, in one the largest orgies of uninhibited sadism ever perpetrated by white people. The torture, mutilation, and immolation of Hose by perhaps two thousand savages—a "Mob Transformed Into Inhuman Fiends" said the Milledgeville *Union Recorder*—sent shockwaves of horror nationwide. Part of the lynch mob that arrived too late to enjoy burning Hose tramped to Palmetto and hung local preacher Elijah Strickland from a tree. Holloway, foreman of a blacksmith shop in downtown Newnan at the time, ignores this event in his autobiography, but he did react publicly at the time. As president of the preachers' association at Mt. Zion AME Church, Holloway and the licensed preachers with their pastor Rev. John Harmon, wrote an indirect response to the events and sent it to the Newnan *Herald & Advertiser* three weeks later. While some white-published newspapers reported that the violence prompted many black residents—even property owners—to flee Newnan and Palmetto, there is no evidence that fear or intimidation possessed Holloway or the members of Mount Zion AME Church.[150]

---

149 Moore, "Southern Field Notes," 357–58.

150 *Union Recorder*, 25 April 1899, 6. The most recent and thorough examination of the Sam Hose lynching is Edwin T. Arnold, *What Virtue There Is in Fire: Cultural Memory and the Lynching of Sam Hose* (Athens, GA: University of Georgia Press, 2009). Arnold, 130, cites contemporary newspaper reports that black residents, even property owners, were moving out of the area. Gregory Mixon argues that some Macon and Atlanta newspapers, after the Hose lynching, hinted that Rev. H. M. Turner had incited a conspiracy of black men to (vaguely) "stand together" against whites—and that this

Perhaps class consciousness—and trust in his carefully cultivated respectability in the eyes of white people—explain Holloway's apparent non-response to the Hose lynching. Holloway's pastor at Mount Zion AME Church, John Harmon, certainly attributed outrageous crimes to a distinct class. On the Sunday morning Hose was captured, Harmon reportedly told his congregation: "[T]he class of negroes that are giving us trouble—who debauch homes—who outrage women, and thus heap disgrace upon our race as a whole, belong to the lazy, indolent, loafing element; that they never visit the Sabbath-school or church; that they never have a decent suit of clothes, because they will not work." Hose was a migrant farm worker probably not personally known to Holloway or any other member of the congregation. The subsequent lynching of Strickland—a local preacher in Palmetto—may have been harder for Harmon to square with his class-based and religious analysis of criminality, but Strickland's lynching received not even oblique reference in later utterances from the church; whereas, Strickland may have been targeted merely because he *was* a black preacher.[151]

The day after the lynching, Governor Allen D. Candler issued a statement through the Atlanta *Constitution* in which he all but blamed everyone in the black community for the atrocity because "they owed it to their race to exhaust every means to bringing Holt [*sic*] to justice." Black leaders, said Candler, "must realize that in order to merit and receive the protection of the community, they must show a willingness to at least aid in protecting the community against the lawless element of their own race.... They must denounce crime and aid in bringing criminals to justice.... To secure protection against lawless whites, they must show a disposition to protect the white people against lawless blacks." In other words, if law-abiding blacks did not police their own communities then they could expect to be lynched with impunity by lawless mobs.[152]

Eleven days after the lynching and ten days after Governor Candler's press statement, at the regular monthly meeting of the ministers of Mt. Zion AME Church in Newnan, H. H. Holloway, association president, and Rev. John Harmon, secretary, drafted and signed a set of resolutions. The resolutions may

---

kind of talk by black preachers had emboldened the alleged rapist and killer Hose ("Henry McNeal Turner versus the Tuskegee Machine: Black Leadership in the Nineteenth Century," *Journal of Negro History* 79/4 [Autumn 1994]: 372–73).

[151] [Newnan, GA] *Herald & Advertiser*, 5 May 1899, 2; Mixon, "Hentry McNeal Turner versus the Tuskegee Machine," 380, n. 24.

[152] Atlanta *Constitution*, 24 April 1899.

incorporate the consensus of Holloway and the local preachers, but the composition is almost certainly the work of Harmon, an accomplished writer who would edit a number of church newspapers and gain a reputation as "one of the most forceful writers in his church."[153] The document they drafted on 5 May 1899 did not mention Sam Hose, lynching, or Governor Candler, but it responded directly to some of Candler's assertions.

Holloway and his local AMEC ministers began, "[W]e condone no sort of crime, neither would we shield the criminal from just punishment. We have no toleration for those who heap disgrace upon our race by the commission of crime, and denounce in strongest terms those creatures who are so depraved by nature and become so reckless as to invade the sanctity of the home and defile the women of our section." Having satisfied Governor Candler's demand for a denunciation of depraved black rapists (with no denunciation of depraved white lynchers), Holloway and his ministers asserted, "We believe the gospel of the Son of God and the teaching of the sacred scriptures by His servants will do more to check lawlessness and crime than all other agencies combined." They resolved to "give more attention to the training of the young—in the school and the home as well as in the church—and that we teach more on the line of industrial and moral training." Finally they called upon "our ministers and teachers to lay aside all petty jealousies of church and race, and that we join our efforts with those of the white race to uphold the majesty of the law, and build up the industrial and commercial interests of our common country, that peace and prosperity may abound within our borders."[154] This plan was pure Booker T. Washington and Christianity.

Less than two years after the Hose lynching, Holloway and Mt. Zion, far from being intimidated and cowed, each invested more permanently in their town and community of Newnan. First, Holloway bought a home for his family in 1900: "I enjoyed good helth and I Bought property no 33 Ray Street."[155] He had built a home in Turin in 1891 that he owned until to his death, but this house in Newnan was probably more convenient while he worked as blacksmith

[153] Biographical sketch of Harmon in Richard R. Wright, *Centennial Encyclopaedia of the African Methodist Episcopal Church* (Philadelphia: Book Concern of the A.M.E. Church, 1916) 108–109, accessible at Documenting the American South, http://docsouth.unc.edu/church/wright/menu.html (accessed 9 January 2015).

[154] *Herald & Advertiser*, 12 May 1899, 3.

[155] The editor visited 33 Ray Street in May 2012 and found an empty lot. Neighbors said the house had been torn down many years ago.

foreman for Dent Manufacturing. The second event, in early 1901, was the proposal by Mt. Zion AME's new young pastor, Rev. Charles A. Wingfield, to build a brick church. Brick churches, in contrast to wooden churches, suggested permanence, strength, and success. Holloway's autobiography tells the dramatic story of how first the money then the building were raised, and how Bishop Henry M. Turner gave the sermon as the church laid the cornerstone. Holloway does not say he was the leading workman for this effort, but his name is first in the list of building committee members on the old stone embedded in one corner of the present-day church building.

Work progressed fast enough on the brick edifice that Mt. Zion AME Church was ready to host the Second Atlanta Annual Conference 17–23 December 1901. The conference minutes spoke with great pride of the new building: "Newnan station is safe for all time. A good brick building with new settees, plastered, with electric lights, with a membership of 128 and all of this work paid for except $765, means very much to African Methodism in this section. For twenty-five years we have done literally nothing at this point. We can but say out of the fullness of our hearts, God be praised and men and women be thanked for what has been done."[156] In the church's triumph, there was no audible echo of Sam Hose's lynching.

Holloway's Last Years

Holloway insisted on demonstrating that he was a concerned and responsible citizen. In 1907 he drafted a letter to the mayor and city council of Newnan to report that "As a law abiding Citisen of Newnan and Coweta County Please allow me to Call your attention to And Evill that had a Small beginning that is growing fast and will Soon be of Trubble if it is not Cheeked That is there is a Soda water and Ice Creem Salune runnng over heare on west washington Street That is groing fast into a nuasance Thre are a Croud of the ruff Element and they are" (the letter fragment ends). We do not know if Holloway actually sent a version of this letter, but it suggests that he may have occasionally corresponded with his municipal government.[157]

---

[156] 2 ATLANTA, 60.

[157] H. H. Holloway letter (fragment) to A. R. Burdett, 19 May 1907, Houston Hartsfield Holloway papers, 1894–1932, MSS84205, Library of Congress Manuscript Division Washington, DC.

After thirteen years as foreman for Dent Manufacturing in Newnan, and after serving as a class leader at Mt. Zion AME Church during the same time, Holloway moved back to Turin in 1909 to work at his blacksmith trade. In early November 1917 the *Newnan Herald's* correspondent from Turin reported, "Rev. P. A. Holloway, a colored minister of the Methodist church and a well-known blacksmith of Turin, died on Wednesday of last week. He was an industrious negro, and well thought of by both races." We cannot now know whether the reporter garbled Holloway's name or the printer's compositor could not read the reporter's handwriting. John Wesley Holloway recorded that his father died on Tuesday, 23 October 1917. He was probably buried in Tranquil Cemetery, near Turin, where lay Cordelia and daughters Mary Jane, Cordelia Aschah, and Eunice Irene; sons Edwin Stanton, Theodore H., and Henry Turner; nephew Tommie Hartsfield, and perhaps others of the family. If there were ever markers for the Holloway graves at Tranquil Cemetery, they are gone.[158]

[158] *Newnan Herald*, 2 November 1917, 6; JWH, 167, lists family members buried in Tranquil Cemetery.

Autobiography of Houston Hartsfield Holloway

Chapter One

Family, Childhood, and Youth in Slavery

Biography of lief of H. H. Holloway. My reader will know that about the time that I bornd scarsley any colord people could read or write and very few whites in the Rurall sections of the cuntry.[1] I was Bord about the first day of May 1845[2] on the plantation of Mr Henry Hartsfield[3] in Upson County Georgia 4 miles north of Thomaston. My grand farthers name was Phillip though he was sould severrall years befour I was bornd.[4] My grand Mothers name was Suasan.[5] She was noted for her energy in evry thing that [she] had to do as a slave. My Mothers name was Louwezer.[6] My Farther was far above the Average slave

---

[1] See p. 20, n.39, for discussion of literacy rates.

[2] Probably 1844. See pp. 10-11.

[3] Henry Hartsfield (1772–1847). Born in Wake County, NC, 30 December 1772. By age twenty-three, Henry Hartsfield had moved to the Clouds Creek community of Oglethorpe County, GA. There he married Mary (Polly) Olive in 1796. After Mary died in December 1827, he married her sister, Elizabeth Olive, in 1829. During winter 1834–1835, Henry Hartsfield moved his household from Oglethorpe to a farm in Upson County, GA. County Tax Digests indicate his death in 1847; a genealogy website asserts that he died on 5 October 1847 but cites no source. See Mrs. Herschel W. Smith, comp., *Historical Collections of the Georgia Chapters, Daughters of the American Revolution, Volume V: Marriage Records of Greene County, Georgia (1787–1875), and Oglethorpe County, Georgia (1795–1852)* (Atlanta: John T. Hancock, 1949, repr. Baltimore, MD: Genealogical Publishing Co., 2001) 173; TUA, Upson County Tax Digests 1846–1848. "Culpepper Connections! The Culpepper Family History Site", "Henry Hartsfield" page at http://gen.culpepper.com/ss/p45961.htm (viewed 2 September 2012).

[4] Philip (b. c. 1798); see pp. 185-186 for biography.

[5] Susan (c. 1800–1862); see pp. 186-187 for biography.

[6] Louisa Hartsfield (c. 1821–c. July 1846), Holloway's mother, was one of Susan's twin daughters probably born about 1821 in Oglethorpe County, GA. Holloway told Floyd the miller that his mother's name was Louisa Hartsfield. Louisa joined her mother's church, Bethesda Baptist, in August 1840 by relating her experience of grace.

Reather Bright complecttion long Black hair about five feet six Inches In hight. he always wore a tall Beaver hat and a Brord Cloth Suat. he was very entertaining in conversation and Reather Impresive in his baring[7] [and] In intellegence whos name was Nepton Holloway.[8] he could read and write and was noted for his high sence of honor and his morrall carrecter. by him my mother give birth to four children, John Westly, Green, Houston and Jacob.[9]

Now about the time of Broo Jacob was bornd Old Henry hartsfeild died.[10] Perhaps inside of 12 mounths after his Death all of the slaves had to be sould and inside of same yeare my Good mother died. The sale came of and the colord folks on the old plantation ware scaterd to the four winds.[11] A man by the name of Charles[12] be longing to old Need Holloway[13] had married my grand mother

---

Louisa died between 27 June and 25 July 1846. See Richard Hartsfield inventory; Bethesda Baptist Church, Minute Book 1, 80, 104.

[7] The manuscript's first page ends here with this note: "N[ota] B[ene] this Page is a reproduction as the first one was lost while I was down with a hard spell of sicness in summer of 1908. H. H. Holloway."

[8] Neptune Holloway (c. 1820–c. 21 August 1861); see pp. 187-188, for biography.

[9] See pp. 188-192 for biographies of John Wesley Hartsfield (c. 1840–prior to 1888), Green Holloway (c. 1842–c. 1884), and Jacob C. Hartsfield (1846–1926).

[10] Jacob was born about April or May 1846, and Henry Hartsfield reportedly died in October 1847.

[11] Henry Hartsfield's heirs seem to have divided and sold his estate without court intervention. I found no public record of inventory, division, or sale of property to tell where each slave went.

[12] Charles Holloway (b. August 1793) was sold by Caleb Holloway in South Carolina to Caleb's brother Edward Holloway in November 1814 for $575; the bill of sale gave Charles's age as "twenty one years old last August." Charles probably married Susan sometime between about 1840 and 1847. He outlived his wife, as shown by a bill for doctor's services rendered on 20 June 1863 ("Prescription & medicine for Charles"). After the Civil War Charles does not appear in any local or federal government record. See bill of sale in loose papers of Edward Holloway estate, Upson County Court of Ordinary, TUA; Upson County Court of Ordinary, Record of Vouchers Book D, 227. See p. 101 for his surname.

[13] Edward Holloway (1787–1850) was born in Edgefield District, SC, 22 February 1787 and served as a US Army officer in the War of 1812. After the war he left the army and moved to Putnam County, GA, in winter 1816–1817. He married Nancy Bryan on 16 April 1818. In 1822 they moved to the newly organized Pike County and established a plantation on land that became part of Upson County in December 1824. Holloway's

and Got his old master to Buy her. After the sale there was 4 little motherless and Fartherless boys left on the plantation with out a singgle relation save a distant cusan. Old mistress[14] was mother and every thing Els for some years, but by the providence of our Heavenly Farther we had our farther to come to see us and come our heades and bathe us and talk to us, tell us how to gat along in the world. He give Broo Westly and [=an][15] old elrementry speeling book who soon learnd his letters and Taught me and Broo Green the same.

My oldes Broo John Westly larned very Rapedly and soon learnd to read and Taught his three little Bothers the same. Now my Recolection goes back to about 12 or 13 mounths of my Birth.

---

plantation where he died 26 August 1850 was seven miles east of Thomaston. His church affiliation, if any, is unknown (obituary in *Georgia Journal and Messenger*, 4 September 1850).

[14] Elizabeth (Olive) Hartsfield (1790–1880) married Henry Hartsfield in Oglethorpe County in 1829. She was sister to his first wife, Mary Olive. A member of Clouds Creek Baptist Church, she took her letter of dismission on 13 December 1834, the same day other Hartsfield Baptists (her husband's property) took their letters. After their migration to Upson County Elizabeth and her five enslaved co-religionists presented their letters to Bethesda Baptist Church on 21 February 1835. When Henry Hartsfield died in 1847, Elizabeth's stepson Washington Hartsfield assumed head of household, caring for his elderly stepmother and managing the work of the estate. Elizabeth's and Washington's slaves, most or perhaps all inherited from Henry, lived on the Hartsfield homestead four miles north of Thomaston. By 1870, Elizabeth ("Miss Betsey") was reportedly insane. She died ten years later, 24 July 1880.

Clouds Creek Baptist Church Minutes 1826–1856, 126; Bethesda Baptist Church, Minute Book 1, 56; 1850 Census, GA, Upson County, Free Pop., p. 325B (stamped), dwell. 579; 1850 Census, GA, Upson County, Slave Pop., p. 201; 1860 Census, GA, Upson County, Free Pop., p. 78, dwell. 613; 1860 Census, GA, Upson County, Slave Pop., p. 28; 1870 Census, GA, Upson County, Pop., p. 120, dwell. 969; 1880 Census, GA, Upson County, Pop., ED 135, p. 22, dwell. 215.

[15] Holloway spelled the article "an" and the conjunction "and" the same way throughout his book, probably because he pronounced them the same way, with the "d" in "and" silent.

In the yeare 1857 my old master[16] stood securrity for some one and had the debt to pay and to rase the money he had to sell 3 of his Negro boys, Cornealus,[17] Green and Houston. This Brings me to the yeare 1858 this 47 years ago. I was 13 years[18] old. I was leved [=levied] on by the High Sherrif and sould for 750 dollars, my Brooher for 900 and some odd dollas, while

---

[16] Washington Hartsfield (c. 1803–1887), born in Oglethorpe County, GA, was the son of Henry and Mary Hartsfield. He joined Clouds Creek Baptist Church by declaring his experience of God's grace on 7 June 1824. He called for his letter of dismission from Clouds Creek on 8 November 1834 and eventually moved to Upson County and united with Bethesda Baptist Church by letter 22 January 1842. A retail merchant in Thomaston, he entered various business partnerships with mixed success. He suffered financial embarrassment and was forced to sell assets in the 1850s. He never married and died 3 November 1887. Cliburn quotes his church obituary and includes a photograph of him (*In Unbroken Line: A History of the First Baptist Church of Thomaston, Georgia, from Its Beginnings at Bethesda to Its One Hundred Fiftieth Anniversary (1825–1975)* [Tallahassee, FL: Thomaston First Baptist Church, 1979] 230–31).

Clouds Creek Baptist Church Minutes 1826–1856 (Oglethorpe County, GA), 8, 125; Edwin L. Cliburn, *In Unbroken Line: A History of the First Baptist Church of Thomaston, Georgia, from Its Beginnings at Bethesda to Its One Hundred Fiftieth Anniversary (1825–1975)* (Tallahassee, FL: Thomaston First Baptist Church, 1979) 230–31, 931; "Davis T. Richardson, et, al., plaintiff in error, vs. Washington Hartsfield, defendant in error" (*Reports of Cases in Law and Equity Argued and Determined in the Supreme Court of the State of Georgia Containing the Decisions at Macon, January Term, 1859...*, vol. 27 [Columbus, GA: Columbus Times Steam Power Press, 1860] 528–35) describes some of Hartsfield's convoluted business partnerships and transactions that led to a flood of lawsuits against him in Upson County courts throughout the 1850s.

[17] Cornelius Weaver (b. c. 1842), born in GA and enslaved to Washington Hartsfield in Upson County, was sold together with Holloway's younger brother Green on 11 December 1858 for $2400, to Travis A. D. Weaver, a Methodist planter and merchant in Thomaston, Upson County. Weaver named Cornelius in his list of shoes bought for 1863. After emancipation, Cornelius Weaver seems to have worked as a hired farm hand in 1870–1871 for plantation owner Calvin Zorn in southeast Upson County, after which his documentary trail is cold. Upson County Deed Book H, 411; Travis A. D. Weaver Account Book (1849–1871), Weaver-Dallas House Collection, TUA, 209; 1870 Census, GA, Upson County, Pop., p. 75, dwell. 620; Upson County Tax Digest, 1871, 589 Georgia Militia District (hereinafter abbreviated GMD).

[18] Holloway believed he was born about 1 May 1845, so he states he was thirteen years old. He was most likely fourteen years old, born in 1844.

Conneailous Brought something over a 1000 dollars, In Thomaston Upson County Georgia.[19]

On the 27th day of December 1858, About one oclock PM, The time came for me to leave the old plantation. Isaac Strictland[20] who bought me in May came after me. Antisepating the time of my Departure from my people I wint down to the widow Holloways[21] Just befour Christmass to see my Farther, steep mother, grand mother the last time. On the day above mentiond was the time for the Brakeing harte strings. With bitter tears I could only gather to gather my little all witch consisted of 2 corse suatis of clothes, one peace of and old Baptist hynn book, one peace of a new Testiment, one McGuffes second reader, one New yourk reader no 2.[22] lisen at the little boy leaveing the old plantation:

---

[19] I explore the complex transactions behind this sale on pp. 22-24.

[20] Isaac Strickland, Jr. (1816–1888), was born Jasper County, GA, 15 April 1816. He married Mary Hartsfield at the house of her father Henry Hartsfield on 20 December 1838 in Upson County, GA. Isaac was baptized into fellowship with Bethesda Baptist Church in February 1840. The 1840 census found Strickland in Upson County, but he probably moved to Pike County about the time he called for his letter of dismission from Bethesda on 27 February 1841. The 1860 census for Pike County enumerated Strickland with eight slaves. After his wife, Mary, died in 1861, Isaac married Martha Andrews on 12 January 1864, in Pike County. He was a Democrat. He died in Pike County 5 October 1888 and was buried in Hebron Cemetery. Nancy Cornell, ed., *Strickland Scene*, 4/2 (1983): 32–33; 1860 Census, GA, Pike County, Slave Pop., p. 17; Cliburn, *In Unbroken Line*, 993.

[21] Nancy (Bryan) Holloway (c. 1799–1866) married Edward Holloway on 16 April 1818 in Putnam County, GA. In 1822 Edward and Nancy moved to newly formed Pike County, GA, establishing a plantation on land that became part of Upson County in December 1824. Widowed in 1850, Nancy lived on the old plantation home place until she died 5 May 1866. Her church affiliation, if any, is unknown.

[22] William Holmes McGuffey, *Eclectic Second Reader*, was first published in 1836; *The New York Reader, No. 2.* was published in New York by Samuel Wood & Sons as early as 1812; both had numerous later editions. Storekeeper Timothy Mullancy sold a *New York Reader* to the Edward Holloway estate for 15 cents on 16 September 1851, almost certainly to educate Edward Holloway's minor children (Upson County Court of Ordinary, Record of Vouchers Book A, 38, TUA). Perhaps Holloway carried this same book, a hand-me-down, when he went to Strickland's place.

Good bye aunt Nancy,[23] good bye aunt Frankey,[24] Good bye miss Betsey,[25] Good bye Brother Jaak,[26] Good by Daniel,[27] Good bye Edmon,[28] fair well to the old plantation. by Good Dark I was at my new home in Pike County Ga.

At this place I had and Aunt, a sweet good woman. with her I hope to live and so I did, but not for long. Mr Strictland who Bought me the previous yeare found out that he could make 225 dollars. On finding out that I could read a little, and likeing a negro that could read no way, Earley in January advertised that he had a fine negro boy for sale and th[e]re was many would be byers over

---

[23] Nancy joined Bethesda Baptist Church in Upson County by letter 25 April 1835, two months after six other Hartsfield Baptists, who migrated from Oglethorpe County, had presented their letters from Clouds Creek. Nancy had not been a member of Clouds Creek Baptist Church, suggesting that she came from elsewhere. When Houston Holloway visited his friends and kinfolk during the 1859 year-end holiday, he found "Aunt Nancy was still alive" and at Christmas 1862 he found her "yet alive." He noted that she weighed nearly 400 pounds. Holloway does not say whether Nancy was related to him. See Bethesda Baptist Church, Minute Book 1, 57.

[24] Frankey (or Franky) was appraised at $350 in the inventory of Richard Hartsfield's property in Oglethorpe County in 1821, but her documentary trail is cold until Holloway visited Upson County at the end of 1859 and found "Aunt Frankey was also a live and glade to See [me]." When he returned at Christmas 1862, "Aunt Frankey was dead." Holloway does not say if or how he was related to Frankey.

[25] Elizabeth (Olive) Hartsfield; see note 14.

[26] Holloway's youngest brother, Jacob, nicknamed Jake.

[27] Daniel Hartsfield (b. c. May 1844), Holloway's cousin and one of the people Holloway saw when he visited his kinfolks during Christmas 1859. Daniel Hartsfield later told a pension examiner: "I was a slave of Wash Hartsfield, of 4 miles north of Thomaston, Upson County, Georgia.... I was born and raised there and lived there until I went into the war. I left the plantation and went to Macon when the yankees came through in April 1865.... I enlisted in May.... I deserted from the regiment...and got home before Christmas of the same year." In 1880 Daniel Hartsfield was a farm laborer in Pike County, GA, and by 1899 through at least 1910 he was farming in LaFayette, Walker County, GA.

See National Archives, RG 15, Veterans Administration Pension files, pension claim of Cesar Davis (No. 1,194,816), Daniel Hartsfield's deposition taken 23 November 1899; 1880 Census, GA, Pike County, Pop., ED 105, p. 33, dwell. 296; 1900 Census, GA, Walker County, Pop., ED 94, p. 11B, dwell. 192; 1910 Census, GA, Walker County, Lafayette, Pop., ED 141, p. 33A, dwell. 292.

[28] Edmund was Holloway's cousin, possibly Daniel Hartsfield's brother. He was one of the kinfolk Holloway visited during Christmas 1859.

the cuntry.[29] And among the many that came to buy there was a rich man by the name of James C Freeman,[30] of the Flat Shoals, Merriwether County, Georgia. This man owend over a hundred slaves. Mr Strictland did not like a negro that could read. Mr Freeman was just the outher way. he liked the reading negro. After severrell Tripp he paid Mr Stricland one Thousand and 75 dollars and your humble correspondant was gorn again from the last relation or frind. I was soon at the flat shoals. one paculia thing about this sale as I Told him [and] his famely Good bye he give me one dollar of the money that he had just reseaved for [me].[31] I did not have the chance to tell my arnta Good bye, I was so soon gorn. The Tripp from Isaac Strictlands was soon made. in one hours time I was at The Flat Shoals in Merriwether County at my new home, new master, new mistress, and I said to be a new negro. I was soon cald Into The Big house to see my new mistress and young masters. C H Johnson[32] of Griffin Georgia was out There and after looking very critically at me for a while he offerd Mr Freman 1200 dollars for me, one hundred and 25 dollars on his Traid for that day, witch was refused.

I was assignd to uncle Floyeds house.[33] Now This man was Mr Fremans miller and The folloing conversation to [=took][34] place after supper in his house.

---

[29] Heather Andrea Williams gives examples of slave masters who hated literacy among their slaves and negated purchases when they discovered that the person could read or write (*Self-Taught: African American Education in Slavery and Freedom* (Chapel Hill: University of North Carolina Press, 2005) 18).

[30] James Crawford Freeman (1820–1885); see biographical summary on pp. 24-26.

[31] In a similar ritual at the sale of Pierce M. Butler's slaves in Savannah in 1859, Butler gave each person one dollar in silver coins "fresh from the mint." See "What became of the slaves on a Georgia plantation?: Great auction sale of slaves, at Savannah, Georgia, March 2d & 3d, 1859. A sequel to Mrs. Kemble's Journal," at Memory Project, Library of Congress, http://memory.loc.gov/cgi-bin/query/r?ammem/murray:@field%28 DOCID+@lit%28lcrbmrpt2305div10%29%29 (accessed 12 January 2015).

[32] Charles H. Johnson, native of CT, about twenty-nine years old, a carpenter by trade, lived in a boarding house in Griffin and owned four slaves (1860 Census, GA, Spalding County, Free Pop., p. 18, dwell. 119; 1860 Census, GA, Spalding County, Slave Pop., p. 12, col. 2, lines 27–30).

[33] Floyd Freeman (c. 1820–prior to 1870), James C. Freeman's miller, was head man in the cabin to which Freeman assigned Holloway. Floyd and Richmond the blacksmith inducted Holloway into their secret reading club; in 1862 his wife, Pherebe, lived on the Thrash Place. Pherebe was possibly his second wife because Floyd was about eighteen years her senior and had children living on Freeman's plantation, the Caldwell Place, in

"Houston where did you come from?" "Upson County." "who was you Farther?" "Nepton Holloway." "my good gracious," said he, "I know you farther well enoufe. he and I was young men togather. what was your mothers name?" "Louiser Hartsfeild." "wy I coated her befour your Farther married her. well well well. I am glade to see you. you got a good master and you must be a good boy."

The next morning I was Introduced to The 12 head of horses and I started off to larn how to keep horsese and carrages and Buggys and it fell to my lot that yeare 1859 to have good Treetment, if such ever was the [case] with a slave. My master allowd me to spell and read and Uncle Floyed encorrage me very much as he could Read some himself.

I grew fast and was very much liked by my master, mistress and David N Freeman[35] and Edward E Freeman[36] his to sones.

Pike County. To have been of an age to court Louisa (b. c. 1820), Floyd was most likely the forty-year-old male mulatto described in the list of Freeman's slaves in the 1860 census. Floyd was best man at Holloway's 1864 wedding, but Pherebe was married to someone else by 1870, suggesting that they had separated or Floyd had died between 1864 and 1870 (1860 Census, GA, Meriwether County, Slave Pop., p. 97, col. 2, line 13).

[34] Holloway usually spelled "took" as "to" probably because he pronounced it that way.

[35] David N. Freeman (1847–1911), son of James C. Freeman and Amanda (Neal) Freeman, was born in Zebulon, Pike County, GA, and grew up at his parents' house in Flat Shoals, Meriwether County. He attended primary school in Flat Shoals College and finished his schooling in Griffin, Spalding County. He was a lifelong bachelor. He remained at the home place in Flat Shoals to manage the family's farming and business interests after 1866 when his father moved to Griffin. David Freeman was still at Flat Shoals in 1900, but by 1910, for reasons not clear, he was living in a boarding house in Cartersville, Bartow County. Suffering from a severe health problem, he entered a sanitarium in Atlanta where he died 9 August 1911. See *Memoirs of Georgia, Containing Historical Accounts of the State's Civil, Military, Industrial and Professional Interests, and Personal Sketches of Many of its People, Vol. II* (Atlanta: Southern Historical Association, 1895) 508, also available at http://dlg.galileo.usg.edu/meta/html/dlg/zlgb/meta_dlg_zlgb_gb0252b.html?Welcome. 1900 Census, GA, Meriwether County, Pop., ED 50, p. 9, dwell. 142; 1910 Census, Bartow County, Cartersville, Pop., ED 5, p. 1A, dwell. 10; *Atlanta Georgian and News*, 9 August 1911, 9.

[36] Edward E. Freeman (1849–1896) was born in Pike County and grew up at Flat Shoals in Meriwether County. He moved with his parents to Griffin, Spalding County, after the Civil War where the 1870 census found him practicing law. In 1873 he was back in Flat Shoals serving as postmaster, but by 1880 he was farming in Bartow County, five miles from Cartersville, where he died on 16 July 1896.

I will not omitt just heare to mention Aunt Ellen who was the milk made and gardener. She to [=took] me for her boy and adopted me for her son. She washed and patched my clothes and was very good to me.[37] She was entencely religious and she had much to [do] withe job of gating me Into the Methodist Church At Flatshoes witch Church I claim to be a member of untill This day.[38] Earley in the spring I was put in the Black smith shoop for a day or 2 to stract[39] for Uncle Richmon,[40] one of the most entelegent men that [I] ever saw, a good smith and Rigedly honist in all of his deailing with men, and was well up withe the principle of the Democra[t]ic, Whigg, Know Nothing and Abolishionite political parties. The polisees of theas parties was well understood by uncle

---

See 870 Census, GA, Spalding County, Griffin, Pop., p. 13, dwell. 103; *Register of Officers and Agents, Civil, Military, and Naval, in the Service of the United States, on the Thirtieth of September, 1873* (Washington, DC: GPO, 1874) 595; 1880 Census, GA, Bartow County, Pop., ED 2, p. 60, dwell. 519; [Cartersville GA] *Courant-American*, 9 July 1896, 1, transcribed at Bartow County GenWeb page, http://www.gabartow.org/Obits/F/obit.FreemanEdward.shtml (accessed 12 January 2015).

[37] Marli F. Weiner, *Mistresses and Slaves: Plantation Women in South Carolina, 1830–80* (Urbana: University of Illinois Press, 1998) 145, uses Ellen's mothering of Holloway as an example of how enslaved women shaped their understanding of womanhood and women's roles, wherein caring for their families, including adopted family members, "helped make the quarters a bearable place to live."

[38] The church at Flat Shoals was on James C. Freeman's land. Meriwether resident Mrs. L. C. Clark reminisced that "There was [a] large two story house [probably Freeman's home] and a small church between the house and the river" (SCC Disallowed claim of James C. Freeman testimony before the commissioners, 6 March 1875, 27; Regina P. Pinkston, comp., *Historical Account of Meriwether County 1827–1974* [Greenville GA: Gresham Printing Company, 1974] 276).

[39] Strike: for heavy forging, a blacksmith used tongs to hold hot iron on the anvil and told his assistant or apprentice (the "striker") where to strike the iron with a heavy sledgehammer.

[40] Richmond (c. 1825–1864) was James C. Freeman's blacksmith and a mentor to Holloway. He kept Holloway's money safe for him. Richmond lived at the foot of the toll bridge over Flint River. He and Floyd the miller inducted Holloway into their secret reading club at the Flat Shoals mill. Richmond was a Methodist class leader in Flat Shoals Church, a teetotaler who also abstained from use of tobacco, and doorkeeper for the big neighborhood ball in 1859. He died 10 September 1864. He may be the thirty-five-year-old mulatto man enumerated in 1860 Census, GA, Meriwether County, Slave Pop., p. 97, col. 2, line 14.

Richmon and he was a man that [was] well thought of by most of the people white and colord of the whole cuntry. I will say more about him farther on. Uncl Jacob also belonging to the same man was a preacher having no Education. Yet he was a power for good among the people. more about him farther on.

On the Second Sunday in August that yeare I had the plesure of hearing Rev Naththenal Jones[41] of Zebulurn Pike County at Salem meeting house as it was Then cald.[42] His sermon Impresed me very much. That yeare was a good crop yeare and I well remember The great corn shuckings, and my reader will never have the fun That we had at Thease frolics. well Do I remember Ranson Freeman,[43] Burl Blackburn,[44] Abe BlackBurn, Dodd Black Burn,[45] and at this

---

[41] Probably Nathaniel Levi Jones (1829–1864), a thirty-one-year-old farmer living within the area served by the Zebulon post office. He was not among the ordained members of the GA Conference of the MECS; therefore, he would have been a locally licensed preacher. Jones was killed in the Battle of Olustee in Florida on 20 February 1864 (1860 Census, GA, Pike County, Free Pop., p. 108, dwell. 766; death info from "GATAYLOR-L Archives" at http://archiver.rootsweb.ancestry.com/th/read/GATAYLOR/2000–10/0971895610).

[42] Local historian and Methodist minister R. W. Rogers wrote that "Salem Church was organized in the early days of Methodism in Pike County, but as the old records have been lost, we cannot give dates." In 1888 the church was moved to Concord and became Concord Methodist Church (*History of Pike County from 1822 to 1922* [Zebulon, GA: n.p., n.d.] 31).

[43] Ransom Freeman (b. c. 1833) had lived in Pike County all his life. Since about 1857 he lived in the 505 GMD that stretched from Concord to the Flint River, where he likely worked on James C. Freeman's plantation called the Brown Place, about a mile and a half from James Freeman's Flat Shoals home until emancipation. He was on the Brown Place when the Yankees came in April 1865. Ransom Freeman was toastmaster at the big holiday dance in 1859. After emancipation, Ransom Freeman was one of the first Pike County freedmen to buy land, a farm in southeastern Pike County, now part of Lamar County. In 1880 he valued his 176-acre farm and animals at $1,850.

See Georgia Archives, Office of the Governor (RG 1-1-108), Returns of Qualified Voters (hereafter cited as GA Return of Qualified Voters), Pike County, Election District 22, Williamsville, 505 Precinct, 10 August 1867, p. 44; SCC Disallowed Claim of James C. Freeman, affidavit of Herod Smith taken 13 March 1872; 1880 Census, GA, Pike County, Pop., ED 104, p. 30, fam. 27; 1880 Census, GA, Pike County, Schedule 3 (Agriculture), ED 104, p. 12, line 5.

[44] Burrell Blackburn (b. c. 1841) was eldest son of Newton and his wife, Hetty. They were all enslaved to Dr. John Lowe Blackburn and wife Martha Ann (Neal) Blackburn. John L. Blackburn's will dated 3 April 1856 listed "Newton and his wife

day, March 24th—1907, I heare The voice of thease genrals on the corn pile giving [out] and Five Hundred Men around the corn pile answering The at the ware heard five miles.[46]

Lisen at them on the Big Corn pile:

[Song no.] 1 heare ratler cone[47] dog
Hare rattle heare heare
Hare Ratleer Blood hound
Haree ratller heare heare
Hogs In my corn feild
Hare rattle Heare Hare
Sick him sick Him heare Hare

And so on

Hetty and their children Burrell, Warren, Adaline, Caroline, Janette, David, Sophronia and Joseph" (Meriwether County Will Book A [1831–1859], 387, Meriwether County Courthouse, Office of Probate Judge, Greenville, GA. Accessed at "Georgia Probate Records, 1742–1990," FamilySearch, http://familysearch.org/search/collection/1999178 [accessed 24 February 2015]).

[45] Abraham Blackburn and Dodd Blackburn were sons of Jordan and Susan Blackburn. They were all enslaved to Dr. John Lowe and Martha Ann (Neal) Blackburn at Flat Shoals. They had a brother, Floyd Blackburn, named elsewhere in Holloway's narrative. John Blackburn's will, dated 3 April 1856, gave to Martha Blackburn: "Jordan and Susan his wife and their children, Dodd, Abraham and Floyd." Abraham Blackburn and his father registered together to vote in Meriwether County on 28 June 1867, although the registrar entered his name as Abram Blackburn (Meriwether County Will Book A [1831–1859], 387; GA, Returns of Qualified Voters, 1867–1869, Meriwether County, Precinct 1213, 23).

[46] This sentence is garbled, but describes a call and response. The general of the corn pile would "give out"—meaning to call out a line of the song the way a preacher would line out the words of a hymn to a congregation in church—and the corn shuckers would answer by singing the words back to the general. Holloway means to say the response was loud enough to be heard five miles away.

[47] John Wesley Holloway transcribed this word as "come," which fits the context. Alternately the word may be a contraction of "come on," pronounced "cō' ȯn" (John Wesley Holloway, "Memoirs of John Wesley Holloway, Thebes Ga., July 3, 1916," 285 [photocopy of unpublished manuscript in author's possession, hereafter cited as JWH]).

[Song no.] 2 I wonder whears the Bugle .E.
Oh Bugle Blow
Old masters got Bugle E
Oh Bugle Bugle Blow
(and so on)

[Song no.] 3 Oh Billy Boundle
Bombe low
Oh Billie Boundle
Bombe low

And Hundreds of similer songs on the above patron [=pattern] wass sing at Thoes Husking Frolice [=frolics], in Thoes days.

This Brings us close to the end of yeare 1859 when I was allow to visit my people In Upson County. I wint by the Culwell plantation[48] Through Zebulurn, pine Mountains and was at my home the widoh Hartsfeilds by 4 oclock and when Broo Jacob saw me ride up to gate I was given and Ovation. My old Mistress And old Master was glade to see me. he made me a presant of a five dollar bill. Aunt Nancy was still alive. Aunt Frankey was also a live and glade to see [me] and to know that I was doing well.

Broo Jack was Theare with Danile and Edmon, tow Cusans, and uncle Harris[49] the foman [=foreman] of the plantation. I spent the night with them and Broo Jak wint with me to the widow holloway. There I saw my grand mother Suasan the last[50] my steep grand farther Uncle Charles And own Deare Farther Nepton and my steep mother Mary[51] and sister Sarah and sister M^{C}, my 2 half sister, and Broo Jones.[52]

---

[48] James C. Freeman bought the Caldwell Place from James T. G. Caldwell in 1857 (Pike County, GA, Deed Book L, 148 [Office of Clerk of Superior Court, Pike County Courthouse, Zebulon, GA]).

[49] Harris Hartsfield (b. c. 1825) was living with his wife and five children next door to Wash Hartsfield in 1870 and stayed in Hartsfield's employ at least through 1871 (1870 Census, GA, Upson County, p. 120, dwell. 970; Upson Tax Digests for 1869 and 1871, 555 District [Freedmen's section]).

[50] Holloway's last time to see grandmother Susan was actually his next visit at Christmas 1861.

[51] Mary was the second wife of Neptune Holloway. On 14 October 1850 Mary was appraised at $600 in Edward Holloway's estate. Mary remained on the Holloway

I mention the John Brown raid that same yeare in November.[53]

My reader will feel a surprised to know that I spint one night with my farther and that was my last for ever so far as this Earth is concearnd. He wint with me more more then 8 miles on the way back to merriwether county. we parted neare Stafford quarter or plantation[54] with many Tears never to meet again, for he died a yeare or tow afterward. I will say This much about my farther, he was a man of some attainments. He was a good scholer for his day. he could read and write and his advice was much sought for by The colord people of his naborhood about many Things pertaining to there well far. he was considered by The Holloways his owners as one of the confidential negros.[55] as such he was alowd [to] By paper and Ink he was alowd also to have a shoot gun and powder and shoot. he was alldw [=allowed] to By Whisker on his own word.[56] And while he was allowd to gat it he drink but little of it at his house

---

plantation with widow Nancy Holloway (Upson County Court of Ordinary, Record of Accounts Book C, 260; Upson County Court of Ordinary, Record of Vouchers Book B, 424, TUA; Upson County Court of Ordinary Record of Vouchers Book C, 696, TUA).

[52] Holloway's half siblings are named again on p. 102 where sister "M^C^" is called "McAma." John Wesley Holloway (JWH, 286) read "M^C^" as "Mac" and offered a reading of "Jonas" for "Jones," but offered no further information about these relatives. Mack Holloway, former slave of Nancy Holloway, married Benjamin Stephens, former slave of William Stephens, in Upson County on 28 December 1868 (*Marriage Record to 1876*, 55, in Probate Court, Thomaston, Upson County, Georgia).

[53] John Brown launched his raid on Harpers Ferry 16 October 1859.

[54] Neptune almost surely knew James H. Stafford as a local ordained Methodist preacher whose plantation was just northwest of The Rock. Stafford quarter in 1860 had three dwelling houses for the twenty-three slaves enumerated there (1860 Census, GA, Upson County, Free Pop., p. 619, dwell. 635; 1860 Census, GA, Upson County, Slave Pop., p. 30; MECS 1859, 155).

[55] "Confidential negro" was a phrase used by some slave owners to describe a servant, often a house slave or driver, whose actions they trusted always to coincide with their own interests, also one who had the masters' ear and with whom they could share private information. (On some large plantations absentee owners used "confidential negroes" as informants against their hired white overseers.) In this context, the phrase may mean simply that the Holloways trusted Neptune to exercise the privileges they granted him discreetly, and not to cause them embarrassment or trouble with their white neighbors.

[56] Sometimes Neptune bought on credit with a written order; for example, on 23 August 1851 storekeeper Timothy Mullancy charged fifteen cents to Nancy Holloway's

and often treeted his frinds to a dram for witch many of them was Thankfull. I got home safe that evirng. My farther lived on untell the [year] 1861. he Took sick and whatever his complaint was among outhers the Tooth ache was one. The Tooth was Exstracted and Blood poision followd and he died with a Eating Cancer a yeare after.[57] My good grand mother died in the yeare 1862.

May the good Lord watch his dust untell the morning of the Resurrection and at the sound of the first Trupit [=trumpet] raise him to lief again to live with God for Ever for he died a Triumphing Christan and his famely Bibbl is in the persseson of my Broo Jacob to day all[so] abook of Westly sermons that was much set by as long as he lived. I cannot say as much about my farther as I wish so for the present I bid him adue.

As for my Mother I very faintly remember her for I was about 2 years old when she died. my youngest Brother Jacob was six weeks old and there is about tow years between our Berths. She and her sister Suasan[58] was said to be about the same sice and ressemble each outher very much. Aunt Suasan was about mediam sice, Buatifull figur, dark Brown Skin with a mircanicall [=mechanical] Turn of mind, good naturd, and intencely Industrous and much devoted to her Husband. My reader will pardon me Just heare to say this nuch about aunt Suasan. Miss Mary Hartsfeild[59] marrid a man by the name of Isaac Strictland

---

account for "1 qt whiskey per order to Nep." Reuben, another Holloway slave, also bought whiskey from Mullancy (TUA, Upson County Court of Ordinary, Record of Vouchers Book A, 39).

[57] Dr. John O. Holloway, Edward and Nancy Holloway's son, began practicing medicine in 1856 at age nineteen. He extracted teeth from "Nep" on 10 December 1860. Between 21 December 1860 and early March 1861 Dr. Holloway visited Neptune sixteen times, prescribing medicines for an unspecified ailment, perhaps related to complications of the tooth extraction. Holloway tells us his father died in summer 1861. On 22 August 1861 coffin-maker John N. Webb billed the Holloway estate $6 for "Coffin for negro man." Coffins were usually ordered, measured, and built within a day after death, suggesting that Neptune died on or about 21 August 1861 (TUA, Upson County Court of Ordinary, Record of Vouchers Book C, 480, 693, 696).

[58] Holloway elsewhere calls her Susan Strickland. She died in fall 1867.

[59] Mary Hartsfield (1821–1861), daughter of Henry and Elizabeth Hartsfield of Upson County, was born 28 January 1821, probably in Oglethorpe County, GA. She married Isaac Strickland at her father's house in Upson County on 20 December 1838. She was baptized into fellowship with Bethesda Baptist Church in September 1839. The Stricklands moved to Pike County in the latter part of 1840 or early 1841. Mary and Isaac were enumerated in the 1840 census of Upson County and called for their letters of

and [some] of the Cendants of this man are quiet prominent in Georgia to day. It very Customary in thoese days when a young white lady married for her farther to present her a young negro woman to starte of with. Aunt Suasan fell to Mis Mary and was carried to Pike County and there she married one of her masters negro men. And in the Corse of years Mr Isaac Stricland took a notion to sell her and her little boy Daniel[60] and in doing This he had to part her from her Husband. He give Uncle Mosses the privalidge of going off withe the speculator, who name was Trice, and let him sell aunt Suasan and her little boy to gather. Uncle Mosses started off with her but did not go far befour he came back home to his Master befour noon. that night his Master did not rest all night. he could see aunt Suasan leaaving her Husband and her mistress and he saw that Miss Marys Harte also was Broken also. The second day and night was still worse for him and it seend that he would never rest any more. A second night with out sleep. He got [up] Earely in the morning, cald for annother white man by the name of Joseph Mountgonery,[61] gave him a letter, put him in a Buggy with a fast mule and he was [to] lose no time on the road but over take Mr Thomas Trice[62] and Bring Suasan and Daniel Back. and it was by hard driveng, Starteing Eearly, and drveing late, he over took Mr Trice who was a Primitive Baptist preacher befour he Broke up Camps in Talburt [=Talbot] County Ga, and presented him the letter befour mintioned. And at first he said

dismission from Bethesda on 27 February 1841. Mary died of diarrhea on 29 May 1861 (*Strickland Scene*, 1/4 (Fall 1980) [Riverdale GA: Strickland Research, Inc., 1980]: 75, 76; Cliburn, *In Unbroken Line*, 993).

[60] "Daniel" was a name given to at least three of Holloway's kinfolk; perhaps the progenitor of the name was a Daniel appraised at $500 in the 1821 inventory of Richard Hartsfield's property. That Daniel may have been Susan's brother or other near kin, and her son his namesake. Holloway also had a cousin named Daniel near his own age, born about 1844, enslaved to the Hartsfield family, who may have been the elder Daniel's son—but Holloway does not explain their lineage (see p. 76, n. 27).

[61] Probably Joseph R. Montgomery (b. c. 1833), who appears in the same district (Zebulon post office) in the 1860 Census, GA, Pike County, Free Pop., p. 42, dwell. 295: head of household, age thirty-five, farm laborer. Isaac Strickland lived not far away, in dwell. 338.

[62] Thomas Calvin Trice (1808–1866), an ordained Primitive Baptist elder, a leader in the Towaliga Primitive Baptist Association and pastor of Concord Primitive Baptist Church (Pike County, GA) for several years in the 1850s. See extended biography in Appendix A, pp. 198-200.

that he would not give aunt Suasan and he[63] boy up but he finally yeald. Aunt Suasan and he little boy was soon in the Buggy and Biding the outhor people in the drove[64] farewell, she on he way back to Pik[e] County. And in about 9 days from the time that she left home she was back to her old home with Mars Ike, Miss Mary and all the children and her Husband to stay untill Parted by the man that rides upon the pale horse whos name is death.[65] In the yard she lived untell after the Emancipation. More about her farther on.

My recolection of Things startes on the rode betwen Mr Thomas Fluellens[66] going to Bethasdy meeting house 2 mills [=miles][67] from home and 2 mills from Thomaston. I was a boy in my Farthers arms and my tow oldest Brothers was walking along behind my farther and mother and my little shoes was too lage for me and I would kick the[m] off and they would pick Them up and I would look over my Farther shulder and laugh. Now this dark Bron skill [=brown skin] little woman was my good mother God Bless her menory.

We got to the meeting. The fist that I ever saw. I was at this time about 13 mounths old. I remember going in the house, my farther seting on the Back seat left for servants. I remember the preachers, gasturs [=gestures] and the singing and the Braking up of the meeting. My Farther came out of meeting house as they ware Then cald, set down on a log and I saw the people mounting the

---

[63] Holloway uses "he" for "her" three times in this passage.

[64] A drove in this sense was a slave trader's human wares moving together as a group. A drove was similar to a coffle, except that people in coffles were usually chained together, but people in droves might be unchained. Trice's drove may have included some of Susan's former neighbors.

[65] Holloway does not date this incident, but it preceded Mary Strickland's death on 29 May 1861. Heather Andrea Williams, *Help Me to Find My People: The African American Search for Family Lost in Slavery* (Chapel Hill: University of North Carolina Press, 2012) 90–116, and Weiner, *Mistresses and Slaves*, 77–78, discuss how some slave owners felt discomfort, embarrassment, or distress over the human sorrow they caused by breaking enslaved families by sale.

[66] Thomas Flewellen (1799–1889) settled in the eastern half of Upson County in 1825, about a mile west of the Holloway farm, but in 1849 he sold that place and bought a plantation in land lot 160, northeast of Thomaston. Bethesda Baptist church meeting house sat on the western edge of this lot, directly south of the Hartsfield plantation. Although Flewellen held the property less than five years before moving to Arkansas in 1854, Holloway still associated this place with Thomas Flewellen more than fifty years later.

[67] Holloway consistently spells miles as "mills" throughout his text.

horsess and going away. And there I surpose I, in True baby fashon, wint to sleep. Now it appears that my lief from this was Blant [=blank] for some mounths. The next Thing that [I] remember seaing was in a little log cabbin cald Louiwezer house, sounthing white streched out a crose the floor on some kind of a form.[68] And my farther was seating at a little windo at the back side of the house with his head down and I Trying shoe hin a gray mair and colt at the back side horse lot. And uncle Edmon low,[69] my farthers Brother, singing of a song. I remember the Tune but have learnd the words since. I will give you the words as best I can from memory:

I came to the place where the lone pilgran lay
and pensively stood by his Thomd [=tomb]
When I[n] a low whisper I heard saunthing say
how sweelly [=sweetly] I sleep her a lone

The Tempest may howl and the Loud Thunder may rore
And gatherring of stormes may arise
Yet calm are her feeling at rest in her soul
The tears ar all wyped from her Eys

He wonderd and Exile and a stranger from home
No kindred nor relatans nigh
he meet the contagion and sink to the Toomb
his soul flw to milron on high.[70]

Oh tell his compaion and childrend most Deare
In a far distant region they dwell
to not week [=weep] for him nown he is gorn
The same hand that lead him Through searnes [=scenes] most severe
has kindly assisted him home.[71]

---

[68] Louisa's death was reported to Bethesda Baptist Church conference on 25 July 1846.

[69] Edmund Lowe (c. 1805–1888) was a locally licensed Methodist preacher. For his biography, see pp. 192-194.

[70] The original poem's words are "My soul flew to mansions on high."

[71] The words are adapted from an 1838 poem by John Ellis, "The White Pilgrim" also known as "The Lone Pilgrim." The song is often associated with Benjamin Franklin

This is as neare the words of the Hynn as I can read it from menory.

I will give one verce and the chorous of annother Hynn sung on the solumn occaision:

And let the feable body fail
And lit it drop or die
My soul shall quit this monefull vale
and sore to worlds on high
  The corrus
I feel like I feel like
I am on my Jurney home
I feel like I feel like
I am on my Jurney home.[72]

A second Hymn was sung I will give you the first verce:

Sweet rivers of Redeeming love
lie just befour mine Eyes
had I the pinions of a dove
I would to those rivers fly.[73]

White's *Sacred Harp* and the "shape note" singing developed and popularized by White. White lived in neighboring Harris County, GA, and organized the Southern Musical Convention in Upson County in 1845, so it is possible that Edmund Lowe learned this song from neighborhood shape-note singers.

[72] The first four lines are from a hymn by Charles Wesley, "And Let This Feeble Body Fail," published in 1759, and commonly reprinted in antebellum Methodist hymnbooks. The chorus cited by Holloway was not part of Wesley's original hymn, but came from another popular religious song, "On My Journey Home." Singers seem to have fitted this chorus to various hymns when the sentiments felt appropriate, including the favorite Isaac Watts hymn, "When I Can Read My Title Clear." For example, see Howard W. Odum, "Religious Folk-Songs of the Southern Negroes," *The American Journal of Religious Psychology and Education* 8/3 (July 1909): 329.

[73] John A. Granade's lyrics, "Sweet rivers of redeeming love," were commonly sung at Methodist and Baptist revivals and widely printed in various popular religious song books, including William Dossey, comp. and ed., *The Choice, in Two Parts; Part I, Containing Psalms and Hymns; Part II, Containing Spiritual Songs, Designed for Public and Private Worship* (Philadelphia: 1836) Part II, 122.

My Children, To whome theas pages are addrest, will know in thoes days 60 years ago there was but few pecturs of any kind and as for photographs they ware very few seen among the rich white people and scarcely any among the colord. I have alredy Told you that I k[n]ew but little about my mother. I have told you also that I was told that my mother and her sister Suasan was Just a like. Taking that to be True, You will permit me to give you a feble desscription of my good aunt Suasan Strickland. Look at a Buatifull shaped Brown sking woman about four feet and sex Inches high, a well propotiond head, reather small hands and feet, a soft Black but reather quick Eye, a mouth in propotiond to her sices, a very pleasand vioce, strangly musical, A plsant converation, dressing well on Sundays, and waering clean clothes every day, and you have my aunt Suasan Stricland whoe departted this lief in the fall of 1867 at the home of Mr Isaac Strictland in Pike County Georgia.

For the presant I must leave my aunt Suasan and my sainted Mother, Though in the progress of this work we will see them again.

Chapter Second

Work, Recreation, and Religious Conversion

In The fall of the yeare 1859, durin of the mounth of november, A man by the name of John Brown made the Celerbrated Raid at Harpers ferry Verginnia and well do I remember The Excitement among the Southern white people when that Thing occord, Patroling from plantation to plantation and woe be unto Negro who was caut without a pass. They could not tell how far the uprising was under stood by the milions of slaves and for a while Excitement ran high.

I[t] was my custom every three or Four mounths to go to see my aunt Suasan. Now that you may understand what I mean by the word pass I will write myself a pass as I often did. after that I would go to my master and ask permision to go to see my Aunt. If he consented, He would write me a pass in the following words:

> Houston has permishion to go [to] Hebrun Church and Thence to Isaac Struckland and back home by sunset.
>
> J. C. Freeman.
>
> This november the 25–1859

Now the above paper would protect me at Church and any wheare in the road between the Church and Isaac Strictcland and at Mr Stricklands and any wheare on the Road between there and home witch was 5 Mills away.

It would be well to say that the yeare 1859 was and unusealy Good crop yeare. Great cropts was made. larger plantations was opend up and slaves was high. 2000 dollars was a comon price to pay for a negro man 22 to 25 years old, and a young negro woman that look well and had one or 2 children Brought readaly 24 to 2500 hundred dollars. Around the Flat Shoals where I lived the land Lords had a Tendancy to Treet there slaves well. they allowed them a chance to make something for them selves and as such they enjoyed selves well, drest well, and was comparivetivly happy.

Through the fall of the yeare corn shucking or husking frolicks was the order from plantation to plantation. At night much merrymet. well do I remember Abe Black Burn, Dodd Black Burn his Broo, Birl Black Burn. theas ware gread men at the Theas Husking Frolicks when a Thousand Bushels of corn would [be] shuckt out by 11 oclock at night. I will give you and Idea of one of theas big to does[1] as you never was at one nor never will be. Think of a pile of corn in the shuck pild up higher then your head, from 15 to 30 feet through, and often 200 feet long, and round this pile from 250 to 500 men mostly, all hollowing at the toop of his great voice with from 3– to 4 genrals or leaders to give out to thoes a round the corn pile to answer:

> Oh Boys I know you heare me,
> oh ho hore oreo
> oh Boy I heare It Thunder
> oh ho hore – or – or

The Leader was all ways able make his song as he wint. On the outher end of the pile there would be annother Big general whooping at the Toop of his voice:

Leade[r]	old aunt Easter moland[2]
	moland corn moland
[leader]	old aunt Diner moland
	moland corn moland
[leader]	Sould my corn to moland
	moland corn moland

Theare was Thousands of theas songs that lived with the people of that day and as long as the Big corn pile was found and they wi[n]t away whith the old plantation corn pile and the faithfull old plantation slave. we could say much

---

[1] A "big to-do" is an extravagant, well-attended, and well-advertised event.

[2] The names in these extemporaneous songs probably referred to real people. Perhaps "old aunt Easter Moland" was Esther, formerly enslaved to Colson Moreland, a marriage gift to his daughter Penniah E. Alexander, wife of William Alexander, in December 1841 when she (Esther) was aged 17 (Upson County Deed Book E, 341); Esther is named again in Colson Moreland's 1862 will in Pike County. Dena J. Epstein, "Slave Music in the United States Before 1860: A Survey of Sources (Part 2)," *Music Library Association Notes* 20 (Summer 1963): 377–78, describes how extemporaneous songs incorporated surrounding places, people, objects and local incidents.

about thos big frolic, but as we did not starte out to writ them out, for the present we leave it off.

On the 28th day of December 1859 I hurried back home from the visit to see my people to be presant at the pairty and fancy ball given by Poline Freeman[3] and Joannah[4] and Auntny Alxander[5] thre of the leading socitey colord people of the Flat Shoals. I got home on time, wint into the Big house and reported to my master and mistres, J. C. Freeman and his refind wief Miss Manda.[6] They asked me how I found my people and former master. I Shurd hin the 5 dollar bill that my old master W H Hartsfeild give me.[7] the partie was on

---

[3] Pauline Freeman was probably born in Virginia around 1842. Holloway called her a "principall house woman" in James C. Freeman's household. Probably the person enumerated in the town of Griffin, Spalding County, as Anthony Alexander's wife in 1870 and 1880 censuses (called "Perlina" and "Antony" Alexander in 1870). Pauline was a rare name; in the whole state of GA in 1870 there were only about 200 people named Pauline or variants like Poline, Perlina, or Perline—and no one else of that name in the 1870 or 1880 censuses is a plausible match for Pauline Freeman (1870 Census, GA, Spalding County, Griffin, Pop., p. 39, dwell. 316; 1880 Census, GA, Spalding County, Griffin, Pop., ED 118, p. 6, dwell. 44).

[4] Possibly "Aunt Joe Annah" who was converted by Rev. Claiborne Neal's preaching at Uncle Richmond's funeral in October 1864 and who died in Atlanta on 19 September 1909.

[5] Anthony Alexander, born in AL likely around 1825, was possibly at one time enslaved to William D. Alexander in Pike County, GA. He was one of five members of the secret reading club that met in Richmond's house near Flat Shoals Bridge during the Civil War. He was married to Pauline Freeman (see n. 3), with whom he may have had at least five children: Augustus, Florence, David, Ola, and James. Within a few years of the end of the war, Anthony Alexander moved his family to Griffin, Spalding County, where he bought $500 worth of real estate and worked at his house carpentry trade. He could read but not write. In 1869 Holloway went shopping in Griffin and asked for directions to Anthony Alexander's house, but was pointed instead to the house of Robert Alexander (no known relation), the AMEC minister who introduced Holloway to the "novell idea" of an "African Methodist Church" (1870 Census, GA, Spalding County, Griffin, Pop., p. 39, dwell. 316; 1880 Census, GA, Spalding County, Griffin, Pop., ED 118, p. 6, dwell. 44).

[6] Amanda M Freeman (b. c. 1825), daughter of James and Frances Neal of Pike County.

[7] There was a practical reason for Holloway to make sure that James Freeman saw the five dollar bill and heard where it came from. Displaying the money could secure Holloway's claim to rightful possession of the bill. Dylan C. Penningroth, *The Claims of*

at the old Johm hase house,[8] admition 25 cts. the house over head was soon fild to overflowing.[9] The White men presant was Mr J. C. Freeman, James M Neail

---

Kinfolk: African American Property and Community in the Nineteenth-Century South (Chapel Hill: University of North Carolina Press, 1993) 91–97, discusses tactics of "display and acknowledgement" that protected slaves' personal property; however Holloway's actions with the bill are an exception to Penningroth's argument that slaves "were discreet with their money" and hid cash from others (97). The scrupulously honest older man called "Uncle Richmond" kept Holloway's money in a box for him.

[8] The old John Hay house was on the same lot as James Freeman's home place, which is why Freeman asserted to the party-crashing patrollers that he patrolled his own yard. John H. Hay (b. c. 1819) and family lived in Pike County in 1850, in Meriwether in 1860, then back in Pike by about 1861 through 1870. Hay made affidavit supporting James C. Freeman's claim before the Southern Claims Commission, in which he said "that he was living at Flat Shoals…when James C Freeman moved to that place and lived with him most of the time until the Second year of the war," presumably leaving the house vacant the rest of the time, and thus available for this party.

See 1850 Census, GA, Pike County, Free Pop., p. 152B (stamped), dwell. 412; 1860 Census, GA, Meriwether County, Free Pop., p. 467, dwell. 941; 1870 Census, GA, Pike County, Pop., p. 96, dwell. 681; GA Return of Qualified Voters, Pike County, Williamsville, Precinct 505, 10 August 1867, p. 45, no.42; SCC Disallowed Claim of James C. Freeman, John H. Hay affidavit of 10 March 1874.

[9] Shade Richards, born 13 January 1846 on the James Neal plantation below Zebulon in Pike County, told a WPA interviewer in 1936 that during slavery times in his neighborhood, "The plantations took turn about having 'Frolics' when they 'fiddled and danced' all night. If it wasn't your own plantation you sure had to have a 'pass.'" James Neal was James C. Freeman's father-in-law, and Shade Richards, close to Houston H. Holloway's age, probably knew Holloway; he may even have attended this very party since James M. Neal (James Neal's son) told the patrollers, "I have 40 or 50 [people] up there" at the party. (Richards named his owner as "Jimpson Neal," and an article by J. H. Mitchell in the *Pike County Journal*, 11 March 1890, reveals that James Neal's nickname was "Uncle Jimpsy Neal.")

Charlie King, born and raised in Woodbury, about seven miles southwest from Flat Shoals, told a WPA interviewer in 1937 of similar parties in slavery times: "Every Saturday night, the Negroes had a 'breakdown,' often dancing all night long. About twelve o'clock they had a big supper, everybody bringing a box of all kinds of good things to eat, and putting it on a long table" (George P. Rawick, ed., *Georgia Narratives, Part 3*, vol. 13 in series 2 of *The American Slave: A Composite Autobiography* (Westport, CT: Greenwood Publishing Company, 1972) 202–203 (Shade Richards interview) and 18–19 (Charlie King interview).

his Brother in law,[10] Mr J C Lovett,[11] Mc.Underderwood,[12] Mr Jack Sutton.[13] white Boys presant D N Freeman, E. C. Freeman.[14] uncle Richmon Door keeper, Uncle Empsey Sutton Fidler,[15] Ransom Freeman Tost Master.

---

[10] James McCormick Neal (b. c. 1839), son of James and Frances Neal of Pike County, moved from Pike County to Meriwether County after the Civil War.

[11] John Cuthbert Lovett (1837–1899), born in Meriwether County, was the son of Meriwether planter Napoleon Bonaparte Lovett. John boarded with James C. Freeman while he clerked at Freeman's Flat Shoals store; his brother Byrd Lovett remembered that John "merchandized" at the Flat Shoals store part of the time that he (Byrd) lived near Flat Shoals. In 1865 J. C. Lovett married and joined the MECS. He died at Woodbury, Meriwether County, 8 February 1899. (1860 Census, GA, Meriwether County, Free Pop., p. 128, dwell. 921; SCC Disallowed Claim of James C. Freeman, statement of Byrd Lovett dated 10 March 1874; *Meriwether Vindicator*, 17 February 1899).

[12] Gaston M. Underwood (c. 1815–1895), lawyer and planter, lived in Flat Shoals neighborhood where the 1860 census enumerated him with thirty-three slaves. At some time before 1855 he set aside his law practice to concentrate on planting. He moved to DeKalb County about 1885 and died 3 September 1895. Holloway doubtless wrote the name as he had heard it spoken ("McUnderwood"), a usage also found in nearby Upson County where the surname of planter Allen M. Walker was often written "McWalker" (1860 Census, GA, Meriwether County, Free Pop., p. 463, dwell. 917; 1860 Census, GA, Meriwether County, Slave Pop., pp. 96–97; John Livingston, *Livingston's Law Register: A Guide for the Every Man of Business and Handbook of Useful Information* (New York: Office of the Monthly Law Magazine, 1854) 84 [list of lawyers; Gaston M. Underwood of Flat Shoals, marked as retired from practice]; *Meriwether Vindicator*, 13 September 1895).

[13] John Sutton (b. c. 1795 in GA) was a farmer enumerated with twenty-six slaves in 1860; he was Houston H. Holloway's next-door neighbor in 1870. A photograph of the Sutton Place, south of Flat Shoals, is in Regina P. Pinkston, comp., *Historical Account of Meriwether County 1827–1974* (Greenville GA: Gresham Printing Company, 1974) 277. (1860 Census, GA, Meriwether County, Free Pop., p. 131, dwell. 940; 1860 Census, GA, Meriwether County, Slave Pop., 99; 1870 Census, GA, Meriwether County, Pop., p. 40, dwell. 296).

[14] David N. Freeman (age thirteen in 1860) and Edward E. Freeman (age eleven in 1860) were James C. Freeman's sons.

[15] Empsey Sutton (b. c. 1820) was born in NC and had lived in GA since about 1850. He moved from Meriwether to Pike County in 1865, where he supported his family as a farm laborer at least through 1880 (GA Return of Qualified Voters, Pike County, Williamsville, Precinct 505 (10 August 1867), p. 48, No. 183; 1870 Census,

The entertainment was on the High order. Such Dancing I had never seen befour and prescious little since. about half past nine oclock It was noised in the house that the patrollers had sourounded the house all was confution within, for a great many had no passes. Mr Freeman enquired of the Trubble. "patrollers," was the answer. he and the outher whitemen wint down and meet the Captain of patrollers:

> "Good eveing Gentlemen"
> "Good eveing Mr Freeman"
> all the outher whitemen likewise spoke to them.
> Mr freeman: "what is the Trubble to night gentlemen?"
> The Capt"we heard that the niggers had a partie down heare to night and thought that there might be some heare without passes and you know the law in such cases."
> Mr Freeman: "I have 50 or up th[e]re. are [you] going to whip mine?"[16]
> Capt: "Mr Freeman you know the law."
> Mr James N Neail: "I have 40 or 50 up there are [you] going to whip mine? not one of them has a pass."
> All that Capt could say was, "you know the law."
> Mr. J. C. Lovett: "My Farther Has 25 or 30 heare & not one of them has a pass. are you going to whip mine?"

Mr Jack Sutton, Mr M^{C}Underwood all spoke to the patrollers on the same line and the Captain seemd dertermand to whip every one that had no pass. To this last white man presant at the Ball Told them that they would have to whip them first and many Rash words past between them and at last Mr Freeman

---

GA, Pike County, Pop., p. 103, dwell. 730; 1880 Census, GA, Pike County, ED 104, p. 50, fam. 159).

[16] Most of Freeman's people worked on two plantations in Pike County, several miles from Freeman's house at Flat Shoals, and GA law required slaves to have passes from their overseers to travel from their home plantations to any other place. For applicable laws see Thomas R. R. Cobb, *A Digest of the Statute Laws of the State of Georgia...* (Athens, GA: Christy, Kelsea & Burke, 1851) 972, 980; also available at https://archive.org/details/digestofstatutel02stat (accessed 9 April 2015).

Remarkt, "This is Christmas time and this is a lawfull[17] meet and the negroes are to enjoy them selves and you are not going to whip one of them to night," and That he patrold his own yard, and he finally drove the whole company of pat rollers off and peace was restord and the fancy Ball went on to the satisfaction of all conceornd.

After the patrollers was gorn many more came and we all had go up to the Big house and forme a ring in the froon of the door wheare the land lady could see the fine dancing and you may Depend upon it there was some fine dancers in thoes days. There was colord Ladys that could skip from one corner of the ring to the outher with a tumbler of warter on her head and [not] spill a drop.[18]

While the Dancing was going untertell [=until] after mid night there was many Beutifull plais [=games] going on. of the many that plade that night I will give you one. of this play any number of cuppuls could gat to gather and forme a ring by Taking hold of Each outhers hand. The Bist singers was alwast put in to the ring and the outhers close in upon him. And the following play song would follow:[19]

---

[17] "lawfull"—Freeman reminded the patrollers that the language of GA's patrol law authorized whipping only for "a slave that shall be found out of the plantation of his or their master or owner…not being on lawful business" (Cobb, *Digest*, 980). In fact, the law required even slaves on lawful business to have passes, but many owners deemed the patrol laws to be a trespass on their rights as masters to "patrol their own yard" and some let it be known in their neighborhoods that patrollers were forbidden to enter their lands. Sally E. Hadden discusses slave owners who tried to exclude patrollers from their land in *Slave Patrols: Law and Violence in Virginia and the Carolinas* (Cambridge: Harvard University Press, 2001) 70, 130–32.

[18] For testimony from two other regions of the Old South where enslaved dancers (including couples and men) balanced glasses or pails of water on their heads to demonstrate their skill, and danced for the entertainment of masters, see Jaqui Malone, *Steppin' on the Blues: The Visible Rhythms of African American Dance* (Urbana: University of Chicago Press, 1996) 42–43. Stephanie M. H. Camp, *Closer to Freedom: Enslaved Women & Everyday Resistance in the Plantation South* (Chapel Hill: University of North Carolina Press, 2004) 65–67, discusses such dances and parties in the context of paternalistic control and surveillance over enslaved people's social activities. Camp's discussion and Holloway's narrative include two common elements: the requirement for the enslaved to dance for the entertainment of the plantation master and mistress and other whites who attended and observed the party, and some whites' attempts to enforce the "pass" system.

[19] My reading of Holloway's description of this game is that the male "Leader" inside the circle would sing out a line of the song, and all the players forming the circle

Leader:

Young ladys dont you pitty me

the whole number would answer,

I am in them Ladys garden

Young gentlemen,[20]

dont pity me
I am In them ladys garden
Ill give a half dollar to get out of heare
I am [in] them ladys garden

at that verce hed shure [=he'd show] a half dollar:

Ill Bet five Dollars Ill get out of hear
I am In ladys garden
If you dont mind I got out of heare
I am In them ladys garden
Hist your hands as high as the sky
I am In them ladys garden

At this place he would run and surge against the side of the garden while they would hold him In:

Give me a pin to pick this lock
I am In them ladys garden

at this point he would act as though he was picking of lock in one of the hands of the young ladys. It required and Expert to get out without Brakeing the ring a round him.

So ends the yeare 1859.

The yeare 1860 ushered In with nothing of Importance that I remember. my Buisniss stay around the home house of a rich land Lord who dwelt a king among his hundred and odd slaves and thousands of Acres of land. His several over seears only subordinates under him on the Exstinsive premises.

---

would respond in unison, "I am In them ladys garden." Holloway wrote the song as one almost unpunctuated block paragraph. To make the game and song easier to read and understand I have separated each line of the song. A similar version of this game is described in Grace Cleveland Porter, *Negro Folk Singing-Games and Folk Games of the Habitants. Traditional Melodies and Text transcribed by Grace Cleveland Porter. Accompaniments by Harvey Worthington Loomis.* (London: J. Curwen & Sons, 1914) viii.

[20] Although Holloway wrote "gentlemen," he likely meant "gentleman" (singular), the same person as the leader or lead singer.

My place to work was with the horses, in the garden, Floyr [=flour] yard at the Big Mill, and now and then at the Blacksmith Shoop with uncle Richmon, and often times no wheare or at least not much any wheare. I had a little [place] to stay in that was a pa[r]te of the Kitchen wheare I stade when I did stay in the Big house. as there was no negro boys to be with me at night I would Read a chapter in my Testament and practice writing on my slate. during of this yeare I wint to school the most of the yeare to Teacher whoes name was Try. he and I wore the same hat or cap as was often the case, The same shoes and pants and coat and that at the same time. Ind [=In the] day I was cald a fool by many of my fellow servants and I gess that was True. That yeare was a very drw [=dry] yeare. The Drouth be gan in May and continurd untill the last of July. there was very poor crops and not a singgle corn shucking that fall. during the mounth of August the sky Turned red red one night in many placeses, it look like streaks of Blood.

It was durin of this yeare that the politicall stome Burst forth that ment to chaing the corse that that cuntry had ben going for neare a hundred years. I passing up a Hill from the shoop on buitfull morning, I pickt a small pam[ph]let containig of a speach deliverd by some congrssman and I will Read you from memory one sentance of that speach. I did [not] understand it and yet I saw that it ment something.

> Gentlemen
>
> The time has come we had as well fase it now as to waight. the chaing will come. this cuntry can stay no longer as it is. evry man must be free or every man a slave.

I carried it to the kitchen. I meet one of my fellow servants there and read it to him. he carried to the mill and Uncle Floyed could read a little. he made out about the same thing. he Brought it up to the shoop and I read it to him and uncle Richmon. And from that time and on I was taken away from the young negro boys into the society of four men. My master was a whig and that party was opposed to secession.[21] I had access to his old papers and as the campain was a speruted on[e], It is needless to say that among the white people politicks ran high. The Election came of in November In favor of Mr Lincoln. South Carlina

[21] Freeman later testified he "was an old line Whig who voted for Bell and Everett" (SCC Disallowed Claim of James C. Freeman, James C. Freeman re-examination of disallowed claim in 1875).

seceeded from the union on the 20th of December. Rev. T. C. Stanley[22] of the Flat Shoals on Christmas day tide a white flag on the lighting rodd of his house shuring that he was with South Carlina.

1861 usherd In [to] find the cuntry politically torn into attoms. pat roleing among the class of white people lookt that work was the order of the day.[23] nothing of special Intress occord that conceard me that I remember, only this, silver money be gan to disappere and in its place a correcy call shinn plasters. Whit men be evry wheare was prepaing to go to ware. we colord people was on to the whole of it and yet remaind loyel to our owners untill the last gun was fired and the last man came home. On the Second Sunday in August It was my good fortune to heare a man prach by the name of Willis.[24] He Read from acts 2 chapter beganing at the 17 verce:

> And it shall come to pass in the last days seth God I will poor out of my sperut upon all Flesh and you sons and your durghtus shall profphesie and your young men shall see vision and your old men shall Dreem Dreems and

---

[22] Thomas C. Stanley (b. c. 1826) was a GA native. The Georgia Conference, MECS, admitted him as a preacher on trial in 1847 and admitted him to full connection as a deacon in 1851. He served as a US Navy chaplain 1848–1853, then located at Flat Shoals in 1854 next to James C. Freeman's land. On 21 September 1852 he married Fredonia E. Blackburn, daughter of Dr. John L. Blackburn of Flat Shoals.

The 1860 census found Stanley (age thirty-four, farmer, with real estate worth $7200, personal estate $25,800) and family still living next to Freeman. Stanley's widowed mother-in-law, Martha A. Blackburn, lived in his household. In 1860 Stanley owned twenty-eight slaves living in nine houses, and Martha Blackburn held thirty-four slaves living in five houses. Stanley eventually left Methodism to become an Episcopal clergyman. See Harold Lawrence, *Methodist Preachers in Georgia, 1783–1900* (Tignall, GA: Boyd Publishing County Ltd, 1984) 524; George G. Smith, *The History of Georgia Methodism from 1786 to 1866* (Atlanta: A. B. Caldwell, 1913) 273; 1860 Census, GA, Meriwether County, Free Pop., p. 128, dwell. 922; 1860 Census, GA, Meriwether County, Slave Pop., pp. 97–98.

[23] Gloss: "Patrolling, by the class of white people who liked that work, was the order of the day."

[24] Unidentified. Probably one of the eight local preachers serving Greenville and Colored Mission; LaGrange District had 56 local Methodist preachers in all. See *Minutes of the Georgia Annual Conference of the Methodist Episcopal Church, South, Held in Columbus, Ga., Nov. 25–Dec. 3, 1863* (Macon, GA: Burke, Boykin & County, 1864) 3–4, 33, available at http://readux.library.emory.edu/books/emory:8gjwg/pdf/ (accessed 7 August 2015).

> on my hand madens I will pore out in thoes [days] of my sperut and they shall profphesie and I well shew wonders in heaven above and signs in the earth beneath, Blood and fire and vapor of smoke. The sun shall be turn into [darkness] and the moon into Blood befour the great and notable day of the Lord come.[25]

It was the custon in thoes days when a servant wish to join a church that he had to gat a recomendation from his owners.[26] But at the conclutions of that sermon Invitations was given for thoes who wished for prayre. I was among the number. the Doors of the Church was Throne oppend. I Staide back for no recomendation but went foward and give my hand and my name witch remaines on the Role untill this day. The civell war was on that yeare in a very mild form untell the great Battle of Bull Run. at that time matters began to gat serious. My Good Farther ded some time during of the sumer of that yeare. I got letter stateing that your Farther Ill, but it was some weeks or mounths when I learnd Throug old farther John day that my Farther was dead.[27]

1862

My Master Mr. J. C. Freeman Give me a pass and a mule to visit my Kindred in the Christmas and [I] past through Zedulurn through the pine

---

[25] Preacher Willis may have been drawn to this passage by news of the First Battle of Bull Run (First Manassas) on 21 July 1861. All his hearers surely expected the outcome of the war to be a great notable day of the Lord—but they probably did not hope for the same outcome, as many white people prayed for Confederate nationhood, while their slaves prayed for freedom. Holloway doubtless remembered the bloody night sky he had seen in August 1860 and interpreted it as one of these apocalyptic signs.

[26] Shade Richards of Pike County, a distant neighbor but probably known to Holloway, confirmed Holloway's audacity: "When a slave wanted to 'jine the church' the preacher asked his master if he was a 'good nigger,' if the master 'spoke up for you,' you were 'taken in,' but if he didn't you weren't." Rawick, *Georgia Narratives*, 203.

[27] Possibly John B. Day (b. c. 1814), son of prosperous planter Lewis Day and his wife, Caroline. John B. Day was a lifelong bachelor who lived at home with his widowed mother in the same Waynmanville, Upson County, neighborhood as the Holloways. Usually unemployed, sometimes laboring on the farm, John B. Day could read and write, and the much younger Holloway might certainly describe him honorifically as an "old farther."

mountains. Took dinner at Mr Thom Allens[28] and Directly to the widowe Holloways that evirng. I had Travell near 50 mills that day witch was along ways.[29] I meet My aged grand mother who was almost Blind. I was never to see her any more. I saw my my steep grand farther Charles Holloway, uncle John Collire and his wief,[30] and Uncle Moseses Holloway[31] who was a methodist

[28] Thomas J. Allen lived in Pike County on Three Mile Creek, about a mile and a half north of the Upson-Pike county line, near the road running south from Zebulon to the tiny settlement of Delray in Upson County. Allen owned twenty-three slaves; it is likely that Holloway ate in the plantation kitchen or at one of three other separate dwellings for the enslaved on the Allen place. Holloway does not explain his connection to Allen's people. Although Allen had lived in Upson County in 1830, he had removed north to Pike County by 1840, several years before Holloway was born. See 1860 Census, GA, Pike County, Free Pop., p. 8, dwell. 52; 1860 Census, GA, Pike County, Slave Pop., p. 2. For location of the Allen Place see Pike County, GA, Deed Books E, 352, 353, and F, 270, 391.

[29] The most useful road map for nineteenth-century Pike County is William G. Bonner's large 1847 map of GA (scale approx. 5.8 miles/inch, or about 1:370,000); the editor found no larger-scale road map of Pike County older than late-20th-century Department of Transportation (DOT) county maps. The earliest large map of Upson dates to 1897, and to 1910 for Meriwether. Roads depicted on the maps in this book are some of the main roads suggested by these older sources and compared with current DOT maps.

[30] Holloway does not explain his lineage from Uncle John Collier and wife. John Collier's wife was Susan, who is documented in probate records of the Edward Holloway estate from 1850 through 1862, including medical attention to her children, Davis and Tula, in January 1862. The estate included a man called John, possibly Susan's husband, but the surname by which Holloway calls him strongly suggests he was enslaved on M. N. Collier's plantation located less than two miles north of the Holloway Place (M. N. Collier held twelve slaves in 1860, including two men about John's age). John Collier and family appear in the 1870 census living near The Rock, Upson County, as John Collier (age forty-nine, farm hand), Susan (age fifty, farm hand), and four children, Davis (age nineteen, farm hand), Tula (age seven), Joseph (age six) and Neptune (age five), all described as mulattos. Neptune, born perhaps four years after Holloway's father's death, was surely named in memory of his late uncle. See TUA, Upson County Court of Ordinary, Record of Accounts Book C, 260, 480; Upson County Court of Ordinary, Record of Vouchers Book A, 474, 690; Upson County Court of Ordinary, Record of Vouchers Book B, 197, 424, 872, 875; Upson County Court of Ordinary, Record of Vouchers Book D, 16; 1870 Census, GA, Upson County, Pop., p. 150, dwell. 1190; 1860 Census, GA, Upson County, Slave Pop., p. 29.

pracher who was the Speri[t]ual guide of my Farther. he was a good man. and many outhers of the many Blacks on the plantation to numurious to mention. and last but least my steep mother and sister Sarah, sister M^c^Ama and little Broo Jones and the sweet Baby in her mothers arms.[32] I do not Remember its sweet name but the good Lord had it upon his Book. I hope to see it and all the Rest on the suny Banks of sweet Delvirance. I spint one night with them and on the next morni[n]g December the 28th I Bid Fair well to my good grand mother, steep grand farther, to my steep mother and My sisters and with a Teare Bedewd Eye we parted to meet no more this side of the grave.

---

[31] Moses Holloway (b. c. 1807). His mother's name was possibly Phillis; his birthplace and early life are obscured, but by age fifteen Moses Holloway was owned by Thomas H. Kendall, who called him Bob. He probably moved with Kendall from Richmond County, GA, to Warren County, then to Hancock County, where Kendall died in November 1822. Kendall, shortly before his death, deeded Bob to his father Henry Kendall, Sr. The elder Kendall knew the enslaved man as "Moses (or Bob)." On 4 October 1826 Kendall sold eighteen-year-old Moses (no longer called Bob) to Edward Holloway of Upson County for $450. Moses lived and worked on the Holloway plantation for the rest of his life. We glimpse him in 1851 cashing a two-dollar order at Timothy Mullancy's store (the same neighborhood store where Houston H. Holloway's father, Neptune, bought whiskey). Physicians treated him for at least four spells of sickness in 1852, 1854, 1856, and 1862. Last mentioned under a physician's care for an undescribed wound in February 1863, Moses Holloway is not evident in post-war records of Upson County.

See Asa C. Alexander & Phereby Alexander *vs* Henry Kendall, Sr., and Henry Kendall, Jr., in loose papers of Upson Superior Court, October Term 1826, Thomaston Upson Archives, wherein he is called "Bob"; will of Henry Kendall, Sr., TUA, Upson County Will Book A, 3, in which he is called "Moses (or Bob)"; bill of sale of "Moses" by Henry Kendall, Sr., to Edward Holloway, dated 4 October 1826, in loose probate papers of Edward Holloway estate, records in TUA, Upson County Court of Ordinary; Upson County Court of Ordinary, Record of Vouchers Book A, 37, 224; Upson County Court of Ordinary, Record of Vouchers Book B, 424; Upson County Court of Ordinary, Record of Vouchers Book D, 16, 227.

[32] Dr. J. O. Holloway attended Neptune Holloway's wife, Mary, twice during accouchement (labor and childbirth); the first time on New Year's Eve 1856, then again on 2 April 1861. These dates may signal the arrival of one of the half-siblings named by Holloway (Sarah, McAma, or Jones) and the unidentified baby, who might therefore have been about nine months old when Houston H. Holloway visited in 1862. I have not found Mary or her children (except Mack Holloway) in post-emancipation records, and Holloway seems to have lost track of them after his 1862 visit.

I Traveld over the Road from the widowe Holloways to the widowe Hartsfeilds, my old Home. I rode up to the gate. my old master reconised me and came down the steeps to shake my hand. by this time Broo Jakcob saw me and he told Edmon and Daniel. they Ran to the Big house to meet me. old miss Betsey was quiet old but was glade to see me. Aund Nancy a woman that would weigh neare 400# was yet alive. Harris was foman of the plantation. Brother John Westly who was a house carperter was at home.[33] Aunt Frankey was dead. Cusan parthema from a small gerl a few years ago had grown into a fine looking young lady.

The fine Velvet vest that my farther married my mother in and also his second wief my steep mother turnd it over to me.[34] I Took dinner with the people on the old plantation and by 2 oclock I Bid the[m] all good bye and on the Road, by Delray, on by Mr Allens [to] home.

---

[33] Holloway may have been unsure whether his brother would be at home because masters often hired enslaved tradesmen to building contractors who employed them at remote construction sites. This had apparently been the case during Holloway's former visit in 1859.

[34] John Wesley Holloway wrote in 1932 that this vest was "still in the family." (JWH, 307) Not located by this editor.

Chapter Three

The Quilting, Courting Cordelia, and Wartime Life

It was some time in the Earley part of this yeare 1862 that I found the white people all away from home one Saturday night. on the same night There was a Big quilting over on the hill witch was BlackBurns quarter. I had alredy learnd to Reaad and write a little. I heard Dallis Black Burn[1] Bloing his quiles.[2] he was and Expert. I steept into the Big house and rote myself a pase. as a matter of corse the pass was a forgery. I had not hardely a mile to go and a very Dark

---

[1] Dallas Redding (b. c. 1844 in GA), enslaved to John and Martha Blackburn at Flat Shoals, Meriwether County, son of Blackburn slaves John Redding and his wife, Mary. His brothers and sisters included James, Chappell, Alice, Frances, John, and George. Holloway calls him by his slavery-time surname, Blackburn, but after emancipation, Dallas used his father's surname, Redding. Dallas Redding registered to vote in 1867 at Flat Shoals, Meriwether County. By 1870 Dallas, his wife, Catherine, and children he had moved east of Flint River into Pike County where he earned a living at farm labor. His brothers scattered to other parts of Georgia, then slowly began to re-unite. By 1880 Dallas and family lived in Griffin where he worked as a domestic servant while his brother Chappell Redding farmed just a few miles north in rural Africa District, Spalding County. By 1900 Dallas Redding and his brothers Chappell Redding and George Redding, with their families, had co-located as neighbors in Union District, Spalding County, where all three men farmed. See Meriwether County Will Book A (1831–1859), 387, Meriwether County Courthouse, Office of Probate Judge, Greenville, GA. Accessed at "Georgia Probate Records, 1742–1990," FamilySearch, http://familysearch.org/search/collection/1999178 (accessed 24 February 2015); GA Returns of Qualified Voters under the Reconstruction Act, 1867, Meriwether County, Election District 36, precinct 1213 (28 June 1867), p 23; 1870 Census, GA, Pike County, Pop, p 97, dwell 687; 1880 Census, GA, Spalding County, Griffin, Pop, ED 118, p 26, dwell 250; 1880 Census, GA, Spalding County, Pop, ED 115, p 1, dwell 1; 1900 Census, GA, Spalding County, Pop, ED 35, p 7, dwells 117, 119, and 121.

[2] The quills, one of the panpipe family of musical instruments, is native to the American South. Made from at least two lengths of canes, usually bound together, one end of each cane stopped and the other end open, you play the canes by blowing across their open ends.

night. I was Soon at Uncle Jordan Black Burns House[3] over on the Hill. the ladys ware all seated a round the quilt stiching away. the Boys was standing a round threeding there neadles.[4] I will mention afew of the most conspiccious among the[m], Emaline Black Burn, Adline Black Burn,[5] Ciller Black Burn, Mertilda Sutton.[6] A mong the girles or young ladys was Miss Debby Thrash,[7]

---

[3] Jordan Blackburn (born in GA, c. 1804) and his wife Susan (born in NC, c. 1805) were enslaved to Martha A. Blackburn. Their children included Dodd Blackburn, Abraham Blackburn, and Floyd Blackburn. By 1870 Jordan Blackburn was a farm laborer in Pike County, GA; Susan was keeping house. Jordan and Susan Blackburn were still in Pike County in 1880, renting a thirty-five-acre farm, worked with the help of their grandson, Jordan, age fifteen, and one horse. See Meriwether County Will Book A (1831–1859), 387 (John L. Blackburn's will dated 3 April 1856); 1870 Census, GA, Pike County, Pop., p. 75, dwell. 528; 1880 Census, GA, Pike County, Pop., ED 103, p. 52, dwell. 492; 1880 Census, GA, Pike County, Schedule 2 (Agriculture), ED 103, p. 31.

[4] Henry B. Holloway (no known relation to H. H. Holloway) who lived in Fort Valley, Houston County, GA, remembered quiltings attended by slaves: "The boys and young men would be there too and they would thread the needles and laugh and talk with the girls, and the women would gossip." See Library of Congress, American Memory (http://memory.loc.gov), *Born in Slavery: Slave Narratives from the Federal Writers' Project, 1936–1938, Arkansas Narratives*, vol. 2, pt. 3, H. B. Holloway, 291. The *Georgia Journal and Messenger*, 15 November 1848, provides another example of a young man attending a neighborhood quilting in Houston County, GA; twenty-four-year-old Jim "had left to go to a negro quilting" when he ran away. Marli F. Weiner, *Mistresses and Slaves: Plantation Women in South Carolina, 1830–80* (Urbana: University of Illinois Press, 1998) 22, discusses the division of labor at quiltings as part of the everyday differentiation between women's work and men's work among the enslaved.

[5] Adaline Blackburn (b. c. 1845), daughter of Newton and his wife, Hetty, all enslaved to John L. and Martha A. Blackburn at Flat Shoals, Meriwether County. Her older brothers were Burrell and Warren, her younger siblings were Caroline, Janette, David, Sophronia, and Joseph. Appraisers of Blackburn's estate on 7 August 1856 valued "Girl Adaline" at $700 (Meriwether County, GA, Will Book A [1831–1859], 387; Meriwether County, GA, Estate Book F [1856–1859], 179, Meriwether County Courthouse, Office of Probate Judge, Greenville, GA. Accessed at "Georgia Probate Records, 1742–1990," FamilySearch, http://familysearch.org/search/collection/1999178 [accessed 24 February 2015]).

[6] Probably Matilda Sutton (b. c. 1840), enumerated in the 1870 Census, GA, Pike County, Pop., p. 104, dwell. 758, age thirty, keeping house, born in GA; married to Sydney Sutton, age thirty-eight, born in NC.

Miss Cordelia Thrash.[8] I stood a round and lookt on at the nimble fingers as they stiched away. time past off very plesantly for some time. as I was looking about I noticed Dallis Black Burn and Floyd Black Burn.[9] Each of them was Threding the neade in Turn for Miss Cordelia Thash. I haerd of her befour but had never meet her nor seen her befour that night. I Took a stand on the opposite side of the quilters and lookt at miss Cordelia for quite a while. I was charmed by her Buety just simply be yound mesure. She caught me looking at her and Turnd her face off with a Bashfull smile. that sweet smile was more then I could Bair. I never spoke to her but I was able to mak and Impression of some sort. there was a penut peddler there selling penuts. he came to me and said that Miss Cordelia Thrash wanted me to Buy her a quarte of ground peas. alright said I "please give me chaing for a five dollor bill," presenting at the same time the bill. He cald out, "gentlemen Mr Freeman wants a five dollar bill chainged. who will chaing it for him?" no one in the house could chaing the bill. So I got in some good advertising and saved my dime also. I will say heare that uncle Richmon the good honest Blacksmith who keep my money for me and I had gorn to him that eveing to get Dollar as I wanted to go to the quilting. After considering a while he give me five dollars and Told me to Bring that money back to morro witch was dun. Shortely after that the quilt was dun and then the supper witch was all ways a good one. Then untill a late hour Dancing was the order of the night. no patrollers turnd up so my first night away from home at a quilting frollic past of plesanty.

The yeare 1863

I know or remember but little pertaing to myself save this. Early In that yeare or late in the yeare 1862, perhaps the latter, Uncle Floyed the Miller said to me late one Saturday Eveing, calling me son, that he wanted me to go up to the widow Thrashes[10] and tell his wief that he would not be th[e]re that night.

---

[7] Debby Ann Thrash (b. c. 1843), daughter of Turner and Rachel Thrash. She married Washington Freeman at Christmastime 1864 (p. 124).

[8] Cordelia Thrash (1845–1894), youngest daughter of Christmas Thrash and Cherry Thrash. See pp. 194-195 for biography.

[9] Floyd Blackburn was son of Jordan and Susan Blackburn (p. 105, n. 3).

[10] Mary (Callaway) Thrash (c. 1789–1869), daughter of John and Bethany Callaway, she was probably born in Wilkes County, GA, about 1789; she married Christopher Thrash on 20 August 1806 in Wilkes County. The couple lived for a few years in Putnam County before moving to Meriwether County by 1840. They settled

he would go to the Cullwell place to see his children. To this I rederly answerd "yes sir." every since the quilting mention befour I had waited for some kind of an Excuse to go Mrs Thrashes. I wanted to see Miss Cordelia at home. all right I wanted it so I had it. I put on my clothes after taking of a bath. goes by Rev T. C. Stanleys, and one of my frends to go with me. And a cross to big feilds half a mile wide Each and we ware at Mrs Thrashes. I soon saw aunt Ferribia[11] and

---

north of the Flat Shoals, overlooking a wide, deep part of Flint River called "The Sea." Christopher Thrash died on 12 October 1844. Mary Thrash died of cancer in June 1869 (Linda Dobbs, Anne Threadgill, Lelia Freeman, et al., eds. *The Heritage of Meriwether County Georgia 1827–2004* [Meriwether Historical Society: n.p., 2004] 403; 1870 Census, GA, Meriwether County, Schedule 2 [Mortality], p. 2, line 8).

[11] Pherebe, Feriby, or Fairby (b. c. 1838) was the fourth child of Christmas and Cherry Thrash, enslaved to Christopher and Mary Thrash at The Sea in Meriwether County. Pherebe was wife to Floyd, James C. Freeman's miller at Flat Shoals. Possibly she was Floyd's second wife, because Floyd was about eighteen years her senior and had children living on Freeman's plantation, the Caldwell Place, in Pike County

In December 1865, six months after emancipation, Floyd and Pherebe were among the first freedpeople in the neighborhood to leave their former owners. Holloway does not tell us where they went or how their marriage ended, but the 1870 census found Phereby ("Farebie") back at Flat Shoals keeping house for Alexander Campbell, a man perhaps eight years her junior. The couple lived very close to Houston and Cordelia Holloway—as John Wesley Holloway recalled: "On the hill-side above us lived my aunt Fairby married to Alex Campbell" (John Wesley Holloway, "Memoirs of John Wesley Holloway, Thebes Ga., July 3, 1916," 9 (photocopy of unpublished manuscript in author's possession, hereafter cited as JWH). The Campbell household included four girls, Mary (age eight), Nice (age four), Eliza (age two), and Cherry (age four months) who was undoubtedly named for grandmother, Cherry Thrash.

Alexander Campbell (b. c. 1846) had lived in neighboring Pike County all his life and had registered there to vote in August 1867, but records do not show when he united with Pherebe. Neither Pherebe nor Alexander Campbell appears in the 1880 census, and Pherebe was presumably dead when Alexander remarried in 1899 to Annie Abrams (*née* Leigh). Alexander himself was dead within a few years. When John Wesley Holloway began writing his reminiscences in 1916 he reported that "Annie...married my uncle (aunt Fairby's husband) and is now living widowed at Griffin, Ga" (JWH, 29).

See Meriwether County, Will Book A (1831–1859), 86 (will of Christopher Thrash); 1870 Census, GA, Meriwether County, Pop., p. 40, dwell. 291; JWH, 9, 29; GA Return of Qualified Voters, Pike County, Williamsville, Precinct 505, p. 45, 10 August 1867; 1900 Census, GA, Spalding County, Pop., ED 92, p. 11, dwell. 190.

Delvered her Husbands message. Dallis Reding[12] my frind he was not long in till [= telling] one of the men that we wanted to see one of the girles and Mr Freman wanted to see the outher. Going as we did from house to house we found Mis Debby and Cordelia in the kitchen. the girles promised to meet at Uncle Turners house.[13] They soon shurd up. Now Doc Thrash,[14] uncle Turners

---

[12] See p. 104, n. 1.

[13] Turner Thrash (b. c. 1803) and his wife, Rachel Thrash (b. c. 1804), were enslaved to Dr. Christopher Thrash and wife Mary Thrash of Flat Shoals. In 1821, a teenaged girl, Rachel, along with a young man named Simon, came into Mary Thrash's possession under a bequest in the will of her father, John Calloway of Wilkes County. Rachel and Turner presumably married sometime after Rachel's arrival in the Thrash household, perhaps about 1825. Turner Thrash had a wooden leg by the time Holloway knew him.

Holloway calls Jim (James Thrash, born April 1826) their oldest son, but we do not know certainly how many children Turner and Rachel had. Christopher Thrash's will, written in 1844, left to Mary Thrash a "woman Rachel and three of her children to wit Jim a boy, Doctor a boy and Debyann a Girl"—implying there were children other than those three. The inventory of Thrash's estate made 21 December 1844 may list other children, but it does not identified their parentage. Turner, Rachel, and their son Jim served as principal advisors to the widow Thrash on how to manage her farm.

In July 1867, two years after emancipation, Turner Thrash still lived in the old Meriwether County neighborhood (perhaps he remained until widow Mary Thrash died in 1869), but by 1870 he and Rachel had moved to Griffin, Spalding County, where he retired in the midst of his numerous kinfolk. He died before 1880. Rachel kept her house while Turner lived, but when widowed, she boarded with a family named Greer. In her seventies she earned her daily bread as a laborer. The 1880 census is the last record of Rachel Thrash.

See Meriwether County Will Book A (1831–1859), 86; Inventories and Appraisements, Returns and Sales, Vol. B, Meriwether County, GA, 373 (available at Georgia Archives, Morrow, GA, microfilm roll DDC 107–108 [drawer 13, box 10]; also at "Georgia Probate Records, 1742–1990," FamilySearch, http://FamilySearch.org/search/collection/1999178 [accessed 24 February 2015]); 1870 Census, GA, Spalding County, Griffin, Pop., p. 78, dwell. 617; 1880 Census, GA, Spalding County, ED 116, p. 4, dwell. 34.

[14] Doctor (Doc) Thrash (b. c. 1840), son of Turner and Rachel Thrash, was enslaved to Dr. Christopher and Mary Thrash of Flat Shoals. After emancipation, Doctor (Doc) Thrash remained in Meriwether County at least through 4 July 1867 when he registered to vote, but by 1870 he and his family—wife and sons, Gus and Dick—had moved to Griffin, Spalding County, Georgia, where Doc worked as a farmhand for many

son, he was a Banger [=banjo] picker. he soon got his old Banger and pickt a Tune while the girles danced. I will give you afew words of his song.

I cum from Tennesee ho ho ho ho
Dar the niger live on clover ho ho ho ho

The girles acquited them selves nicely, at least I thought so. I got a chance to see Miss Cordelia and have a Talk with her. She agreed to be my sweet harte and I was to be heres on the followng conditions. I was to be her company from that time and on where ever we met, a meeting or els where, and I was to be hers. She could dance with [whomever] she would but that was to be the end of it as I did not dance.[15] Miss Cordelia and I had a very plesant cort ship for neare tow years. I keep my word. She did the same. The girles soon left me of[f] since I did not notice any one particular but Miss Cordilia and noticed no one but her.

---

years. Census-takers recorded Doc's wife's name as Cinda in 1870 but as Scynthia in 1880.

Doc Thrash's son Gus Thrash was the father of Dox Thrash (ca. 1891–1965), the artist and printmaker whose national recognition grew from innovative work in Depression-era Philadelphia with the Federal Art Project. Dox Thrash depicted everyday scenes in the lives of black Southerners, "impoverished but strengthened by family, community, companionship, and religion." Perhaps reminiscent of his musical grandfather, one of his best-known etchings depicts a banjo player.

See Meriwether County Will Book A, 1831–1859, 8; 1870 Census, GA, Spalding County, Griffin, Pop., p. 60, dwell. 476; 1880 Census, GA, Spaulding County, Griffin, Pop., ED 118, p. 56, dwell. 511; 1880 Census, GA, Spalding County, Griffin, Pop., p. 18, dwell. 161; 1900 Census, GA, Fulton County, Pop., ED 45, p. 2, dwell. 20; quotation from Philadelphia Museum of Art, "Dox Thrash: Revealed; a companion site to the Philadelphia Museum of Art exhibit: 'Dox Thrash: An African American Master Printmaker Rediscovered,' 1893–1907," p. 1, (at http://www.philamuseum.org/doc_downloads/education/ex_resources/doxThrash.pdf (accessed 17 February 2015).

[15] Holloway probably did not dance because he had joined the Methodist church. Members were prohibited from dancing. Cordelia was free to dance until she joined the MECS in August 1864, four months after she married Holloway. Holloway's son John W. Holloway recalled the day his father forced him to join his church in the late 1870s: "The next Friday night there was a big 'swinging dance' at Perry McAlister's and because I had become a member of the church and everybody knew it I couldn't dance. All I could do was to hop around alone" (JWH, 40).

About this time the Civill War was on with all of the Horror that goes with a Bloody ware. many a time we have devited the last potatoo with a passing Confedrate soilder. Many of then would tell us that they ware poor men and thery fighting for the rich men and they did not care if the yankees did whip them. And as strang as it may appeare many Thousands [of slaves] had learnd to love there owners and under no considerration would they have lifted up there hands against them. Many Thousands of the slave holders ware kind to there slaves. Many of them would not under any considerration parte a man from his wief or a woman from her husbands. Theas however ware the Exseption and no[t] the rule.

Our Reading Club was care for [=careful]. Sheareman with one Hundreed Thousand fedrall Trups had envaded the northerburn part of the State. Much Distress was on every hand. the March from Chattanoog of Shermans Army and the Fleeing Refeges from northern Gorgia ware ever on on the road.

times ware gating worse every day. About this time Honable John Bell[16] who ran for the presedency againt Mr Abrehan lincoln was a Refege at the Flat Shoals, stooping at Mr J. C. Freeman. It fell to my lot to wate on him. he was a very clever man, also his Daughters Miss Gennie and Miss Sallie. The winter of this yeare was Reather mild and many Thought it was Gods mercy on on the Confedrate souldiers in the feild. In the fall of 1863 I think great Battle of Chickamaga was fought. genral Rosuncrans and genrul Johnson on the Confedrick side was the Topics for conversation every wheare.[17] The Southern

---

[16] John Bell (1797–1869) born 15 February 1797 in Nashville, TN; educated as a lawyer; elected to seven terms in the House of Representatives (1827–41); began his political career as a Democrat but switched to the Whig Party; served briefly as President William Henry Harrison's secretary of war in 1841; served as US Senator (Whig Party) from Tennessee 1847–1859; in 1860 ran as the presidential candidate of the Constitutional Union Party on a platform to preserve the Union above all other issues. Bell garnered 13 percent of the popular vote and 13 percent of the Electoral College in the race that elected Abraham Lincoln. After South Carolina fired on Fort Sumter, Bell retired from politics and returned to his home state. His business assets were heavily damaged in the ensuing conflict. Bell lived as a refugee at James C. Freeman's house about twelve or fourteen months from 1864 until the end of the war. His two daughters, Sally and Jenny, lived there about six months of the time. John Bell died in Dover, Tennessee, on 10 September 1869. For Bell's time as refugee see SCC Disallowed Claim of James C. Freeman, affidavit of Sally Bell Keeble, dated 8 April 1875.

[17] At the Battle of Chickamauga, 19–20 September 1863, Confederate commander Braxton Bragg soundly defeated Union commander Brig. Gen. William Starke

people proclamd a day of fasting and prayre for Gods help in the great struggle.[18] The widow Thrash lived one mile above the flat shoals. I could slip off from home when ever the white people was away from home to see my good girl God Bless her. having access to my masters writting table I would go into the Big house some Sunday after noon And write myself a pass after this maner:

> Houston has permishion to go to Mrs Thrashes and back home by sun down.
>
> J. C. Freeman.
>
> Sept the 6, 1.8.6.2.

I would go out and stand beside the Big rode and wate for some white man to pass and have him to see if my pass was right. This being dun a crose the feilds and up the river swamp and I was soon at Mrs Thrashes. Mis Cordelia was always looking for me. Thease white people as a rule was humane to wards there slaves. they clothed well and fed well and they did not often whip bad. Uncle Turner was a man with a wooden leg. He was noted for his good comon sence. Old miss as they cald her would spind many sabbath after noon with uncle Turner and aunt Rachel and Jim there oldest son[19] Talking about the plantation and how every thing aught to goo on. I would take a walk down on

---

Rosecrans. Holloway's "genrel Johnson" might be General Bushrod Johnson, who served under Bragg at Chickamauga, but is more likely Bragg's superior officer, General Joseph E. Johnston, who commanded the Department of the West in 1863.

[18] President Jefferson Davis issued two proclamations in 1863 calling for days of fasting, humiliation, and prayer. The designated days were Friday, 27 March 1863 and Friday, 21 August 1863.

[19] James Thrash (b. April 1826) registered to vote 4 July 1867 in the same Meriwether County neighborhood as other former Thrash slaves. He then moved to Griffin in Spalding County by 1870, where he and his older sons worked as farm hands and his wife, Clarissa, worked as a domestic servant. By 1880 he and son Simon (probably named after his uncle, Simon Thrash) still farmed in Spalding County, although James was temporarily disabled by paralysis. His wife ("Clara") cooked for another family. The couple had adopted three very young children surnamed Caracker. James Thrash is not found in the 1900 census.

See GA Return of Qualified Voters, Election District 36, Meriwether County, Precinct 1213, p. 28, 4 July 1867; 1870 Census, GA, Spalding County, Griffin, Pop., p. 32, dwell. 269; 1880 Census, GA, Spalding County, Pop., ED 115, p. 2, dwell. 11.

Sea[20] witch was wide place in river we would set down on the Bank and Talk sweetly to gather. This sweet corrispondance wint for neare 2 years. Some time during of the yeare 1863 I went over to Mr Isaac Strictland to see and [=aunt] Suasan and to tell her about my good girl. And Suasan told me not marry that gal untill she could see her. the time was set and she walkt five mills down to the Flat Shoals. I had my sweet harte notified and she was on hand. Aunt Suasan saw her and was please with choice for a wief.

My Recolection is this. It was in the fall of the yeare 1863. The civill war was Rageing on all sides so much so that patroleing was discontinurd. Infact the young white men and many of the old men was in the Army. evry man between the ages of 16 and 60 years was enrold. this left the wh[i]te women and gerles at home with the slaves and I have got to hear of the first one yet that betrade his or her Trust.[21] Colord men was often placed over all the outher slaves as the white men was all away from home In the army and thoes formen often Turnd out to be the hardest kind of over sears over the rest. The winter of the yeare 1863 was noted for tow things that is it was very dry and cold.

The end of the yeare came. we all as a rule had a plesant Christmass. The pricissis of corn ran from 8 to 10 dollars per Bushell and the next yeare it wint to ten and twelve dollars per Bushell in Confedrate money. a good pair of shoes would readaly Bring from one hundred and fifty dollars and a pair of Boots would Bring 200 dollars. most any mule would Bring 500 dollars a calico dress patron, if you could find one, was worth ten dollars per yard. If a man had a[n]y thing to sell and any body wanted it he could gat any pr[i]ce that [he] asked for it. a Brase watch worn out was worth one Hundred dollars. A good Buggy was worth from tow to three Thousand Dollars.

The yeare 1864

Ersherd In.[22] The cuntry was in a very gloomy state. The fedrall Army with genrall Sherman at its head was alredy on the north western Border of the state. Our folk as we cald them was hard put to it for men. every man from 16 to 60

---

[20] The Sea is a deep place about 250–300 yards wide on Flint River, one mile upriver from Flat Shoals bridge. When Holloway knew the spot, Christopher Thrash's widow, Mary (Polly) Thrash, owned the land on the west bank of The Sea.

[21] Weiner, *Mistresses and Slaves*, 177–78, compares Holloway's comment with other contemporary testimonies of loyalty, and discusses possible reasons for slaves' apparent loyalty to their white mistresses during wartime absence of the households' white men.

[22] Gloss: "The year 1864 ushered in."

years of age was compeld to Enter the army. Every foot of ground between Chattanooga and Atlanta was bone of contention between our folks and the envaders. That yeare about the first of Febuary My master and [=one] Sunday morning cald me and Told me to hitch his horse to the Buggy. the order was promtly fild. I drove the horse up to the froont gate where he always came out and there I meet one of the plantation young men Whoes name was Floyed.[23] He and [I] chatted untill Mars James came out and The following conversation took place. "houdy mars James." "Houdy Floyed what are you down heare after." "I came to see you." "what do you want." "I wants to marry." "who do you want to marry?" "one of Mr Sam Parks[24] Girles." Mars James replied, "you shall not do it. I have right there on the plantation as good or galls as any Mr Parks has and you go back home and marry one of my galls right heare."

I will Exsplain this matter. in theoes days when a negro man, old or young, wanted a wief, even If the woman belong to the same man that he did, he had to ask his master for her. If she belonged to annother man and his master consented for him to marry her, he asked his master per mishion. If he consented He rote to the man who owned the woman on this manner:

[23] Floyd Freeman lived on the Caldwell Place, James C. Freeman's plantation northwest of Concord in Pike County, about seven miles by road from J. C. Freeman's house. In 1845 James Neal gave Floyd and his mother Amanda as gifts to Neal's daughter Amanda Freeman, J. C. Freeman's wife. (James Neal's 1845 deed named eight people: "Negro man Jim commonly known as Jim Brown, negro woman Amanda and her child a boy by the name of Floyd, also a negro man by the name of Claiborn, negro man named Sandy, negro woman named Amy and her two children Harriet a girl and Edmund a boy" (Pike County Deed Book G [1843–1850], 464).

Many years after the Civil War, freedman "*James Campbell* better known as *James Brown*" (emphasis in original) named Amanda Freeman and Floyd Freeman as witnesses to events in April 1865 when Yankee soldiers visited the Caldwell Place (SCC Disallowed Claim of James C. Freeman, affidavit of James Campbell dated 13 March 1872).

[24] Samuel C. Parks (b. c. 1801), farmer, had newly moved into Pike County with twenty-seven slaves when enumerated by the 1860 census-taker (1860 Census, GA, Pike County, Free Pop., p. 60, dwell. 413; 1860 Census, GA, Pike County, Slave Pop., pp. 24–25).

Mr. J. H. Hines,[25]

My negro boy John wishes to have one of your negro women for a wief. He is a good boy. I have no objection.

G. W. Head.[26]

The above certificate was all the Licens Isherd to a collord man in thoes days and they wore not binding on eather side. The land Lord Had the right to sell the woman while the outher had the right to sell the man when ever he chused.

Returning to Mr. J. C. Freeman, Floyed, and myself at the froont gate. Floyed was denide the privealidge of marrying The girle whoes harte he had won. I was planing to do the same thing. with a cupple pretty girls in the yard with me, I was planing [to] ask permishion to marry Miss Cordelia Thrash. I was the house boy and I Thought at once If Mars James would not let Floyed marry off from home, and he a plantation boy, I stood no chance at all to mary Mis Cordelia Thrash. Now what mist I do. I will Tell you In the next chapter.

---

[25] J. H. Hines was possibly planter James Hines, enumerated in 1860 with twenty-three slaves (1860 Census, GA, Meriwether County, Free Pop., p. 72, dwell. 515; 1860 Census, GA, Meriwether County, Slave Pop., p. 68).

[26] George Washington Head (b. c. 1813), in 1860 was a farmer owning thirty-three slaves; he and family lived next to James C. Freeman. According to Head's testimony to the Southern Claims Commission, he moved onto lands adjoining Freeman's place in January 1860 (1860 Census, GA, Meriwether County, Free Pop., p. 128, dwell. 920; 1860 Census, GA, Meriwether County, Slave Pop., p. 281; see Disallowed Claim of James C. Freeman, affadavit of G. W. Head, 10 March 1874).

Chapter Four

Conjure Men and Marriage

In thoes days we had men among us in all partes of the cuntry that was surposed to do wonders with diferrant kinds of roots and outher ingrediants known only by the Indiviguall. he was surposed to chaing your mind from one theng to annother. They could blind [=blend] certain roots to gather and put them down some wheare about The door where the person lived, be he white or b[l]ack and Influance him as he chused. Sum was Surposid to be sharpe Enoufe to make a hand that would work a white man this way one Hundred Mills. So it was in this case. Uncle Henry Baley was a new comer from Clark County. he was the slave of Connell Samyell Baley.[1] haveing not lived very long about the Flat Shoals and had already advertised himsell as and Expert in the misterious arte of making hands as theas th[i]ngs ware cald and Jacks and so forth. I will tell you more about theas men in a seperate chapter.[2]

In my case I wint up to see my chums Dalles reading and Scott Baley. The[y] Recommendid uncle Henry baley as one of the best men in casesis of that kind. There was severrall men in the nabborhood that could do wonders on that line befour uncle Henry got th[e]re.

---

[1] Samuel Bailey (c. 1804–1879), reportedly a native of Virginia, moved as a youngster to Clarke County, GA, where he lived for a few years, then moved to Meriwether County where he was twice elected to the Georgia House of Representatives. He lived in Griffin from 1865 "and by a life of honesty and fair dealing had worked his way into the highest esteem of everybody" becoming "one of [Griffin's] wealthiest and most public spirited citizens." He was for some years president of the Griffin Banking Company. A member of the Methodist church, he "lived the life of a consistent Christian." He died aged about 75 in Griffin at the residence of Dr. J. J. Caldwell, on 15 July 1879 (Atlanta *Daily Constitution*, 17 July 1879 [obit.]). He was the namesake of Griffin's Samuel Bailey Male Institute, constructed in 1870. (The building exists today as part of the Griffin High School campus (City of Griffin, GA, "Samuel Bailey Building," http://www.cityofgriffin.com/visitors/PlacesofInterest/SamBaileyBuilding.aspx [accessed 17 February 2015]).

[2] Holloway never completed the chapter organization of his book.

On Sunday or monday night I think the latter I wint over on the Hill which was Connell Baleys plantation. I had a private Intervew with uncle Henry. I Told him all about my Trubbles and what I wanted dun. He lisend very close to my storry untell it was finished. He afterward grond a long grone and a deep sigh befour he said any thing and He spoke. And heare is about what he Said: "Well my son you case is a hard one and I think that I can work it for you but will take at least three mounths to do it. You are your masters house boy and he thinks a great deel of you and then you are young. If you was older I could work it better. it well cost you right smart of money to have it dun. Now the first thing dat you do, go and get me some whiskey and some shugar. I will have to have dat in de hand and it will take tow weeks to make de hand. And Mars James will have to walk over it tow or three monts buffour you can say any thing to him about it."

My reader may gess how I felt over the Situation. When you consider that this was in the latter part of febuary 1864 and I had pland to marry Miss Cordelia in Aprile. You will know that whiskey was worth fifty dollars per galon in Confederate money and I was not allowd to buy it at all, but suceeding however to gat uncle Henry half pint of whiskey. A pound of dog tail shugar cost me tow dollars. it took me neare tow weeks to get theas assenuals [=essentials] for uncle Henry to began the audest [=arduous] Task of makeing my hand or Jack to chaing Mr Freemans mind in my favor. I Turned it over to him. On Turning over to Uncle Henry my whiskey and Shugare he told me that it would take him at least three mounths to do what it would have to do in that time.

Jush heare I will say that I had sum doubts about the Arte that was often beleaved in by the best colord people and many of the comon whites. One week after I left uncle Henry I Took a notion that I would go to my master and ask for the sweet privaledge of marrying. this was in March 1864. I saw annother cunjurror who was said to be very smart on this lime [=line]. I will not tell my reader what he did. not much; however, He charged me four dollars in Confedrate money wich was not much. Mars James spoke reather Kind to me that Sunday morning about the Second Sunday in March and I Took a notion that I pick my chance that day and ask him to let me marry. the whole day past off untill night and I could not catch him alone so after supper I said to my Room mate John Aron and asked him to steep in the House and tell mars James to please steep to the door, I wanted to see him. he Told me in so many words "I will not do any such a thing. what do you want with him?" I would not tell him what I wanted and [he] would not serve me. After words I Saw Mertilda[3] the Nerce and she refused. After her I saw Sarah a small gerle and she refused to go. about this time I went back to John Aron and offord him five dollars to go and see Mars James. After a while he promised me he would witch he did and charged me nothing. In short while Mars James came out and walkt down to the gate I made him a short speach I[n] theas words: "Mars James you have owend me for six years. I have tried to be a good boy all the time and put you to no Trubble. now I wants to marry." to this he replid loud enofe to [be] heard back up in the yard: "wants to marry." all the servants up in the yard laught, Booth women and men. I did not want them to know any thing about it. Mars James as he was at that time told me after teasing me not a little, told that he Thought that I was to young But I had been agood boy since he ond me. he would have to let [me] marry. I cannot tell how full of Joy I wast at that time. I leave that part of my story to be Told by some one that have had simular Exspereances on that line, for my feble pen Is enadequate to the Task. From my fellow servants in the yard from one to annother I[t] was all over the naborhood That Houston Freeman was going to marry Cordelia Thrash. His master had consented. uncle Henry Baley heard of it. He was my cunjuror who was to work the case for me by some way pecular to himself. He came and Told me that he found away to work on me and my master booth at the same time and put the matter right Through and he wanted his money for His servesses and, If I did not pay It, I would have bade luck, when I knew that I had always been In hard Luck any way. I did not beleave him no way and I surpose the worst of it came to him for he lived to gat free but not long afterword.

At this time I had been made Teacher in a Sunday School wheare colord children ware catachise on the Sabbath wheare the Land Lords would allow it as I could reade a little. I soon had many children that could answer every question in the first catacism.[4] The Great civell war was Raging. many a time have I

---

[3] Holloway tells us Matilda the nurse was a "principall house woman" [p.131] for James C. Freeman.

[4] Never before had the MECS Greenville Circuit & Colored Mission provided formal religious instruction for enslaved children. Georgia Methodists called non-white Sunday school students "catechumens" because they were orally drilled to memorize a simplified catechism. In this way the church conformed to state law forbidding anyone to teach a slave or person of color to read. In contrast, white MECS Sunday School pupils learned from books. The book from which Holloway drilled his pupils was some edition

divided my meales with a Confedrate soulder and I would have my reader to understand that in the Confedrate Army that was the very embodement of Humanity. I came in contact with Thousands of them and all ways found them to be considerrate and very seldum overbarring. But more about this farther on.[5] The time for my marrag drew nie which was bild to take place on the 9th of Aprill 1864. on a cirtain friday in the first of the same day th[e]re was proclamation, the people meet at the several churche[s] and fast and pray for Gods help In drveing back the Invaders of the soil.[6] this fast day was observed at Salem Meeting house over in Pike County. I had gorn over in Pike and seen aunt Suasan and had her to meet my Bride at the Flat Shoals. She likt her very much. She was a prety girl and a smart one. I had alredy gotten a paper from My master to carry to the [widow Thrash]:

> Mrs. Christian Thrash,
> My boy desires to have one of your negro gerles for a wief. this is to enform you that I have no objection.
> J. C. Freeman

My pass to Mrs Thrashes read as followers:

> Houston has permission to go to Mrs Thrashes.
> J. C. Freeman
> This March the 30th 1864

There was one thing that will be quiet amuseing to my reader. There was afew men haredely ever more then tow in a narborhood that was cald tow

---

of William Capers, *Catechism for the Use of the Methodist Missions. First Part* (for example, see third edition [1853] at http://docsouth.unc.edu/church/capers/capers.html) composed in simple words "for the mass of colored people" (quote is on p. 3.), Statistics for Greenville & Colored Mission 1860 through 1863 show zero catechumens (1864 did not include a statistical table), but the Statistical Table for 1865 shows fifty catechumens, presumably Holloway's class. (*Minutes of the Georgia Annual Conference of the Methodist Episcopal Church, South, held in Macon, GA, 15 November 1865* [title page missing], Statistical Table).

[5] Another indication that Holloway envisioned a larger book than the one he wrote.

[6] President of the Confederacy, Jefferson Davis, proclaimed Friday, 8 April 1864, a national day of "humiliation, prayer and fasting."

headed men. Men that was surposed to have the ability to chainge the mind of most any one to suat themselves.[7] Such a man was uncle Henry Baley referd to befour. I went to Mrs Thrashes that night gating my good frind Dallis Blackburn to go with me. it may be needless to [say] more then this. on that night evry thing went well. Sailing was smoth and plesant. Mrs Thrash give her consent for me to marry Cordelia. Matters moved on nicely for ten days or more, witch brought me to the ninth day of Aprill 1864 and on a buitifull stare light Saturday night at nine o clock, I [was] befour the widow Thrashes door. I was marched with uncle Floyed Freemen who was the Brother in law of my Bride[8] and read the ceremony from the Disciplin of the M E Church South and pronounce Me and Cordelia Thrash man and wief in the name of the farther and of the Sun and of the Holy ghost, ading thoes whome God had Joind to gather let no man put assunder. Though it was a dark day and a dark night but I fail to Exspres the Joy that Thrild my soul that night. I had nothing but my wief and not even her more then a name and yet I had all that I wint for no colord man nor boy got any thing more in that day.[9]

---

[7] Two-headed men or women, sometimes called two-headed doctors, also called conjurors, attributed with "second sight"—able to sense things that ordinary people cannot see, able to influence others by magic. See Albert J. Raboteau, *Slave Religion: The "Invisible Institution" in the Antebellum South* (New York: Oxford University Press, 2004) 275–88.

[8] Floyd Freeman was married to Pherebe, one of Cordelia's older sisters.

[9] Holloway reminds his readers that Georgia law did not recognize marriage among slaves, so that the title "wife" did not invoke more protection than any other name or word. Floyd Freeman highlighted Georgia law's moral bankruptcy when he included the words, "Those whom God hath joined together, let no man put asunder," in Holloway's wedding ceremony.

Chapter Five

Richmond's Funeral, Yankees, and Emancipation

I was 19 years old about that time the civill [war] was Raiging then on all sideds. The Fedrall armey had alredy envated the north western part of the State. The Confedrate goverment was straining its self to the utter to raise men to replinish the ranks of its armey at the froont. about this time evry man between the ages of 16 to 60 years was cald out and conpeld to enlist and shoulder a musket and go to the war. About this time there was but few citisens at home. about the flat shoals there was but 4 white men and they ware plased at the Shoals and the Cross Roads to chalens evry man that past to know who he was and where he was bound. There was in a Radus of 3 mills a round not less then 800 slaves with the white women and children. Comon corn was sould at ten dollars per bushell, Bacon at tow dollars per pound, Floyr at 25 cts per pound, meall 12 dollars per Bushel in Conferate money. Genrall Sherman with and army of 200,000 men was contending with genrall Johnson a right of way to Atlanta. Sorgum syrrup sould at one dollar per quhart. most any kind of home spun sould at ten dollars per yard. a good suat of Jeanes bring from 250 to 300 d[oll]ars. a good pair of shoes was Easley bring one Hundred dollars. a good pair of Boots sould at 200 to 250 dollars. a good Buggy would Bring 3000 dollars. Most any kind of a horse would Bring five hundred to 1000 dollars.

During of that yeare 1864 in the mounth of August Uncle Richmon, Mr Freemans old Trusty Blacksmith mending [=mentioned] in a former chatter [=chapter], took sick down at the foot of the Bridge. Mr Freeman and his wief and Mrs Stanley[1] and evry body Els did what they could for uncle Richmon but after a lingering of 3 week or more uncle Richmon, who was a class leader in the flat shole church, and much saut by among all the people, at 8 oclock 30 minutes, past over the Hills I trust into cuntry from witch un [=none] has ever retund.

Uncle Richon was a most Exemplary man as you will see when we consider the prevaleing custims of thoes days. there was very little considerration given to

---

[1] Fredonia E. Stanley (b. c. 1834), daughter of Dr. John L. Blackburn of Flat Shoals, had married Rev. Thomas C. Stanley on 21 September 1852.

the subject of temprence. most every body would take a drink of whiskey. Uncle Richmon would not drink a drope of whiskey nor use tobacco in any forme. He stood upon his morrill carrecter. he would not lie. on this line there was no question if uncle Richmon said any thing it was true.

He was well up in the politicks of thoes days, the Democratice partie, the Whigg partie, the no nothing partie, the nulifires[2] and the anteno nothing parties.[3] He understood the principals also of the Abolishionite partie.[4] He was on to the stuburnness of of the Whigg partie in the North and its sympathisurs on the one hand and the Democratic partie of the South that Brought on the civile war. Many an everng have I spint in a close Room of his house at the foot of the flat shoal Bridge Reading of Mr Freemans last paper the Savannah Republican.[5] while I read he understood better then I did the contents of the papers. Into this Roon there was but four men allowed to meet, uncle Richmon, uncle Floyrd the miller and Anteney Alxander and myself and uncle Jacob the preacher[6] who belong to Mr J C Freeman. as the civell war progrest we was on to every movement small and large Ingagement from the beganing untell the End of that Bloody Struggle.

---

[2] Although the Nullifier Party, a short-lived political party of the 1830s, did not participate in 1860s politics, John C. Calhoun's stance on nullification still resonated with members of the most pro-slavery branch of Georgia's Democratic Party; thus Richmond would have heard and understood the term.

[3] The Anti-Know Nothing Party was an alliance of Democrats, Whigs, and Freesoilers who opposed the xenophobic and anti-Catholic American Party (nicknamed the Know-Nothings).

[4] The Republican Party.

[5] *Savannah Republican*, published from about 1802 until 1865, had a statewide readership. Politically partisan like most newspapers of its day, it was a mouthpiece for the Whig Party in Georgia until that party's functional demise in the early 1850s.

[6] Probably Jacob Freeman (b. c. 1817) who most likely worked on James C. Freeman's plantation, "the Brown Place"—he was named as a witness there to Wilson's Raid in April 1865—one and a half miles from James Freeman's home at Flat Shoals. Voting registrars in August 1867 recorded that Jacob Freeman was born in NC, had lived in Georgia for fifty years, in Pike County for twenty-two years, and in the 505 GMD (wherein lay the Brown Place) for twelve years. He does not appear in the 1870 or 1880 censuses. See SCC Disallowed Claim of James C. Freeman, affidavit of Herod Smith taken 13 March 1872; GA Return of Qualified Voters, Pike County, Williamsville, Precinct 505, 10 August 1867, p. 45, no. 67.

as we said on a former page uncle Richmon died on the tenth day of September 1864 and was Buried on the next day. Most all of the colord people was Turnd a lose to go to his Berring. He give Mr Freeman a 50 dollar bill in Confederate money to sind to the plantation down in Pike County Alabamma for Uncle Claibon[7] to come to Georgia to preach his furnall.[8] My Reckolection is that memorable Furnall was preached on the secon Sunday in October 1864. on that day no patroleers was out for more then ten miles a round and my reader may depend upon it the people was out. The Rev. W. A. Parks[9] the circut rider

[7] Claiborne Bush (b. c. 1807), enslaved to James C Freeman's wife, Amanda, by deed of gift from James Neal in 1845, was a locally-licensed preacher in the MECS during slavery; after emancipation the MECS ordained him deacon, but he joined the AMEC in 1870. See biography in Appendix A, p. 200-202.

[8] It was customary in this part of Georgia for a person to be buried the day after she or he died, but a funeral might be preached about thirty days later.

[9] William Asbury Parks (1834–1910) was first licensed to preach in August 1856 and elected deacon 1858. He was appointed to Athens Colored Mission (1859) where he inducted future CMEC bishop, Lucius Holsey, into the MECS. Parks was next appointed to Oglethorpe and Traveler's Rest (1860). In November 1860 he transferred to the Texas Conference, where he was appointed to LaGrange Station, TX, for 1861. He was elected elder in November 1861 and appointed to Gonzales for 1862. Parks described himself as "overburdened with his appointment," and in a fit of "despondency" he enlisted as a private in Waul's Texas Legion in March 1862 (*Wesleyan Christian Advocate*, 14 December 1898, 2). General Waul appointed him chaplain. In 1863 Parks transferred to Barton's Georgia Brigade (also known as Stovall's Brigade), serving as chaplain to the 43rd and 52nd Georgia Regiments where he rejoined his Georgia friends. Decades later Parks wrote a series of reminiscences about his military service up to the Atlanta campaign in July 1864 (*Wesleyan Christian Advocate*, 18 January 1899, 3; 15 March 1899, 2; 5 July 1899, 3).

Holloway places Parks at Richmond's funeral, but the published GA Annual Conference rolls do not include Parks until November 1865 (and conference minutes do not tell when he rejoined). Possibly the LaGrange District presiding elder placed Parks in the Greenville Circuit and Colored Mission to replace J. W. McGehee, who had gone as missionary to Stovall's Brigade sometime before January 1865. After the war Parks served as pastor at Cuthbert and Georgetown (Lumpkin District), then served the MECS North GA Conference as agent of the American Bible Society from 1870 to 1876.

See Harold Lawrence, *Methodist Preachers in Georgia, 1783–1900* (Tignall, GA: Boyd Publishing County Ltd, 1984) 409; MECS 1858, 60, 63; MECS 1859, 159; MECS 1860, 262, 274, 277; MECS 1861, 349, 351; MECS 1863, 473; MECS 1864, 511, 528; MECS 1865, 572.

preached to the white people at eleven o clock, and at one oclock a multitude was on hand to heare uncle Claibon. There was present that day Rev David Harris[10] of the Baptist Church, And Rev Mr owens[11] of the Methodist Church South who was Brotheren law to uncle Richmon.

The Rev Clairbon Neale arose and after singing the Hynn and let this Boddie Die this well wrort Frame decay,[12] falword by one of the most solum

---

[10] David Harris (born in NC, c. 1803), a local Baptist preacher before 1865, was ordained after the Civil War in Hebron Baptist Church, Pike County. In 1867 with Rev. Dan Williams he founded Rocky Mount Bethel Baptist Church to serve black Baptist sharecroppers in northeastern Meriwether County, east of Luthersville. The congregation built their small wooden church on an acre donated by a white landowner. Harris registered to vote at the Greenville precinct, Meriwether County, in 1867. The 1870 census enumerator found him ("David Hariss") living near Flat Shoals in Meriwether County, a farm hand, sixty-four years old, with his wife Harriet, age fifty-six, keeping house. By 1880 Harris lived in the 665 District (near Greenville), worked as a farm laborer; his new wife, Isabella, keeping house.

See Dobbs, Threadgill, Freeman, et al., eds. *Heritage of Meriwether County*, 39; GA Return of Qualified Voters, Pike County, 48 (David Harris); Georgia Archives, Office of the Governor, RG 1-1-108, Reconstruction Registration Oaths Books, 1867–1869 (hereafter cited as GA Reconstruction Oath Book), Meriwether County, Election District 36, Election Precinct 665 [Greenville], 4 July 1867, (David Harris); 1870 Census, GA, Meriwether County, Pop., p. 35, dwell. 257; 1880 Census, GA, Meriwether County, ED 87, p. 35, dwell. 113. (Possibly the same person, a man of similar age named David Harris, not correlating with any Pike County resident in the 1870 census, registered to vote in Pike County on 10 August 1867, stating that he had lived in Georgia sixty-four years and in Pike County, Williamsville precinct, for two years.)

[11] Probably a non-ordained local preacher. Printed minutes of the Georgia Conferences 1865–1869 list no one surnamed Owens or Owen. Being uncle Richmond's brother-in-law Rev. Mr. Owens was presumably black (since Georgia law forbade marriage between white and colored races).

[12] A Wesleyan hymn common in antebellum Methodist hymnbooks. The first verse, below, is quoted from Rev. Cyrus Prindle, comp., *A Collection of Hymns, for the Use of the Wesleyan Methodist Connection of America* (New York: O. Scott, 1846) 425: "And must this body die, / This well-wrought frame decay? / And must these active limbs of mine / Lie mould'ring in the clay!"

prayrs that I ever heard, He announce for his text Hebrews the 4th chapter and 9 verse, There Remaneth Therefor a rest for the people of God.[13]

My reader will Hardely understand me when I say I heare no such preaching in this our day as that Truly Logicall and Eloquent sermon was that day. In speeking of the deceast he said among many outher things "he was Honest, he was a greable, he was Industrius, and was bloved by all good people.

"He Came into the world as all outher people. he past through the world in such away as to make good people love him. Thought often times it was dark He had his trubles as outher men but he knew how to over come them. How did he pass through the dark wast houlding wilderness of the world. Th[e]re was a light that shome on his path way that was not seen by evrybody. Some times he would pluck a bunch of sweet graps heare and he would find annother bunch there. Now and then he would find a cluster sweet grapes."

He spok in such away as to move the people white as well as the colord. not all that Hell or sin can say shall tempt me for gat that day. During of the time Uncle Claibon was out heare Aunt Joe Annah was converted who just a short while ago died This September 19 1909 in the City of Atlanta.

This yeare 1864 was fast passing away. there was nothing of particular Importance occuring the remaing tow mounth save this, the old Fashan Corn Shuking past away. not one was had in the cuntry that yeare. The confedrate goverment waggan was out for[a]ging for corn and cattle to feed the men in the Armey. we would see at times five Hundred waggon and six mules to Each waggon on the Road forgeing for provision. The yeare ended with a big weding at the widow Thrashes. Miss Debby Ann[14] was married to Washington Freman[15] in the Chrismass. So ends the yeare 1864.

---

[13] Hebrews 4 compares God's rest on the Sabbath after Creation to the heavenly rest of the righteous after life's labors. Hebrews 4:9 was a popular text for funeral sermons; for example, at the funeral of Christian educator Mary Peake at Hampton, VA, in 1862. See Rev. Lewis C. Lockwood, *Mary S. Peake: The Colored Teacher at Fortress Monroe* (Boston: American Tract Society, n.d.) 48.

[14] Debby Ann Thrash (b. c. 1843), daughter of Turner and Rachel Thrash.

[15] Washington Freeman probably lived and worked on Freeman's Caldwell Place plantation in Pike County because James Brown named "Wash Freeman" as one of the witnesses to the invasion there by General Wilson's Yankee cavalry in April 1865 (SCC Disallowed Claim of James C. Freeman, affidavit of James Campbell, a.k.a. James Brown, dated 13 March 1872).

The yeare 1865

The Darkest days of the civell war was seen in the first four mounth of that yeare. The yeare went out with a Turberl ciclone pasing over a part of Merriwether & Pike Countys. A white man by the name of Frank kindell and his mother[16] was kild in Merriwether while Con [=Colonel] Samyell baleys Barn and Jin house was Blown away. Mr J C Fremans Jin house and much cotton stord away there meet the same fate. Nothing of particular Importance Happend of Intress. there was but few white men in the cuntry at all. evry man that could shoulder a musket was at the froont and Els wheare at the service of the government.

It was my day to stay at home on the 3 Sabbath in March. My sweet little wief came down to the flat shoals to stay with me. about that time a Happyer cupple then myself and little wief would have ben hard to find. there was a Toll

---

[16] Frank Kendall (c. 1823–1865), judge of the Court of Ordinary for Meriwether County, died in the tornado. His mother Mary Kendall (1780–1868) was seriously injured but lived another three years. Frank Kendall joined Greenville Methodist Church as a probationer on 29 August 1858 but was dropped from the church roll in 1859. The 1860 census found him living with his eighty-year-old mother in the Greenville District. The Richmond, Virginia, *Daily Dispatch*, 27 January 1865, reported, "F. Kendall, Ordinary of Meriwether county, Georgia, was killed by the tornado which recently passed through that country. His residence, a two-story building, was lifted from its foundation and carried about one hundred yards. His neck and legs were broken. Others of the family were seriously injured" ("List of Male Members 1857," Greenville Methodist Church [in possession of Greenville United Methodist Church, Greenville, Meriwether County, GA]; 1860 Census, GA, Meriwether County, Free Pop., p. 372, dwell. 276; [Richmond VA] *Daily Dispatch*, 27 January 1865, 3).

The 1860 census enumerated Mary Kendall, head of household, with twenty-one slaves and $3,000 worth of real estate. Her obituary in the *Southern Christian Advocate* reported she was born in Wilkes County, GA, 24 July 1780: "She was married twice, and her last husband the late Major E. Kendall she survived more than twenty-five years. She was the mother of eleven children, all of whom she survived but three." She had been a faithful member of the Methodist church for perhaps fifty years. "She was poor—she became rich by unwearied industry and economy, and in the Providence of God she saw it almost entirely destroyed in an instant by a terrible hurricane, her son killed, and she crippled for the remainder of her life, and in a few months her negroes set at liberty." She died near Flat Shoals, Meriwether County, 24 April 1868, "after an illness of but a few days having very nearly completed her 88th year" (1860 Census, GA, Meriwether County, Slave Pop., p. 65; *Southern Christian Advocate*, 10 July 1868, 112).

Bridge a cross Flint river. this particular Sabbath past untill noon. In the after noon there came [someone] a cross the Bridge. I meet him to collect the Tole. at the same time there came along 2 Conferate souldirs and the following conversation came up.

> The citesin: "Good evirng gentlemen"
> [soldiers:] "Good Evirng sir"
> citesen: "Gentlemen whare are you from?"
> souldire: "Alabamma"
> citizen: "I have started over to Opalicka to see about some hats that I had making over there"

The souldiers replied that "we heard that the yankees was there yesterday morning." the gentleman past on his way. So did the 2 souldiers.

On Tuesday the 23 day of March[17] about day light I came [out] of the yard on my way to the lot to feed the stock. I lookt down towards the foot of the Bridge and saw many cattle and mules and Black people and some few children and one old white man who had charge of whole outfit. upon I[n] qurey I found that they were Refegees from Trupe County Borduring on Alabama. They was soon a cross the Bridge and gorn. Just Bout this time I look up the Rode and a colord b[o]y coming down the Road upon a mule in a sweeping gallop. I made my self a little Inquisitive:

> "hello ther, hold up, whare are you goin?"
> "after Jim"
> "what do you want with Jim?"
> "Mars Rhubin[18] says we got to Refegee"
> "whats the matter?"
> "the Yankees are coming"

---

[17] Holloway is off by about a month. Gen. James H. Wilson's raid through Georgia happened in late April 1865, not March.

[18] Probably Reuben C. Strozier (c. 1839–1914), whose residence and farm, operated with twenty-one slaves, was on the road west from Flat Shoals. See 1860 Census, GA, Meriwether County, Slave Pop., p. 96; and 1860 Census, GA, Meriwether County, Free Pop., p. 463. Strozier had married James Freeman's daughter Sarah Elizabeth (1843–1887) on 18 May 1860.

I repled back to him, "your are a lier." he passed on to the mill and soon Jim and his fellow servant was on there was [=way] back and I saw them no more for a while.

There was much gri[n]ding at the mill that day and I had to leave the shoop and go to the assistance of uncle Floyed at the mill. I could work in the mill and see the people passing over the Bridge also. about ten oclock I saw about mounted confedrate souldus with three magazine wagon and 3 cannons. the horses was weet with sweet. They spook to no one as they past. I goes to the house to gat our dinner and goes back by the shoop about helf past one oclock. I lookt up the Road and saw about 50 white boys cumming in hast. I knew one of them. I Call to him, "Hellow Mr Bonney, What is the matter?" He replied, "Stay heare untell night and the yankees will shure you whats the matter." "Sir, is the yankies coming shure enoufe?" he replied, "they shoot at me twice coming out of greevill [Greenville] about 12 oclock." and on they went. I ran by the mill to tell uncle Floyed the miller and back up to the house to tell Mars James as we Cald him. ran into the Big house and told him what the white boy told me. He unly replid, "I cannot help it." I then ran one mile up the river to the widowe Thrashes to tell them and I had not been th[e]re but a short while befour I heard the Yankeys shooting at a fleeing white boy about a mile up on the big rode. I told my wife that I would not leave her and go with the yankeys but just now I would go back to the shoals. on pasing through the feilds I lookt some distance a cross the feilds and saw 4 men going down towards the shoals. I was soon there also. from the shoop door I saw 4 men and Mr Freeman who was a union man at his froon gate talking with 4 men who had on Blue clothes. I soon found out that they were the advance gard of the main armey of 8 or ten Thousand mounted men, to say nothing about the Thousands of Black people who had ran away and Joind them.

The 24 day arley in the morning the whole command was on th[e]re fast march Bound for Macon. I meet Mr Freeman at the gate and [he] Told me with a laugh that all the horses was gorn. he told me also to go down to the Lower Shoals and wade a cross the River and see if I could not beat the yankeys to the Culwell place and tell Nels[19] to hide out the mules. I undertook the Task. It

---

[19] Nelson Freeman (b. c. 1830) was born in the 505 GMD of Pike County and lived there for at least the first thirty-seven years of his life. Enslaved to James C. Freeman by the 1860s, if not earlier, he worked on Freeman's plantation, the Caldwell Place, and was a witness there to Wilson's Raid in April 1865. He registered to vote in Pike County 10 August 1867. See SCC Disallowed Claim of James C. Freeman, affidavit

ment at a nine or ten mile and the yankey was a head of me at the starte. I ran about 5 mills and meet Nelson coming down to the Shoals to see if the yankeys was coming. Shure enoufe I told him that they shure there, also what Mars James told me to tell him. he turnd around and ran back towards the plantation as fast as his feet and legs would carry him. he got there time Enoufe to meet the yankeys coming out of the lot with the mules.

I was releaved of going any farther. Mr Lorrance tried to gat me to take the woods with his folks.[20] I preferd gat back to the River and then a cross If pasable and see what had be come of my sweet wife. I was soon at Mr Coggin greeggs.[21] there I meet uncl Prince Poop[22] who had bin down to the shoels to see if the yangies was th[e]re. th[e]re was sevrall Black ons with him. Mrs Greegg asked him if they ware there. He replied "yankeys, Yankeys, yankeys, world without [end!]."[23] Mrs Gregg Brouk out with a loud cray. I give uncle Smart 2 dollars in Conferate money to carry me down to the river and put a crose in his cannou. He did So. he was a man that was never known to do any thing in a Hurry and he was not much of a Hurry this time but got there Just the same. when I got from Mrs Greggs down to Flint river Down under a bluff in a deep Junggle I found a celebrated Methodist preacher who dun all that he could to Bring on the war. he spoke the cuntrey over telling the people that it would be a kind of a

---

of "*James Campbell* better known as *James Brown,*" taken 13 March 1872; GA Return of Qualified Voters, Pike County, Williamsville Precinct 505, p. 44, 10 August 1867.

[20] Jesse Lawrence (b. c. 1806), enumerated in 1860 Pike County census, age fifty-four, farmer, real estate worth $4625, no slaves; with his wife Cynthia Lawrence, age fifty-seven, and three minor females, probably his daughters (1860 Census, GA, Pike County, Free Pop., p. 45, dwell. 315).

[21] George Crogan Gregg (b. c. 1831-65), found in 1860 census, age twenty-eight, a farmer, owned eleven slaves, lived with wife Fetney A. H. Gregg, age twenty-five, and family. Gregg lived very close to Jesse Lawrence (Census, GA, Pike County, Free Pop., p. 44, dwell. 311; 1860 Census, GA, Pike County, Slave Pop., p. 15). George C. Gregg was with the Confederate army in Virginia, where he was killed about this time.

[22] Prince Pope (b. c. 1823) was enslaved to Cadesman Pope prior to emancipation in 1865. Prince Pope's widow, Fanny Pope, and children (including Prince Pope, Jr.) were enumerated in the 1870 Census, GA, Pike County, Pop., p. 43, dwell. 304.

[23] John Wesley Holloway suggested the bracketed word and exclamation mark, which are a persuasive emendation (JWH, 335). "World without end" is a Biblical phrase roughly synonymous with "forever" or "without limit." The phrase is part of the hymn "Gloria Patri," sung weekly in most Methodist churches. In this context the words would have suggested a seemingly endless number of Yankee soldiers.

rat killing and the common white people Beleavd him. but on that memorable day the 24th day of March he could not find a Junggle thick Enoufe to hide in.

In a cannou Uncle Smart put me on the merriwether side of the river. a cross the feild of the big plantation I [ran] and I was at the widow Thrashes and the yard was full of yankeys and the women ware cooking and they wore Eating and a connell was siting on his horse Eating and duscussing the causses of the war with the wihite women.[24] when they left they took away all of the stock that they could gat hold of and among them, old Jess, Mrs Thrashes favorite horse. In the after noon I went down to the shoals to see what was going on. th[e]re was about 20 yankeys left th[e]re while the main body of the army like a devasta[t]ing storm had gorn on a cross the cuntry having no opposition in its way. on the 25 day of March, 2000 more yankeys was th[e]re, Genrall McCook[25] and his staff. the men spent the night on the Hills a round but the genrall and his Staff put up at the Big house. we got our first drink of coffie and saw some shugar for the first time in 3 years as they had all of thease things with [them]. Hon John Bell the Whig cannodate for the presidency against Mr Lincoln was th[e]re and a big time they had th[e]re that night as Mr Freeman was a Union man and had a protection from Mr A Lincoln.[26] very soon after the Rade led by genrale Wilson[27] had capturd Macon there was an Armmistress proclamd witch was a cessation of Hostillities for some time looking to a close of the war.

---

[24] This ironic twist on Southern hospitality, where enslaved plantation women cooked the plantation's food for General Wilson's troops while the plantation mistress looked on and conversed with the officers, was repeated elsewhere in April 1865: see p. 29, n. 58.

[25] Edward Moody McCook (1833–1909), a brevet brigadier general, commanded the First Division in Gen. James H. Wilson's cavalry raid through Alabama and Georgia in March and April 1865.

[26] Probably a neighborhood or slave quarter rumor. James C Freeman's claim before the Southern Claims Commission from 1871 to 1875 includes no hint of presidential protection; on the contrary, the commissioners denied Freeman's claim on grounds of documented disloyalty to the Union.

[27] James Harrison Wilson (1837–1925), a brigadier general commanding a cavalry force that raided through Alabama to Macon, GA, in March and April 1865.

April was heare and it was during of this mounth we heard that genrall Lee had surrenderd at Appomattox.[28] There was no news papars published of account. news wint slow in the last of the mounth. I had a bout 100 dollars in Confederate money. I went to Mr J C Freeman to Buy 10 dollars worth of floyr. He let me have the floyr but would not take the money. I soon meet a white woman who had some pantloon cloth to sell, common cheeks [=checks] at 10 dollars per yard. I took 3 yard at 30 dollars. I got off 10 more dollas some how and the next day in the morning [as] I was going down to the mill I saw a Conferate soulder making gun wading of 5 & 10 dollar bills. I saw at once that the money [was] dead.

about the 10th of May [came] a gentleman drest in a connells uniform Leading a bay horse and riding [one] of dapall Iron gray. He wand a horse shood. we went to work to shoe the horse. the shoes had to be made. Nales also. we got a long slow having no tools. Hen [=He] Inquired if the was any yankees any wheare in the cuntry. D N Freeman replied the [=he] heard there was some out on the old plank road about 8 mills away. The gentleman got all at once in a Hurrie. we got his Job dun as quick as we could. Hon John Bell was siting on the Root of a tree in the front of the shoop. the connel wint to him and Talkt with him a while. he wore a pair of colord glasses with side Eyes. assoon as his work was dun I asked a colord boy who led a gray horse and rode a bay who the gentleman was. He said that was connell green of Missippie. the connell just heare mounted his horse and was gorn. Hon Mr Bell cald Mr Freeman to him and asked him did he know that man. he told him he did not. he replied in a lowe voice, "that was no body but Jeff Davice.[29] I knew him assoon as he rode up."

Soon after this the confedrate souildes began to return home and the great civill war was over. we could see that something was comeing. what was [it?]. there was something in the air. Mr Freeman wint to the lot and caught his horse and saddle it. I had never know him to do that befour. the mounth of May past and as June come neare Poline & Mertilda t[w]o of the principall house woman

---

[28] Robert Edward Lee (1807–1870), general-in-chief of the Confederate States Army, surrendered on 9 April 1865 at Appomattox Court House, VA.

[29] Jefferson Davis (1808–1889), president of the Confederacy, along with the Confederate Cabinet, left Richmond on 3 April 1865 as federal forces approached to take the city. Davis was the object of an intense manhunt by the US Army. Until his capture on 10 May 1865, his whereabouts sparked wild rumor and speculation.

and I took a notion to go Mount Carmell Methodist Church to meeting.[30] I asked for the use of the carrage & horses. they wore granted. I got a man to dr[i]ve by the name of Nelson. I got the Black saddle ho[r]se and my mastus saddle and off we shoot to meeting. we asked for a pass. He told us that we would not need one. this was the last time that [I] ever asked for a pass, June the 4 1865.[31] It would be needles to say we had a big time that day. this Brings us to the greatest day that I had ever known up to that day. Earley Monday morning Mr J C Freeman told me to hitch his horse to the Buggy. I promply obeyed. he wint to the Culwell place, cald all of the slaves up and set them free and frome there to the More place[32] and set them free and was at home by noon. passing by the shoop he told me to go to the mill and tell Floyed and lewis[33] to come to the house. this ord[er] was my last or[der] as a slave. it proomtly obayed. At the house Dinner was served and about 20 of us was cald up to the house doore and set free.

Amen Amen Amen

---

[30] Built in 1842, located about eight and a half miles north of Flat Shoals by road, the same Carmel Church sanctuary in which Holloway worshipped now serves as Carmel United Methodist Church.

[31] This event on Sunday, 4 June, and James C. Freeman's subsequent emancipation of his slaves on Monday, 5 June, coincides with publication of President Andrew Johnson's "Proclamation 134–Granting Amnesty to Participants in the Rebellion, with Certain Exceptions" on 29 May 1865. The proclamation granted "to all persons who have, directly or indirectly, participated in the existing rebellion, except as hereinafter excepted, amnesty and pardon, with restoration of all rights of property, except as to slaves." To claim benefit of the pardon, ex-rebels had to swear the following oath: "I,______,do solemnly swear (or affirm), in presence of Almighty God, that I will henceforth faithfully support, protect, and defend the Constitution of the United States and the Union of the States thereunder, and that I will in like manner abide by and faithfully support all laws and proclamations which have been made during the existing rebellion with reference to the emancipation of slaves. So help me God" (see www.presidency.ucsb.edu/ws/index.php?pid=72392).

[32] Holloway usually calls Freeman's two plantations in Pike County the Caldwell Place and the Brown Place; this is the only instance where he calls one "the More Place."

[33] Lewis Freeman lived at James C. Freeman's home place during the Civil War. He and Jones Harald, a fellow-slave, "dug a cave, when the Confederate authorities got after Mr Freeman to put him in the army, and urged him to hide in it and they would feed him and take care of him" (SCC Disallowed Claim of James C Freeman, affidavit of Jones Harald taken 13 March 1872).

He Told us that he was Free to[o]. he felt like a burd out of a cage.[34]

Amen Amen Amen

I could hardely ask to feel any better then I did that day. the Thought thrils me at this day. Just think of it. I had been sould 3 times, once at Sheriff sail and twice privetly.

The week past off in a Blse of glory. on Saturday everng I left off work for the first time in lief and gos over in Pike to see my ant Suasan who yet belong to Isaac Strickland for he had not yet set his slaves free. on my way over there I meet and old poor whit woman. She asked me who I belong to. I Told that I blong to myself. She blard her eys[35] and ask, "who did you use to be long to?" I told, "James C Freeman." "Has he sat all of his nigges free?" was the next question. I answed "yes mam" and walkt on. tow mills farther on and I was at Mr Strickland. Ant Suasan was in the feild. neare night she came home. she embrace me in her arms and when I told her that I was Free she Embracet me again and said, if you ar free. I had a Talk with Mr Strickland. he requested me to come back and live with him.

Some time in august that yeare I got my first letter as a freeman, my Second let[ter] in lief.[36] The letter read as follows

Benney Manes Mill.[37]
Talbert County Georgia
August the 6 1865

Deare Broo Houston,

I writ this to let you know that I am free. have you received your liberty yet?

your Broo,

---

[34] Eric Foner, *Reconstruction: America's Unfinished Revolution, 1863–1877* (New York: Harper & Row, 1988) 77, has Holloway exclaiming, "I felt like a burd out of a cage"—but Holloway was quoting Freeman, not himself: "he [meaning Freeman] felt like a burd out of a cage."

[35] To "blare one's eyes" is to stare with eyes wide, almost bulging, to show disapproval or hostility.

[36] The first letter, received in 1861, had told him of his father's fatal illness.

[37] Benjamin Manes (b. c. 1798) lived in the Pleasant Hill District of Talbot County; his mill was probably on Lazar Creek.

J. W. Hartsfield.

On the 28th day of July that yeare at one oclock in July my first child who is now at this writting is paster of Bethleham Congregationall Church Newark Newjersey was bornd on the plantation of Mrs Christopher Thrash neare the Flat Shoals in Merriwether County Georgia on the 28th day of July 1865. He was the first child bornd in the naborhood after Freedum. Dr Dellosprayr[38] wated on my sweet wife and received my Free bornd Son into the world. This boy seemd To have come into the world a lover of Book. while it is comon for children while Infants to tare papers and books, This baby was and Exseption to the rule. whe[n] he was Eight days old I cold him John Westly[39] for my oldest Brother about whom more will be said farther on.

Some time in the mounth of December, beganing about the first, the colord people began to Brake up and leave There former owners. So it was with me and Brother Floyed who had my wiefs sister for a wief. He moved his wief first. I followard on afew days later. My first home was in the Room in the yard of Mr. J. C. Freeman whare I had been for 6 years. The outher people who did not contract to stay on the place moved away. My first Christmas spent as a free

---

[38] James C. DeLaperriere (1832–1916) was born 7 June 1832 in Jackson County, GA, son of Dr. Angel (or Ange) DeLaperriere, an immigrant from France but longtime resident of Jackson County. James C. DeLaperriere, graduated in 1853 from Graffenburg Medical College in Alabama. He moved to Flat Shoals neighborhood in 1858, where the 1860 census-taker enumerated him as a physician living two houses away from James C. Freeman. He enlisted as a private in Company F, GA 55th Infantry Regiment, serving May–November 1862. After the war he seems to have subordinated his practice of medicine to agriculture because the 1870 census lists him as a farmer. (The census taker spelled his surname "Delaprier," a close phonetic match for Houston Holloway's spelling, probably reflecting how the name was pronounced in the neighborhood.) The 1880 census found DeLaperriere practicing medicine back in Jackson County where he was reportedly "for several years a leading physician" but later "devoted his attention to farming, banking, real estate and manufacturing." He died 9 December 1916. All quotations are from J. C. Bennett, "The Medical Fraternity of Jackson County," originally printed in *The Jackson Herald*, 14 December 1905; republished online at http://www.victorianmaysville.com/history/jchistory/jcdoctors.htm (accessed 20 January 2015); 1860 Census, GA, Meriwether County, Pop., p. 128, dwell. 923; 1870 Census, GA, Meriwether County, Pop., p. 34, dwell. 248; 1880 Census, GA, Jackson County, Pop., ED 2, p. 2, dwell. 6.

[39] John Wesley Holloway (1865–1935). See biographical sketch, pp. 196-98.

man was at the flat shoals. We knew nothing in thoes days about Buisness. Hence the provost marshail had to see after and approve all of the contracts made betweean the colord people and there former owners the Incoming yeare. this Brought on much confution and to the whit people It was very Humiliating to have to go to the then Hatefull yankey to aprove or disapprove his contract with his former slave.

Now at this time the goverment of the state was almost Intirely military. There was a garrison of Fedrall soldiers at Evry county seat and in all Town to keep order, For we colord people did not know how to be Free and the white people did not know how to have a free colord person about them.[40] at that time it was often so that many colord men and colord women also did not know his wief or Husband, On account of previous sales and seperrations groing out of the old order of things. But the yankey was Equel to the Amergancy. So when ones old wief, who had bin sould away, came back to the old naborhood Hunting for her ferst Husband, leaving a man that [she] had marrid while away from her ferst, finding her husbnd marrud to annother woman, It took a yankey to straten the matter out. and you may depend upon [it] he had much of this kind of work to do for a yeare or tow. The chief of the Freedman Buroes word was Law in all matters of that kind and there was no appeal beyound his decission and strang as it may appeare his decission was always satisfactory untell a provsional goverment was Establishe by the Goverment at washington.

And assoon the Legeslator of the State of Georgia past an act declaing all colord men and woman liveing to gather on a certain day to be man and wief by law.[41] in outher states they had to take out lisens and marry straight out.

---

[40] The last half of this sentence, beginning "For we colord people did not know how to be Free," is frequently quoted in books and on the Internet. Writers usually use this sentence to make arguments about economic conditions in the early days of Reconstruction, but the full sentence in context shows that Holloway was explaining the need for federal military presence to keep peace and social order.

To view the proliferation of this quote on the Internet, enter this sentence fragment into any search engine: "For we colored people did not know how to be free." The original site from which the others copied may have been Library of Congress American Memory, African American Odyssey, at http://memory.loc.gov/ammem/aaohtml/exhibit/aopart5.html.

[41] On 9 March 1866 Georgia's governor approved *An Act to prescribe and regulate the relation of Husband and Wife between persons of color*. By this law pre-existing monogamous marriages between persons of color did not need marriage licenses and did not need to be

So Ends my Story for 1865.

recorded. The law stated that "persons of color, now living together as husband and wife, are hereby declared to sustain that legal relation to each other, unless a man shall have two or more reputed wives, or a woman two or more reputed husbands. In such event, the man, immediately after the passage of this Act by the General Assembly, shall select one of his reputed wives, with her consent; or the woman one of her reputed husbands, with his consent; and the ceremony of marriage between these two shall be performed. If such man, thus living with more than one woman, or such woman living with more than one man, shall fail or refuse, to comply with the provisions of this section, he or she shall be prosecuted for the offence of fornication, or fornication or adultery, or, fornication and adultery, and punished accordingly" (*Acts of the General Assembly of the State of Georgia, Passed in Milledgeville, at an Annual Session in December 1865, and January, February, and March, 1866* [Milledgeville: Boughton, Nisbet, Barnes & Moore, 1866] 240).

Chapter Six

Preaching and Working

The firs six mounth of Freedum Brings us to January the first 1866. we all went to work some how. I wint to work in the old Blacksmith shoop neare the foot of the Bridge In copartner ship with George Freeman.[1] Bacon meat was 25^cts^ per pound, corn meal 1.50^ct^ per Bushell, Floyr 5 dollars per Hundred. As for Luchuries outside of meat and Bread there was nun and we wanted nun for we was Free. Glory be to God was our daley cry and the same aught [to be our cry] to day.

Things moved along very well the whole of that yeare. I was [al]ready a member of the Methodist Church South and felt that [I] was cald of the good Lord to preach. The white man who was appointed to preach to the colord people in that section was a good man if there was any in the world. His name was W. A. Parks.[2] He it was who recomend me to the greenvill circut

---

[1] I found two candidates for George Freeman, freedman, Holloway's partner at the blacksmith shop in 1866. The elder George Freeman (b. c. 1827) was native to GA and had lived in Pike County since about 1847 and in the Flat Shoals neighborhood since about 1850, and worked on the Brown Place, one of James C. Freeman's plantations at the time of Wilson's Raid in April 1865. He registered to vote in Pike County with some of his Flat Shoals neighbors on 10 August 1867. The younger George Freeman (b. c. 1840–1843) lived at James C. Freeman's home place at the time of Wilson's Raid, but registered to vote in Greenville District in 1867 and farmed as a sharecropper near Greenville in 1870 and 1880.

See GA Return of Qualified Voters, Pike County, p. 44, precinct 505 Williamsville, 10 August 1867; 1870 Census, GA, Meriwether County, Pop., p. 36, dwell. 270; 1880 Census, GA, Meriwether County, Pop., ED 87, p. 30, dwell. 84; 1880 Census, GA, Meriwether County, Schedule 2 (Agriculture), ED 87, p. 10; GA Return of Qualified Voters, Meriwether County, p. 60, precinct 665, 6 July 1867; NARA, RG 233, Southern Claims Commission, Disallowed Claims, Office 244, Report #7, No. 2783, claim of James C. Freeman, hereafter cited as SCC Disallowed Claim of James C. Freeman, available in NARA Microfilm Publication M1407, fiche 2463–2365, affidavits of Jones Harald and Herod Smith, taken 13 March 1872.

[2] See p. 122, n. 9.

M E Church South as a suatable person to be lisind [=licensed] to Exhort, the quortely confernce convend at mount plesant M E Church South six mills above greenvill Eighteen mills from the flatshoals. Rev Claibon Bush[3] and I left The Flat Shoals afoot on Friday some time in the morning. we past throug greevill Aprill the 17, 1866 [actually, Friday was 13 April] and we spent the night with a good man by the name of Charles penson in the naborhood of mount plesant. Saturday morning Aprill the 18th [actually, 14 April] The presiding Elder Rev D J McGhee[4] and the paster of the greenvill circuit and quiet a number of the white pople began to arrive. I had never seen a presiding Elder befour. At the hour of Elevenoclock Devine Service was opend by Rev Mr Smith the Circut Rider.[5] The presiding Elder arose and Took for His Tex [blank]. It would be

---

[3] Claiborne Bush (b. c. 1807) was a formerly enslaved farmer who became Holloway's co-worker in preaching to the neighborhoods near Flat Shoals 1866–1870. See biography in Appendix A, pp. 200-202.

[4] Holloway mistakes the name; presiding elder of LaGrange District in 1866 was John Boykin McGehee (1833–1917). Born in Perry, Houston County, GA, on 6 September 1833, McGehee was licensed to preach on 7 November 1852. After several annual appointments in various places, Bishop Pierce appointed him to Greenville Circuit and Colored Mission (Meriwether County) for 1863 and 1864. In January 1865 the bishop appointed him presiding elder of LaGrange District, a position he filled until December 1867 when the MECS Georgia Conference split into North GA and South GA conferences. McGehee served the rest of his sixty-five years of ministry in the South GA Conference. He died 22 July 1917. See John Boykin McGehee, *Autobiography of Rev. J .B. McGehee, of South Georgia Conference* (Buena Vista, GA: n.p., 1915) 5, 43, 133–36; MECS 1862, 404; MECS 1863, 458; MECS 1864, 511; MECS 1865, 572; MECS 1866, 28; MECS 1867, 121.

[5] J. Blakely Smith (1820–1872) was born in Charlotte, NC, and reared as a Presbyterian. Smith converted to Methodism in 1843 at Newnan, GA, and was admitted to the MECS ministry on trial in 1847. He was elected deacon in 1850; appointed to various stations and positions until elevated to presiding elder of LaGrange District from 1861 to 1864. Fellow-itinerant John Boykin McGehee described Smith as "well rounded in body, soul and spirit" (McGhee, *Autobiography*, 56–57). In 1865 he was appointed to LaGrange District's Greenville and Colored Mission—the capacity in which Holloway would have known Smith as the circuit rider. He was appointed to Greenville in 1866, then to Macon 1867–1870, and finally to Americus District as Presiding Elder 1871–1872. On 30 September 1872, after staying overnight at the home of a church member Smith arose early, walked into the front yard, collapsed, and died.

Impasable for me to give and out line of his masturly Effort. Dinner was served on the grond. the quartely confernce convend at 2 oclock our Recomendations faild to gat there But we ware authorised to Exercise untill the next quartly confernce.

During the next 3 mounths we held many meeting as we wore not use to being free. things wint well. Rev Bush was at his farme. I was at the Black smith shoop during the week. we came some Exposed to a case of small pox[6] over on the Hill as it cald Backmans [=Blackburn's] quarter. in a short time th[e]re was many cases of small pox over there and tow at my house. I had a very slight attact. And our Baby who is now Rev J W Holloway paster of the Congregationall Church at Theebs georgia his attact was slight. Now as straing as it may appear my good wief sleep with us Throug the Entire spell and never caugh the disease.

That spring was very weet. provision was casta [=costly]. Bacon was 25 ct per pound, Mail 150[c] per Bushell, Floyr 500 per hundred and no money to Buy any. our old forner master Advanced us surplise on credit. it may be safe for us to say that we got along some how. the 3 munths soon gorn and July was heare and the quartly confernce convend at Trinity M E Church not far from the warm springs and off again afoot on Friday Eveing for 20 mills we had to walk. we spint the night At Mr James Reace with one of his tenants by the nane of James.[7] the quartely confernce convend after noon and The session was Largely attended by the white people as there was no colord seeking Amission but Rev Claibon Bush and myself. Rev Bush was Relisend [=relicensed] or in ourther words his Lisens was renewd. At the same time I was Licend to Exhort. And heare I will say the Church made a mistake for it surdenly lade hands on us when Saint Paul had warnd then many centuries bfour to lay hands surdenly

---

See MECS 1860, 260; MECS, 1861, 343; MECS 1862, 404; MECS 1863, 458; MECS 1864, 511; MECS 1865, 572; MECS 1866, 29; MECS 1867, 124; MECS 1868, 225; MECS 1869, 326; MECS 1870, 434; MECS 1871, 557; MECS 1872, 680–681, prints a detailed biographical obituary.

[6] Gloss: "We became somehow exposed to a case of small pox."

[7] The Meriwether County Tax Digest, 1863, 704 GMD, records a James Reese returning taxes on four slaves and a lot of land in 2nd Land District (same locale as Warms Springs); but no James Reese appears in the 1860 or 1870 censuses for Meriwether County. No better identification found for tenant "James."

upon no man.[8] That summer we had many conferts of there kind. we had many glorious revivals At Salem Flat Rock in Pike and at the flat shoals.[9] I can heare now in my humble Imagernation Sister Minta Collins[10] shouting, "Glory to God and the Lamb for ever."[11] There was not a singgle ordaind colord minister in that section of the state. what Baptiseing that was dun it was dun by white men.[12]

The yeare 1866 was now neareing its close. Afew of us all over the cuntry cleard a little money. the largest potion came out in debt. I remember uncle Toney Babeley workt for the fift that he mad[e] and Borded himself and cleard 15 dollars. I cleard something over 200 dollars but was never able to colleect it all. The yeare 1867 came on and I was the only colord person That could read and was Easley perswaded to leave the Blacksmith shoop and take a school witch I Taught 9 mounth in Pike County a mile and a half from The Flat Shols. we had but one Book. That was websters erementry Spelling Book. my Role of

[8] 1 Timothy 5:22, "Lay hands suddenly on no man…." Biblical commentators usually explain this verse as a warning against placing inexperienced Christians prematurely into positions of responsibility, a meaning in harmony with Holloway's assessment of his own ministry later that year: "I…preached in my Humble way on Sundays I do not all pretend to say it was properly."

While Holloway criticized the action of his local MECS quarterly conference in licensing him, members of Georgia's fledgling AMEC connection would voice a similar complaint against their own church the next year (discussed on pp. 45-46).

[9] See map "Holloway's Neighborhoods, 1844-1870," for Salem Methodist Church and Flat Rock Methodist Church.

[10] Minta Collins (b. c. 1830) and similarly named Minta Collin (c. 1842–1869) both lived about this time in the 505 GMD, Pike County, served by the Williamsville (Flat Shoals) post office.

The elder Minta Collins was enumerated in the 1870 Census (GA, Pike County, Pop., p. 79–80, dwell. 567), where she kept house with Franklin Collins and five children.

Twenty-eight-year-old Minta Collin was married and keeping house when she died of hepatitis in September 1869, as shown in the 1870 Census, GA, Pike County, Schedule 2 (Mortality). See also 1870 Census, GA, Pike County, Pop., p. 97, dwell. 686, for the family in which she died.

[11] "Glory to God and the Lamb forever"—a common exclamation among evangelical Christians in the English-speaking world, derived from Revelation 5:13.

[12] Normally only an ordained minister could administer baptism in the Methodist church.

pupills was small at the start, Lonzey George, Sidney George,[13] Charrity Mail [= (probably) Neal], Ellen Neail, Henrietter Freman and befour the yeare was out my Role grew to fifty or more. our Revivals was great also that yeare. Our same whitman meet us on Every 2 Sabbath in the mounth, Baptised our converts, And we ware Happie. In the mounth of September my second child was Bornd who we give the name of Mary Jane[14] for her aunt Mary Jane.[15] The yeare soon past away and the yeare 1868 was soon was soon on. my School as I Taught 50 cts per mounth as might have been Exspected did not pay me The past yeare.

---

[13] Rev. Madison N. George's sons, Alonzo and Sidney, were nine years and twelve years in 1867 (1870 Census, GA, Pike County, Pop., p. 100, dwell. 706).

[14] Mary Jane Holloway (1867–1893) was born 31 September 1867. Holloway paid for his daughter to study at Tuskegee Institute, but there she contracted consumption. In 1892 her father recalled her to convalesce at home, where she died on 12 July 1893.

[15] Mary Jane Thrash (b. c. 1832) was the eldest daughter of Cherry Thrash and Christmas Thrash and sister to Cordelia Thrash (Houston Holloway's wife). They were all enslaved to planters Christopher and Mary Thrash at Flat Shoals, Meriwether County. Mary Jane married a man many years her senior, Simon Thrash (b. c. 1803), who was one of two slaves received in 1821 by Mary Thrash from the estate of her father John Calloway of Wilkes County. Nephew John Wesley Holloway recalled that Simon "was gray haired when I first remember" in the late 1860s. Mary Jane and Simon had only one child, Susan (b. c. 1860).

Mary Jane and Simon Thrash remained in Meriwether County for the first years after Emancipation (Simon registered to vote there on 28 June 1867), but moved across the Flint River to Pike County by 1870. In Pike County Mary Jane's recently widowed father, Christmas Thrash, lived in the family but apparently died before the next census. The family moved to Spalding County where, in 1880, Simon Thrash cultivated a 30-acre one-horse farm on shares. Mary Jane and Susan helped on the farm. I found no record for Simon after 1880. John Wesley Holloway tells us Simon's and Mary Jane's daughter "cousin Susie" "came to Turin and staid with us a while, during my mother's illness" (Cordelia was ill from 1887 to 1894). In 1900 the widowed Mary J. Thrash worked on a farm rented by her younger brother, Eli Thrash, and wife, Sarah, in Monroe County, GA.

See JWH, 1, 416, 417; GA Return of Qualified Voters, Meriwether County, Election District 36, Precinct 1213, p. 23, 28 June 1867; 1870 Census, GA, Pike County, Pop., p. 10, dwell. 717; 1880 Census, GA, Spalding County, ED 117, p. 1, dwell. 3; 1880 Census, GA, Pike County, Schedule 3 (Agriculture), ED 117, p. 1, line 2; 1900 Census, GA, Monroe County, ED 72, p. 9, dwell. 170 (The age given for Mary J. Thrash, fifty-nine, must be an error, or this is a different family with exactly the same names.) I estimate Simon's birth year from the 1870 census (sixty-seven years).

I give up my Calling as a Teacher, Took my hammer in hand and became a Travling Blacksmith. The Reconstruction acts had past in Congress puting the Ballot in the hands of the Blacks.[16] It feil to my Lot to take not a little stocks in the politicks of the day and was nomernated to run for the Legislator, But I refused to run because I knew nothing about what was needed to be dun for cuntry and in my place a man by the name of Peter Chambers who was Elected and served in the Constutionale Convention of 1868 with annother man, a baptist preacher by the name of M J Keeth if I am not mistaken.[17] The enfranchising of the Black prodused the Union Ligh [=Union League] a secred society of that I became a member and in Pike County not a few white men that was union men at the out Brake of the [war], was opposed to secession, But under the Confedrate goverment was compell to go to the war, united with the abolishtionite party and with Thousands of theas and all the Blacks governor Bullock was Easley Electted governor of Georgia and he came to be head of what was cald the Radicall Partie.[18] politicks got in our midst and our revivall or Religious work for a while began to wan[e].

The yeare 1868 Began [to] neare its close and not afew of us had began to know what money was made for and began to mak a little more then we had ever had. Some began to Byland and around the citties not a few had bgan to by lots and Build them small housses.

The yeare 1869 founds [=found us] in a very Demorrellised condition from and Eccleseasticall point of vew. The M E Church Sounth had Largely dropt us. The M E Church had sent mishionarys from the north down heare and they ware Attracting not a little attention among our people. Thousand of our people win into that church. now some time late in the fall or the first of the winter [I went] up to griffin on a trading Expedition And while [there] I enquired for a

[16] Holloway registered to vote 28 June 1867 in precinct 1213, Meriwether County (GA, Returns of Qualified Voters and Reconstruction Oath Books, 1867–1869, Meriwether County, Middle 9th Dist., 24).

[17] Peter W. Chambers (born in GA, age forty-nine, of Sulphur Springs) and J. M. Key (born in GA, age forty-nine, of Luthersville) represented Meriwether County at the 1868 Constitutional Convention. See *Journal of the Proceedings of the Constitutional Convention of the People of Georgia, Held in the City of Atlanta in the Months of December, 1867, and January, February and March, 1868* (Augusta, GA: E. H. Pugh, Book and Job Printer, 1868) 611–12.

[18] Rufus Bullock (1834–1907), a Republican, was governor of Georgia 1868–1871.

man by the name of Auntney Elexander.[19] Some on told me wheare I would find him. On going to the house I found Rev Robt Alxander[20] paster of the African Methodist Church. I had never seen such a man befour. He was a small yeler man who had some Edgucation. he was not the man that I was hunting for but he was the man I found. But and African Methodist Church was quiet a novall Idea to me. I learnd that a church of that kind was in griffin. posably six mounth after that In the summer I went up to griffin again to carry my wief as she had never seen a town of no sort and as and oppotuninty presented Its self to see a Town and the cars also.[21] I met a man by the name of Albert McGhee[22] who was paster of the same church in griffin. I found him to be a good talker, one who was able to make himself felt. I went out that night to one of his meetings on Hill Street. that his meeting Impresed me would be puting it very very mild. the same man promised me that he would visit my sextion of the cuntry witch he did do in the spring of the next yeare and set up the A M Church at the Flat Shoals and Bush Chapple neare willamsvill witch is neale now. We had but few

---

[19] Anthony Alexander, p. 92, n.5.

[20] Robert Alexander (b. c. 1840) was licensed by Henry M. Turner in 1866 to help evangelize Georgia and Alabama for the AMEC. See biography pp. 204-205.

[21] "The cars" was a nineteenth-century colloquial term for a railroad passenger train.

[22] Albert McGhee (1822–1882) was born in Abbeville District, SC. He converted to Christianity at a South Carolina camp meeting in 1847 and was admitted as a preacher on trial, then two days later elected and ordained deacon, at the South Carolina Conference, April 1867; appointed to Griffin GA, for three years (1867, 1868, 1869). A pioneer for the AMEC in Georgia, he traveled over most parts of the state. He was ordained elder at the second session of the Georgia Conference in 1868 and appointed to Washington, Wilkes County (1870). He served as presiding elder of the Americus District (1871, 1872), was appointed to Cartersville (1874), to Putnam County Circuit, No. 1 (1875), and back to Washington, Wilkes County (1876, 1877); to Greensboro (1878, 1879); to Rome (1880); and to Kingston Circuit (1881, 1882). The 1870 census stated that he could read but not write, but by 1880 he could do both; his wife Lucinda (b. c. 1832), also a native of SC, learned to read and write in the decade up to 1880. Albert and Lucinda McGehee adopted a girl named Mary (b. c. 1869). McGhee died at his home in Cartersville, GA, on 7 August 1882.

Minutes of the South Carolina Conference of the African M. E. Church, 1865, 1866, 1867 (Charleston, 1867), 12, 14; 9 NGA, 49, 54; 10 NGA, 23, 37; 1870 Census, GA, Wilkes County, Washington, Pop., p. 17, dwell. 108; 1880 Census, GA, Bartow County, Cartersville, Pop., ED 1, p. 17, dwell. 171.

things of perticuler Importance to happend. Rev David Harris[23] was ordaind In hebron white Baptist Church by the white paster to the ministrey and Rev David Alxander[24] was ordaind at Mount Zion Baptist Church in Marriwether and theas Tow men began to Build up one of the most numerrious associations in the state, The people Being Ignorat and carried very Easey in a Direction that promised them liberty.

Our presiding Elder was a very good man though short of the nessorry qualification for such a Responsable position in the church or out.[25] He was the Best man perhaps that the bishop had in his reach. had he been competent to fill the place He no dout would have dun much good that needs to be dun to day. A work mighte have been dun that day that would be hard to do to day in that section of cuntry.

That yeare quiet a number of Blacks be gan to Bie land in diferrant parts of the cuntry. Ransom Freeman[26] bought a plantation in pike County not far from Zebulurn. Uncle Robin Avery[27] a Blacksmith Bought a lot of property In old

---

[23] See p. 123, n. 10.

[24] David Alexander (b. c. 1834) was born in AL and came to GA as a child about 1843, arriving in Pike County about 1851. He was almost surely born enslaved, probably to W. D. Alexander. In the aftermath of the Civil War and emancipation, the white pastor at Mt. Zion Baptist Church in Meriwether County ordained him to the ministry in 1869. In the hard-hit economy after the Civil War, preaching and church building were necessarily a part-time avocation, and the 1870 census taker in Pike County recorded that David Alexander (age thirty-six) and his wife Harriet (age forty-three, born in SC) were both farm laborers. By 1880 the Alexander household seemed more prosperous. He had moved across Flint River to Meriwether County where the enumerator recorded his dual occupations, "Ministry & Farming," while Harriet had exchanged full-time fieldwork for "Keeping house" (GA Return of Qualified Voters, Pike County, Election District 22, Hollands District, 534 Precinct, 9 Aug 1867, p. 40; 1870 Census, GA, Pike County, Pop., p. 78, dwell. 556; 1880 Census, GA, Meriwether County, Pop., ED 82, p. 4, dwell. 35).

[25] Seymour B. Jones (1868–1871), Presiding Elder of Marietta District, was quite aware of his own shortcomings; see p. 145, n. 31.

[26] See p. 80, n. 43.

[27] Robin Avery (b. c. 1805), blacksmith, was born in VA. He was a resident in GA since about 1850, and lived in Pike County (580 GMD) since about 1860. By 1870 he had accumulated real estate worth $300 and personal estate valued at $150. In 1880, at age seventy-six, he was still working at his trade in the town of Zebulon, Pike County (1870 Census, GA, Pike County, Pop., p. 48, dwell. 332; GA Return of Qualified

Zebulurn. Rev willam Fincher[28] one of the most Eloquant colord ministers to be found any wheare, he had alwas from the time that [he] was lisend [=licensed] attracted much attention, began to Build The Methodist Episcopall Church In that part of Pike County around Zebulurn. he was a great politician also. I did not live close to him and cannot say much about [him] be yond this, he was far be yond his day In knowlage. Some time during the Earley part of the fall of that yeare Rev Albert McGee paster of the A.M.E Church in Griffin came out there about the Flat Shoals and organised the A.M. Church.[29] I was left in charge of the same untill confernce whitch conved at Amerricut [=convened at Americus] in Sunter County the next yeare. A collection was Raised to Build Bush Chapple neare Willamsvill. That work moved on very nicely untill the End of the yeare.

My Recolection is I[n] the mounth of December I was notified that the quartely confernce of the Griffin Station would conveain at Griffin on Saturday. Rev M N George[30] and Farther Bush was a mainable and was Exspectted to be

---

Voters, Pike County, Election District 22, Precinct 580 [Zebulon], 12 August 1867, p. 33; 1880 Census, GA, Pike County, Zebulon, Pop., ED 107 p. 1, dwell. 11).

[28] William Fincher (b. c. 1822); see Appendix A, pp. 202-204.

[29] Holloway seems to contradict his earlier statement that McGee visited his neighborhood in the spring—here he says the fall—but the year was certainly 1869, McGee's last year as pastor at Griffin. Holloway says he (Holloway) was in charge of Flat Shoals until the Fourth Session AMEC GA Conference met at Americus on 28 January 1870, confirming 1869 as the year McGee organized AME churches at Flat Shoals and Bush Chapel. Unfortunately, minutes of that session are unavailable; earliest statistics for Williamsville and Flat Shoals are reports for 1870 printed in the Fifth Session GA Conference minutes (1871). Bush Chapel today dates its founding to 1867. Perhaps the church sprang from Claiborne Bush's preaching in 1867 after the MECS licensed him and appointed him to Pike County and Flat Shoals.

[30] Madison N. George (c. 1828–1873) was probably born in Pike County, GA. From about 1857 he lived in the western part of the county between Zebulon and Flat Shoals, the same neighborhood as Claiborne Bush and near the school briefly taught by Houston Holloway in 1867. He was "trained in religion from his youth; entered the ministry in 1867" (1 NGA, 18). The AMEC Georgia Conference in January 1870 admitted George on trial and appointed him deacon; the census taker for Pike County reported him "Minister of Gospel," able to read and write, and with personal property totaling $400. The AMEC Georgia Conference appointed him to Williamsville (Bush Chapel), Pike County, for 1871; in January 1872 he was raised from probationer into full connection and appointed to Flat Shoals. He had no church appointment for 1873 and

presant. I and Rev M N Georgia, Farther Claibon Bush, and I left the Flat Shoals and our Humble homes Saturday moning there was no way for us to gat to Griffin But that of walking. We Thought nothing of it 21 miles was not much to walk and by one Oclock we had arrivid at the A M E Church in Griffin. The quartely confernch was cald to order About 3 oclock. Rev Albert McGhee occupeing the chare as S B Jones[31] the presiding Elder of the Marietter

---

died that year. His church obituary recalled him as "a man of solid piety; was a good husband, father, and a peaceful neighbor. He died cheering his family in the words of the 23d Psalm, 'The Lord is my shepherd,' and singing, 'How happy every child of grace'" (1 NGA, 18). He left his widow Elva with eight children.

His birth year is uncertain; his AMEC Conference obituary states 1835, but the voters registrar on 10 August 1867 recorded him as born in GA and having lived in both GA and Pike County for thirty-six years, suggesting a birth no later than 1831; the 1870 census put his age at 42 (thus born c. 1828).

See Wesley J. Gaines, *African Methodism in the South; or Twenty-Five Years of Freedom* (Atlanta: 1890) 26; 5 GA, 18; 6 GA, 61, 63; 1 NGA, 18; GA Return of Qualified Voters [1867–1869], Pike County, precinct 505, p. 44; 1870 Census, GA, Pike County, Pop., p. 100, dwell. 706; Pike County tax digest, 1868, Freedmen section, 505 GMD.

[31] Seymour B. Jones (b. c. 1833) was born in Taliaferro County, GA, and raised in Houston County; he one of the original 14 preachers presented by Rev. Henry M. Turner to the South Carolina Conference at St. Andrew's Chapel in Savannah, 14 May 1866. Jones was admitted preacher on trial and elected deacon that same day, his rapid advancement due to the African Methodist Church's urgent need for ordained ministers to spread the Word. He vividly recalled Bishop Payne instructing conference members to nominate only qualified men for the ministry—but when the bishop admonished, "Don't bring any men to me who do not know what the canonical Scriptures are," Jones remembered murmuring in consternation, "My God, what is that!" (Gaines, *African Methodism*, 116–17). Notwithstanding shortfalls in his theological education, Jones was advanced to elder in April 1867.

Holloway's precocious four-year-old son, future author and poet John Wesley Holloway, retained a happy memory of Jones from 1869: "I remember the coming of the first [AMEC] presiding elder into the community, S. B. Jones. He came loaded down with books and pictures for sale" (JWH, 12).

Jones was first appointed to Athens (1867) where he registered to vote on 7 August. Subsequently he was appointed presiding elder of Marietta District (1868–1871), presiding elder of Atlanta District (1872, 1873), Eatonton Station (1874), Augusta Station (1875), Sparta Station (1876), and presiding elder of Marietta District (1877), Clinton Station (1880), transferred to the Georgia Conference in 1881 where he was

District faild to arrive. I disremember The Statistcks of Stoward report Though I Seveved [=served] as Seccratarey. All There [=three] of us however was Recomended to the Anuall Confernce as suatable persons for Decons orders and also to be Admitted Into the Itinerrate work. I will Say Just This much, If the same work had to be dun over, It would not be dun as it was then. My obsovation is among our people since the Rite to confer such orders has been Delegated to our people they have conferd them to There Thousand, Boath Methodis and Bappist.[32] In doing so, much harne has been dun The people and scarcely any good untill this day.

Farther Bush was a preacher of great power in that day. At Eleven oclock on Sunday he was appointed to preach. at the proper time He a rose and took for his Tex, "he that hearthe thees Things of mine and doeth them I liken him to a man that Bilt his house upon a rock. And the raines decended and the winds Blew and the Beat upon that house and it fell not because it was founded upon a Rock." Mathew [chapter 7] 24 & 25 verces. "And he that hearth thees sayings of mine and doth not I will liken him to a man that Built his house upon the Sand and the Rains decended and the winds Blew and the Beat upon that house and It fell and great was the Fall of it." Mathew [chapter 7] 26 & 27 verces. we returned home monday. the winter past rether mild. The Anuall Confernce convend At A Merricuss [=Americus] Georgia about the 20 of

---

appointed presiding elder of Columbus District (1881–1884), presiding elder Americus District (1885–1886). In 1889 Jones was sent to the North GA Conference. (Incomplete sets of conference records make his record of appointments patchy.)

See Registers of Signatures of Depositors in Branches of the Freedmen's Savings and Trust Company (1865–1874), NARA Publication M816, roll 6, page 137, account 1041 (Seymour B. Jones); *Minutes of the South Carolina Annual Conference of the African M. E. Church, 1865, 1866, 1867* (Charleston: 1867) 8, 20; Wesley J. Gaines, *African Methodism in the South; or Twenty-Five Years of Freedom* (Atlanta: 1890) 26, 110, 116–17, 143, 217; GA Return of Qualified Voters, Clarke County, precinct 3, p. 25; *Christian Recorder*, 15 June 1867, 2; *Christian Recorder* 4 April 1868, 1; 3 GA, 13; 5 GA, 18; 6 GA, 63; 7 GA, 23; 1 NGA, 23; 2 NGA, 15; 3 NGA, 15; 4 NGA, 24; 7 NGA, 17; 1 MACON, 24; 2 MACON, 30; 3 MACON, 29; 4 MACON, 39.

[32] Gloss: "...our people have ordained their thousands, both Methodist and Baptist." See discussion on pp. 59-60 of Holloway's criticism of uneducated Methodist and Baptist clergy and his wish (expressed in the *Christian Recorder*, 10 May 1877, 1) that the church strip incompetent preachers of their licenses.

Janurary 1871 [actually, 1870].[33] we remaind there neare ten days. we ware ordaind Decons about the forth Sabbath in January and our Appointment was read out on monday following and off we put for home. I was Assignd to the Flat Shoal Cercut and Rev M N Georgia was assinged to the Bush Chapple Circit.

It would be useless to say that many people ware added to the Circuts that yeare. I Baptised many people in Flint River and many In the proper way by pooring At the church.[34] I also set up a church at a place cald Ebeneser and one at a place cald penhook. I also married many cupple whitch was Big things for a black man to do in thocs days. During of the week I followed my Trade and preached in my Humble way on Sundays. I do not all pretend to say it was properley. Rev. S. B. Jones presided at all of our quartely Confernces. Bush Chapple A.M.E Church was Bilt That winter and Dedicated on the first Sabbath in June and A great day it was. This was on the Pike County Circut, Rev M N George paster. Many united with the Church. At the same time I was taken with chills and fevers That lasted me untill the fall of the yeare and weacond me down very much.

Collections in thoes day was not to be compaird to the collections now. My surport for the yeare was something like one Hundred and 30 dollars. I took sumething like 1 one Hundred and 50 members into the Church. I Discoverd that taking one Into the Church then did not amount to much in that day and but little more now for our people could not read then whil the[y] can Read now but they fail to do it.

The Georgia Confernce the yeare 1870 [actually, 1871] conveained in Big Bethell Chuch Atlanta[35] Bishop John M Brown[36] presideing. Great proggress

[33] The events Holloway describes happened at the Fourth Session, GA Annual Conference, in January 1870; however, I have found no copy of the minutes. Gaines, *African Methodism*, 25–28, includes a summary of the conference.

[34] Holloway's preference for pouring was not a Methodist doctrine; unlike Baptists, Methodists required no specific mode of water baptism. See Christopher H. Owen, *The Sacred Flame of Love: Methodism and Society in Nineteenth-Century Georgia* (Athens: University of Georgia Press, 1998) 85.

[35] The Fifth Session of the GA Annual Conference of the A.M.E. Church convened 14 January 1871 at Bethel Church, Atlanta, GA.

[36] John Mifflin Brown (1817–1893) was born in Canwell's Bridge, DE, on 8 September 1817. When ten years old he moved to Wilmington, DE, then later to Philadelphia, receiving secular and religious education along the way, and learned the

had been made on all lines for The work had Expanded every wheare. after Reading out the appointments I was assignd to The Ringgold circut away up in the mountains. I was sorry after some years that I knew not what I was doing. I spoke to the people at the Flat Shoals the last time about the first of March 1871 and was soon of to my New feild. I arrived there on on Thirsday In the Afternoon. The first night I spent was with a very good man a Blacksmith by the Name of Gilbert vincin.[37] I meet annother good man there by the name of Mosese Darian[38] and his good wief. At grasevill, Just on the line of Tennesse, I

---

barber's trade. He joined Bethel AME Church in 1836. To prepare for the ministry, he attended Wesleyan Academy for two years. Brown's first pastoral appointment was to the church in Detroit, MI, 1844–1847; he was ordained deacon in 1846, then elder in 1847. After various assignments, North and South, he was elected and ordained Bishop in May 1868. Brown succeeded Bishop Wayman as bishop of Georgia from 1868 to 1873, turning over the GA Conference to Bishop T. M. D. Ward at its seventh session in January 1873. Bishop Brown died 16 March 1893. See Richard R. Wright, *Centennial Encyclopaedia of the African Methodist Episcopal Church* (Philadelphia: Book Concern of the A.M.E. Church, 1916) 47, accessible at Documenting the American South, http://docsouth.unc.edu/church/wright/menu.html (accessed 9 January 2015).

[37] Gilbert Vincent (died c. 1888) successfully eluded census enumerators in 1870 and 1880, but could not escape death and taxes. A self-employed blacksmith in the town of Ringgold, Catoosa County, he was named on the 1866 federal tax list for Ringgold. He registered to vote in Ringgold on 2 July 1867, paid local taxes on a valuable town lot in the 1870s—but was dead by 1889 when his administrator filed a county tax return on his estate. See Internal Revenue Assessment Lists for Georgia, 1865–1866, July 1866, Collection District 4, Division 14 (Ringgold, Catoosa County), p. 35 [NARA M762, roll 8]; Georgia Archives, Office of the Governor (RG 1-1-108, Reconstruction Registration Oaths Books, 1867–1869 (hereafter cited as GA Reconstruction Oath Book), 1867, Catoosa County, p. 185, oath no. 369; Catoosa County Tax Digests 1872–1877, 1889 (Georgia Archives, Revenue-Property Tax Unit, County Property Tax Digests [RG 34-06-001], viewable at http://ancestrylibrary.com in *Georgia Property Tax Digests*, 1793–1892, collection.).

[38] Probably Moses Dearing (b. c. 1825). Registered to vote on 2 July 1867, in the 930 GMD of Catoosa County, Dearing was living in 1870 as an apparent bachelor in the household of Jacob Carmichael near Graysville in the 1084 GMD, occupation described as "hireling." By 1880 he and wife Rosa (b. c. 1840) had a four-year-old son, and they had relocated to the vicinity of Ringgold where Moses farmed and Rosa kept house. 1870 Census, GA, Catoosa County, Pop., p. 46, dwell. 334; 1880 Census, GA, Catoosa County, ED 12, p. 12, dwell. 100.

had annoth Cald Aunta Ork.[39] at this place I found a very good man by the name of Willsams. he was one of the most gifted men at prayr I most Ever meet. Also Broo Sidney Woods.[40] we meet annother man there by the name of Richard Anderson.[41] H[e] was one of the most Trubblesom men that we found up there, had no learning, yet he Thought himself cald to preach. we had him to Expell from the church befour the yeare was out. we was very successfull on that circut. In the fall of The yeare on account of the wether being so cold I requsted to be moved forther down the cuntry.

Our Anuall Confernce seting In Savannah some time in January 1872, I had 418 mills to go to gat there. money was scarce but some how we made it and [observed] good Improvement In all parts the State. I was assignd to the Kingston and Adasvill [=Adairsville] Circut. I got my good wief and 3 children moved to my new [assignment] which was 22 mills long. My first night on this work was spint with Broo Burnet Herrington and his Broo Inlaw James Dungan.[42] I found some very good men on this work, Rev Shade Holly,[43] Broo Verge wolly[44] and severyll outh at Kingston. we Took hold of this work with

---

[39] Gloss: "At Graysville, just on the Tennessee line, I had another church called Antioch."

[40] Sidney F. Woods (b. c. 1841), described by the 1870 census as a farmer, lived with his family in the Cross Roads District of Catoosa County, bordering TN. He had registered to vote 2 July 1867 (1870 Census, GA, Catoosa County, Pop., p. 31, dwell. 220; Return of Registered voters, Catoosa County, 1084 Precinct, oath cert. No. A172).

[41] Richard Anderson (b. c. 1821) was born in TN, described in the census as a farmer, a substantial property owner with real estate worth $1400 and personal estate valued at $210. He could not read or write. Besides his wife, Rachel, and immediate family, his household included a hired woman employee. This may be the man of whom Holloway wrote in a letter to the *Christian Recorder*: "[I was] sent to Ringgold, staid one year and had a slight difficulty with a Democrat Negro" (1870 Census, GA, Catoosa County, Ringgold, Pop., p. 110, dwell. 54; *Christian Recorder*, 4 July 1878, 2).

[42] James Dungeon (or Dungion) (born in VA, c. 1846) was a cooper by trade, could read and write, and lived with wife, Virginia-born Harriett, and their children in or near Kingston, Bartow County (1880 Census, GA, Bartow County, Kingston, Pop., ED 5, p. 30, dwell. 272).

[43] Shadrack Holly (born in VA, c. 1822) was a carpenter. He lived with wife and children in or near Cartersville, Bartow County, about eleven miles from Kingston. He could both read and write (1870 Census, GA, Bartow County, Pop., p. 184, dwell. 7).

[44] Virgil Wooley (born in GA, c. 1824) lived near Cartersville, Bartow County, with wife, Sarah, and seven children; he was a farmhand who could neither read nor

Booth hands. On the Second Sabbath in Ma[r]ch 1872 we left Kingston on the Second Sabbath morning. I heard that It would cost ten cents to cross the [Etowah] River. the wether was bad. I had 12 mills to walke to gat to drumerns Hill[45] meeting. I did not have a dime. I faild to gat one in Kingston Saturday Eveing, so Earley Sabbath morning I Took my gripp and cane and way bill[46] and was off. I walkt 4 mills or something like that and pickt up a 15 cent bill in a horse Track as it bin a heavey rain the[re] over night I held [it] up and dried it in the sun by the time I got to the river. I cald the ferry man and [he] Took [me] over and suspissioned that I was preacher, only chage me 5 cts. I walke tow or 3 mills and I was at Broo Hall Milands.[47] After Introduceing myself to Him and Broo Aron porter,[48] who was a Blacksmith, they had many hard things to say about my predesesor, Broo W H Harris.[49] He did not preach to them but 3 times the past yeare. It seemd like that thire was nothing that I could say to them to gat there confedence. we got a small congregation at Broo porters house and spoke to them as best we could that night. we asked them for a collecttion

---

write, but he owned an unusually large amount of personal property ($120) for a farmhand with such a large family (1870 Census, GA, Bartow County, Pop., p. 213, dwell. 75).

[45] Drummond Hill was about seven miles due south of Kingston, GA.

[46] His *grip* was his traveling bag; his *way bill* was his directions to his destination.

[47] Hall Milam (b. c. 1810), farm hand, and his wife Chaney (b. c. 1823), keeping house, were born in SC. In 1870 they lived near Cartersville; by 1880 they had moved west to Floyd County (1870 Census, GA, Bartow County, Pop., p. 263, dwell. 45; 1880 Census, GA, Floyd County, ED 72, p. 14, dwell. 139).

[48] Aaron Porter (b. c. February 1837) and wife Mary, son James, and adopted daughter, Sarah, lived near Stilesboro. Porter had previously lived near Cartersville and would later return to that neighborhood. Although Holloway recollects that he was a blacksmith, the 1870, 1880, and 1900 censuses enumerate him as a farm laborer; perhaps he smithed part-time (1870 Census, GA, Bartow County, Pop., p. 263, dwell. 42; 1880 GA Bartow County, Pop., ED 3, p. 17, dwell. 150; 1900 Census, GA, Bartow County, Pop., ED 2, p. 13, dwell. 215).

[49] This was not the similarly named W. H. Harris, later Presiding Elder Harris, with whom Holloway would have an unpleasant encounter in 1881. According to AMEC GA Conference Minutes for the Fifth Session (1871), the appointee to Kingston and Adairsville for 1871 was W. H. Harrison—but the conference membership roll has no one by that name. However, there were two men with names similar to William H. Harris, and one of them seems to have been erroneously put down as Harrison (5 GA, 5, 15, 18, 25; 6 GA, 39, 40, 61).

telling them how hard we ware up. not one cent was forth coming. I said to them, The Good Lord knew how you was going to do o[v]er heare to night and caused some one to drop 15 cts in a Horse track for me to pick up and pay my fair cross the river and back again. And that faild to reach them. I had one five cents left. I savd that for my next trip over there one mounth Afterward. I spoke to them in a little Log house at a place cald Drumons hill. Broo Hal Milan lifted a collection. He did well. when he got through He turnd over to me 20 cts.

By this time the Spring was opeing up. a good congregation was out and we spoke out of Doors to a very good congregation and the lifted a collections of one dollar and 20. I tended to them all that yeare. Took into the [church] a good many and on my last visit to them befour going to confernce witch meen [=met] in Macon they give me a collection of 20 dollars. Kingston and Adairsvill was my main points that yeare. I sucseded well at the Church at Kinston. Rev Shaderack Holly, a good Locall preacher, was my assistant. he did good work. also Broo James Dungon,[50] Burnett Herrington and James Brown.[51] That yeare 1872 I Taught schoole in connection with my ministeriale work.[52]

The confernce meet In Macon [11–20 January 1873], Bishop T. M. D. ward[53] presiding, Bishop J. M. Brown Assisting. The wether was very cold in

[50] Holloway's eldest son would allege, "[James] Dungeon borrowed most of the money" his father earned from teaching school in Kingston and never repaid it (JWH, 361).

[51] John Wesley Holloway recalled, "We lived in Kingston two or three years. Part of the time in the house with a shoe-maker, Jim Brown a yellow man. He had two daughters of his own, Jane, a grown-up and Ellen a girl perhaps ten or twelve years old. What I remember most vividly is the immorality of these girls.... They were good-looking but grossly immoral. So were most of the people there then.... Ellen married a young fellow by the name of [blank] Later he killed a white fellow by the name of Harris about her and had to run away" (JWH, 19–21). The 1870 census, taken two years before Holloway moved to Kingston, found James Brown (b. c. 1840) living near Cartersville, a thirty-year old farm hand, head of a family that included Martha age twenty-eight, Jane age thirteen, George age twelve, and Ellen age eight; all native to GA. I did not find this Brown family in the 1880 census (1870 Census, GA, Bartow County, Pop., p. 192, dwell. 83).

[52] J. W. Holloway wrote, "Mrs. Herrington, a yellow woman, was his assistant" (JWH, 267).

[53] Thomas Marcus Decatur Ward (1823–1894) was born in Hanover, PA, 28 September 1823. Converted in 1838 at Philadelphia, he joined the AMEC, was licensed to preach in 1843, ordained deacon in 1847, and ordained elder in 1849. He was

January. many of the young men, I among them, was Ordaind Elders. I was returnd back to the Kingston and Adairsvill circut. Sucseded far be yound my Exspectations. Tood a great many into the church. Baptised a great many by Emerchion at Adairsvill, Drumons Hill and at gore Spring [=Gore Spring]. I was assisted by Broo Joiel Stevens[54] a very Good man who finally became a Travling preacher.

The yeare 1874

The confernce conveaind At Augusta, Bishop T M D ward presiding. The confernce having been Devided at macon into the Macon and North Georgia Confernces, the North Georgia meet at Augusta. At this confernce After all the reports had got [submitted] the parsonage was Burglerised on Saturday night.

---

appointed missionary to the Pacific coast. He arrived there in 1852 and served several years. Elected and ordained bishop in 1868, he served as bishop to the Pacific coast for four years before being assigned to the southeast United States. He presided over the Seventh Session, GA Annual Conference, in January 1873 and presided over the first three sessions of the North GA Conference (1874–1876). He would also serve the AMEC church in AL, FL, and MS before his death on 10 June 1894.

See Wright, *Centennial Encyclopaedia*, 237; Charles Spencer Smith, *A History of the African Methodist Episcopal Church, Being a Volume Supplemental to a History of the African Methodist Episcopal Church, by Daniel Alexander Payne, D.D., LL.D., Late One of Its Bishops, Chronicling the Principal Events in the Advance of the African Methodist Episcopal Church from 1856 to 1922* (Philadelphia: Book Concern of the A. M. E. Church, 1922) 32; 7 GA; 1 NGA; 2 NGA; 3 NGA.

[54] Joel Stevens apparently attended the Third Session of the North GA Conference (November 1875) as a layman where he paid $1 to the Missionary Association. In December 1876 he was admitted as a deacon on trial and appointed to Lexington, Oglethorpe County, for 1877. His later appointments included Hogansville (1880), Haralson Circuit (1881), Griffin Circuit (1882), Fayette County Circuit (1883), Greenville Circuit (1884, 1885), Logtown Circuit in Upson County (1886, 1887), Pine Grove Circuit (1888), and Oglethorpe Circuit (1889). His presiding elder reported that "Bro. Stevens…is too good and easy to ever be of much service to himself and church while he is in the ministry" (17 NGA, 25). Despite that harsh assessment, the bishop appointed Stevens to Hartwell Mission for 1890 and to Harmony Grove Mission for 1891.

See 3 NGA, 16; 4 NGA, 4, 14, 23; 7 NGA, 17; 9 NGA, 54; 10 NGA, 55; 11 NGA, 48; 12 NGA, 37; 13 NGA, 41; 14 NGA, 68; 15 NGA, 60; 16 NGA, 64; 17 NGA, 59; 18 NGA, 58.

fortuanatly Rev J. H. W. Burley[55] our Connectionall Financioul Secretary [had] carried the 15,000 dollar money Down Town and Depositted the same in the Bank. The Theeves got the Bishops gold watch and 30 some odd Dollars, all of the contingant money Belonging to the Confernce, And all outher valuables that they could gat hold of.

Thay yeare 1874 I was appointed to the palmetto circut In Campbell and Coweta and fayet countys. on that work we succeeded Be yound any man that had ever served on it. We Took into the Church that yeare Sumthing over 150 members. The Locall prohibition question found many followars among the white people and many of our people. I Tood sides with it And the Barrooms was Brok up in Palmetto. Rev Lacy Beck[56] was my presiding Elder. He was not And Edgucated [man] and It was on this circut that I began to see things going on among the App[oint]ing powers that I could not endors. Rev Lacy Beck

---

[55] John W. H. Burley (d. 1879), member of the AMEC Baltimore Conference, appointed at the AMEC General Conference in 1872 to the new office of Financial Secretary. His main duty was to collect and account for the Church's "dollar money" (see pp. 51-52). Burley died in office in 1879. Smith, *History of the African Methodist Episcopal Church*, 95, 103, 135, 344.

[56] Lacy Beck (born in VA or MD, c. 1815 or 1820; censuses disagree) was admitted on trial to the Georgia Conference in February 1869, was first appointed to Greensboro, next to Thomasville for 1871. By 1872 he had been elected elder and appointed to Griffin for 1873. At the formation of the North Georgia Conference, he was appointed presiding elder of the LaGrange District for 1874, but at the January conference in 1875, he was reported "for failure to return the Griffin Dollar Money last year, $26" (2 NGA, 5). The Conference members voted to give him one year to settle the debt. The bishop removed Beck from his post as presiding elder, took his name off the itinerant list, and left him without appointment for the coming year. In December 1875 the Conference listed Beck as a local elder, appointed to Cedartown Circuit for 1876. The December 1876 Conference left him "in the hands of the Bishop" (4 NGA, 17) without appointment for 1877, but the minutes do not explain why. In 1878 Elder Lacy Beck seceded from the AMEC, reportedly in protest against burdensome church taxes levied on Southern AME congregations to support the mainly Northern AMEC bishops. Beck led three other disgruntled former AMEC members to found their own short-lived Methodist denomination, the Independent Southern Methodist Church.

See 1870 Census, GA, Green County, Greensboro, Pop., p. 19, dwell. 180; 1880 Census, GA, Fulton County, Atlanta, Pop., ED 93, p. 10, dwell. 51; 3 GA, 5; 5 GA, 19; 7 GA, 25; 1 NGA, 24; 2 NGA, 5; 3 NGA, 1, 15; 4 NGA, 3; *Christian Recorder*, 9 May 1878 and 30 May 1878.

knew that I was his superior in Lerning And He got the Idea into his head that I was trying to get His place as presiding Elder. he told Broo Leak Durand[57] what he was going to do with me At the confernce when it convend at Athens. That is, he was going to send me as far back up the State Rode[58] as he could. And Shure Enoufe when the Appointements was read out I was assignd to Cave Springs.[59] To that place I refused to go. That stand that I Took Brought on more Trubbles.[60]

I wint to work at my trade for a while but soon reflected and winto work and got up a new work cald the Campbell County mishion. The Anuall Confernce siting in 1875 in Cartervill,[61] I reported 12 dollas Dollar money and 3 very good preaching placesses, 2 of them in the naborhood of Red oke Station

---

[57] Doctor Leak Durand (or Duran) (c. 1854–1890) was a layman aged twenty or twenty-one from Coweta County in 1875 when he warned Holloway of Elder Beck's intentions. He was living in his father's house in 1870, apparently unmarried, but ten years later in 1880 he was a widower, living next door to his father and with his ninety-six-year-old grandmother. In January 1880, he was licensed to preach "on trial" by the North GA Conference; he was elected deacon in 1884 and elected elder in 1886. His appointments included Atlanta City Mission (1882), Greenville Circuit (1883), Jonesboro Circuit (1884, 1885), Woodstock Circuit (1886) Elberton Circuit (1887), Athens Circuit (1888), and Ringgold Circuit (1889). At the November 1889 conference his presiding elder reported him to be in very bad health and requested the prayers of the conference. Durand died four months later on 2 March 1890.

See 1870 Census, GA, Coweta County, Pop., p. 61, dwell. 447 (mistakenly enumerated as female); 1880 Census, GA, Coweta County, Pop., ED 37, p. 29, dwell. 261; 11 NGA, 4, 11; 9 NGA, 4, 53; 10 NGA, 55; 11 NGA, 48; 12NGA, 37; 13 NGA, 42; 14 NGA, 69; 15 NGA, 60; 16 NGA, 64; 17 NGA, 24; 18 NGA, 44, 57. Durand's full name is given in Gaines, *African Methodism*, 155.

[58] The Western and Atlantic Railroad, commonly called the State Road because it was built and owned by the state of Georgia. It ran 138 miles between Atlanta, GA, and Chattanooga, TN.

[59] Cave Spring Circuit was a newly established appointment in the Marietta District of the North GA Conference. The circuit bounds were in Floyd County between Rome, GA, and the AL border.

[60] At the Griffin District quarterly conference on 27 June 1875 Bishop Ward reprimanded Holloway for failing to go to his appointment (*Christian Recorder*, 5 August 1875, 8).

[61] The Third Session of the North Georgia Conference met at St. Luke's Chapel, Cartersville, GA, 16–20 December 1875.

About 12 mills From Atlanta.[62] That Session of the confernce was noted for the Display of Learning That was Brought to bare in the pulpit, Bishop ward presiding,[63] Rev Francis J. Peck,[64] And Rev Roberson,[65] Being the leading lights.[66]

I was Assinged to the Newnan Circut. on this work I [served] 1876 and 1877. We left the work in the fall of 1877 we think much Improved. the confernce siting in Griffin, I was assigned to the Sharpesburro Circut. I made Senoia my home. on this work I began to learn that our people was not making the head way In a sperretuall [way] that many good people was lead to think. I discoverd that they ware very Ignorant and at the same time Thought they ware very wise. If they liked a man they would Join him, But as for the good Lord

---

[62] Holloway's self-appointed project does not appear in the conference statistics, but his work does appear in the list of dollar money receipts, listing him as pastor for eleven named members and an anonymous friend of the church who each gave one dollar (3 NGA, 27).

[63] Bishop Ward delivered his opening message to the conference on 16 December, but did not preach thereafter at conference due to illness. Anticipating Bishop Ward's sermon scheduled for eleven o'clock, Sunday, 19 December, a dense congregation packed St. Luke's Chapel, but the bishop send word he was too feeble to preach. Dr. Theophilus G. Steward, one of the church's leading intellectuals and a prolific writer, spoke instead (3 NGA, 3, 7).

[64] Francis J. Peck (1834–1898), at this session of conference served on the Education Committee, Missions Committee, and the Committee to Examine Fourth Year Candidates (in the AMEC's four-year theological studies program for preachers), and the Committee to Publish Minutes. On the fourth day, Sunday, 19 December, Peck preached the ordination sermon "forcibly, feelingly and sensibly" (3 NGA, 7). Peck was freeborn in Baltimore, MD, in 1834. His father, Nathaniel Peck, was a powerful local elder in Baltimore's Bethel African Methodist Episcopal Church. See Appendix A, pp. 205-206, for a biography.

[65] Scipio H. Robertson (b. c. 1840–1896) served the Third Session North GA Conference in 1875 on the Charges and Complaints Committee, the Electoral College, the Committee to Examine Fourth Year Candidates, the Committee on Last Year's Minute Money, and as conference reporter to the local Cartersville newspaper. Born in AL, Robertson grew up enslaved on a plantation in MS. He was ordained deacon at the AMEC GA Conference 1869. See Appendix A, pp. 207-208, for a biography.

[66] H. H. Holloway led devotional services on the third day of the conference, singing the hymn, "Try us, Oh God, and search the ground of every sinful heart," reading Romans 13, and praying (3 NGA, 4).

they knew nothing about him, but thought they knew it all. I servd Senoia, New hope, Sharpsburro, Brokstation and got up a new point cald Shilo.[67]

We Reported a considerable Encreece [to] The Confernce seting at Maderson Georgia Bishop J P Campbel[68] presiding. This session was reather a stormey one. Bishop Cambell and the presiding Elders not a greeing, severrell presiding Elders was taken down and new men was put up. I was Transferd to the Florda Confernce and appointed to the Ferndener Station. by some means I never got my papers so I had to work here in Georgia annother yeare. 1888 [actually 1879] the Confernce seting in Cotton Avenue AME Church Macon Georgia I was appointed Tempora to the New hope and Harralson work untill the Ala Confernce conve[ne]d. I was to be Tranfernd to the Alabama Confernce. on takeing charge of the new hope The work Receaved me with open arms. I wanted to remain with the work, not for what I could gat out of it, for I had Bilt up a considerable Reputation as workman at Turin.

And my oldest son J. W. Holloway had began to display quiet a Tellent for learning. We for got to Say that my Oldes Broo J. W. Hartsfield and His famely

[67] New Hope AME Church is in Senoia. Brooks Station was about five miles east of Senoia in the southern tip of Fayette County. The editor did not discover the location of Shiloh.

[68] Jabez Pitt Campbell (1815–1891), eighth bishop of the AMEC, was born in DE to free persons of color Anthony and Catharine Campbell. His father was a licensed AMEC preacher. At about age thirteen, Campbell ran away to PA to avoid being sold into indentured servitude for his father's debt in DE; instead his father sold him into servitude in PA. He bought the rest of his own term of service at age eighteen and became a free man. He was converted and joined the AMEC at age ten, licensed to preach at age twenty-four in 1839, ordained deacon in 1841, and ordained elder in 1843. In the late 1840s he taught school and preached in Hudson, NY, and affiliated with the Wesleyan Methodist Church as pastor of Second Wesleyan Church in Albany in 1850. Later the same year he reconnected with the AMEC and was appointed to a series of churches in NY, PA, NJ, and MD through 1864. Self-educated and intensely interested in theology, he served for a time as the AMEC book steward (1852–1860) and edited the *Christian Recorder* (1854–1860). Elected bishop in May 1864, he went to the west coast of the United States and organized the CA Conference of the AMEC in 1865. Bishop Campbell presided over the North GA Conference from December 1876 to January 1880. He died in 1891 (Wright, *Centennial Encyclopaedia*, 15, 58, 294; 4NGC, 1; 15NGC, 45).

came and stade with me in Senoia quiet a while in the Summer of 1878.[69] During of that yeare My little boy Houston H Holloway died, Sunday June 23, 1877. he was bornd at powellvill Sept the 5th 1876. He was a sweet good little boy.

In the yeare 1889 [he means 1879] I told the Breathern who mett me if they wanted me to stay with them they would have to go to work. I appointed a Rally for the Trustees and give them my pland to Bild a good house of waship. I Apointed Broo Simon Adday,[70] Trup McCalley,[71] A[nd] several outhes a mong them severall working ladys, sister Amanda white,[72] Sister Phinton Dennis,[73] and outhers and off I was for Turin.

Tow weeks after that I wint Back and found 3000 feet of Lumber on the ground and it paid for. the Rally came off with 23 dollars on the table. and one man who had a large famely and a good wief And all of them in the Church but himself. In appointing Beggirs to Raise money I did not appoint him at all. on the Rally day he Turnd up with 60 dollars. Thoug he did not Belong to the Church he be came Dictator who should be Tresura and pay master. And It

---

[69] Holloway's son J. W. Holloway recalled, "One day who should come walking up but my uncle Wesley and his whole family? They were with us several months" (JWH, 34–35).

[70] Simon Addy (b. c. 1850) was about age twenty-nine when he volunteered to help Holloway build the church; he was a GA native, farmer, husband of Laura Addy (b. c. 1854), and father of four (1880 Census, GA, Coweta County, Pop., ED 39, p. 55, dwell. 498).

[71] Troup McCally or McCauly (b. c. February 1832), farmer, and Cindy (b. February 1845), his wife since 1864, lived in the Rocky Mount District (657 GMD) of Meriwether County, near the Coweta County line. At forty-seven, he was the oldest of the volunteers named by Holloway who helped build the church (1880 Census, GA, Meriwether County, Pop., ED 82, p. 42, dwell. 339; 1900 Census, GA, Meriwether County, Pop., ED 41, p. 16, dwell. 282).

[72] Amanda White (b. c. 1853), GA native, farm hand and mother of four, married to farmer Ellis White (b. c. 1845), was about twenty-six when she volunteered to help Holloway build the church (1880 Census, GA, Coweta County, Pop., ED 43, pp. 44–45, dwell. 375).

[73] Diligent research turned up no woman named Phinton Dennis, but a man named Fenton Dennis ("colored") is listed in the GA Return of Qualified Voters, Coweta County, 691 Precinct (Senoia), p. 4, on 15 July 1867. I could not locate him in any census. Perhaps the church sister was Fenton Dennis's wife, but Holloway could not remember her Christian name.

finally Turnd out to be a white man, a member of the primitive Baptist Church To hold the money And pay it out.

On the seconday in march the Job was let out To The Lowest Responsable bidder. one colord man sent in his, he wonted 125 dollars and bord and Lodgern for himself and helpers. one outher wanted one 100 dollars for the same work. A white man by the name of Clark[74] from Senoia Bid 75 dollars And Bord and Lodging for himself and helpers.[75]

[There are five pages, about 660 words, missing from the manuscript here.]

they wanted to Bluff the young women In that way. By the help of the good Lord we wound up our work all around satisfactilory. [In 1881] the Anuall Confernce meeting at Big Bethell Church in Atlanta, Bishop W F Dickerson[76] presiding. I was appointed to serve on the Comittee on the State of the Cuntry.

---

[74] Probably James G. Clark (born in VA, c. 1827), who was a carpenter and about age fifty-two at the time he may have bid on the contract. He lived near Newnan in 1880. Clark may have been Lutheran; he married his first wife and baptized his children in Mt. Pilgrim Evangelical Lutheran Church, at Haralson, Coweta County (1880 Census, GA, Coweta County, Pop., ED 42, p. 74, dwell. 660; 1870 Census, GA, Coweta County, Pop., p. 40, dwell. 280 [1870 census gives birthplace as SC; 1880 says VA]; Mt. Pilgrim Church information provided by Margie Roop Pearce at http://wc.rootsweb.ancestry.com/cgi-bin/igm.cgi?op=GET&db=mpearce&id=I08020).

[75] Presiding Elder Richard Graham was highly pleased with Holloway's work, writing to the *Christian Recorder* (5 August 1880, 1), "I can truly say he has done the greatest work I ever saw done in the country in so short a time. He has built a nice church 30x40 [feet]. It beats a good many of our city churches. They are preparing to lathe and plaster and carpet the aisles, and inside the altar and pulpit. That is out in the country 7 miles from Senoia. The best of all he has a good set of men to work with him."

[76] William Fisher Dickerson (1844–1884) was born in Woodbury, NJ, on 15 January 1844. His parents were both members of the AMEC. He received his primary education in the common schools of Woodbury, and graduated from Pennsylvania's Lincoln University. He would earn a D.D. from Wilberforce University. Dickerson converted to Christianity and joined the AMEC in New York in 1861, was licensed to preach while a student at Lincoln, ordained a deacon in 1868, ordained elder in 1871. After being elected the thirteenth bishop of the AMEC in 1880, he oversaw the church in SC and GA. Bishop Dickerson died in Charleston, SC, on 20 December 1884 and was buried in Woodbury, NJ (Wright, *Centennial Encyclopaedia*, 83–84).

His Excelency governor Colquit who was governor of the State[77] was presant when I read in our Report as I was secratary.

After the flight of 30 years and the Rise I will Read as best I can our report from memory witch Read as followas.

> To the Bishop and Confernce. we your Committie wich was appointed on the State of the Cuntry Beges leafe to Reporte we have met and considerd to the Best of our knowaage. And we are glade to report that The cuntry every wheare is in a prosperrous condition. peace and prsperidy abounds on evry hand. Our people are also are prespering. The 2 great perliticall parties seems to understand Each outher better then ever be four.

Our people at that time owned over 20 000 acrs of land in Georgia.[78] The Report was Highely spoken of by His Excelancey governer Colquit and also Rev Dr Evenes paster—of Westly Chapple, ME Church South, peach tree Street, Atlanta.[79] the Appointment read out on monday night. I was assignd to Eatonton Station. I wint staght to Eatonton from Atlanta. Rev Andrew Brown,[80] The out going paster Introdusing me to the Church and Recomending me to the people. This was my first appointment in this part of the state.

---

[77] Alfred H. Colquitt (1824–1894) was governor of GA 1876–1882. Colquitt was a licensed Methodist preacher, active in his own MECS church, a frequent visitor at Methodist conferences, and for many years taught Sunday school in black churches.

[78] I could locate no copy of the minutes of the Eighth Session of the North GA Conference (1881) or any copy of Holloway's committee report.

[79] Clement Anselm Evans (1833–1911) was pastor of First Methodist Episcopal Church, South, on Peachtree Street in Atlanta, from 1880–1883. Before 1870 the church's name was Wesley Chapel.

[80] Andrew Brown (born in SC, c. 1825–1887) said he had waited for a black people's church since 1844: "The day the M. E. [Church] South split from the M. E. Church, while in the woods upon my knees, God showed me this church.... In 1865 I met in Atlanta a poor, barefooted, bareheaded man, named Jas. Lynch; he told me of the A. M. E. Church" (7 NGA, 24). Brown first preached in the AME Church at Union, SC, then preached throughout TN before appearing at the SC Conference's second session in Savannah where he was ordained deacon 14 May 1866. His first appointment was to Dalton, GA. In September 1866 the MECS sent a white preacher "to preach to the colored people in Dalton." Brown recalled, "He sent for me and told me he was sent there.... I told him...we must look for ourselves. He said if I was going to take the people, to take them and leave. I thanked him and we left" (7 NGA, 24).

I became Exposed to the mumps on going back to Turin. I got down with the mumps and my whole famely and many outher people caught them. It was late In Febuary befour I could move to my new faild. on or about The first of March I was on the ground And planing for the years work. I did not do well all the way a round. After runing a protracted meeting in the last of may and the first of June Taking Into the Church more 100 members,[81] my oldest Daughter Mary fell with tifoird fever. She was not down long befour I fell and then one of my boys and then my youngest Daughter Cordelia.[82] I got so lowe that I lay three weeks and five days unconcious. after a mount or t[w]o, I was able to go out but [not] able to do any thing in the line of Church work untill late in the fall.

My presiding Elder In the person of W H Harris[83] was not at all a strong man and was far from the pious line to say [the least]

Brown's subsequent appointments were presiding elder of the Atlanta District (1868–1871), Macon District (1872), Columbus District (1873), Macon District (1873–1877), Atlanta District (1879, 1880), Lexington Circuit (1881), St. Paul Circuit (1882), White Plains Circuit (1883, 1884), Griffin District (1885, 1886), and, finally, Jonesboro Circuit (1887). On his way to a preaching appointment Rev. Andrew Brown suffered a stroke and was found lying on the road. Carried to his home, he lingered a few days but died 16 May 1887. A man of action, he had told the North Georgia Conference, "I would rather wear out than to rust out" (15 NGA, 35).

See *Minutes of the South Carolina Annual Conference of the African M. E. Church, 1865, 1866, 1867* (Charleston: 1867), 8, 20; *Christian Recorder*, 15 June 1867, 2; 4 April 1868, 1; and 10 February 1881, 1; 3 GA, 14; 5 GA, 17; 6 GA 61; 7 GA, 23; 1 NGA, 23; 2 NGA, 16; 3 NGA, 15; 4 NGA, 24; 9 NGA, 55; 10 NGA, 50, 56; 11 NGA, 49; 12 NGA, 37; 13 NGA, 41; 14 NGA, 68; 15 NGA, 35; 1870 Census, GA, Whitfield County, Pop., p. 94, dwell. 339; 1880 Census, GA, Putnam County, Eatonton, Pop., ED 113, p. 19, dwell. 177.

[81] The *Christian Recorder*, 26 May 1881, 2, published Holloway's report: "Our protracted meeting has closed. We have had ninety conversions and received ninety-seven into the church."

[82] Cordelia Achsah Holloway (1870–?) was born 23 August 1870, "married a roust-about and died of neglect" (JWH, 2, 167).

[83] William H. Harris (b. 1845) was born at Hartford, CT. Kidnapped and sold into slavery in GA in 1858, he escaped in 1860 and later entered the Union army. In 1866 on the corner of Peachtree and Whitehall streets, Atlanta, Rev. Henry M. Turner licensed Harris as an exhorter in the African M. E. Church. Turner presented Harris at the March 1867 South Carolina Annual Conference in Wilmington, NC, where he was admitted on trial as a local preacher. Harris received some schooling at what would later

[The next three paragraphs substitute for a missing page. The text is from John Wesley Holloway's 1932 paraphrase of his father's manuscript (JWH, 369–70). Because J. W. Holloway's paraphrase does not match his father's original sentence structure, content of the two texts overlaps at beginning and end.]

Rev. W. H. Harris who was neither strong nor pious, came to me and said, "Holloway, I want a broad cloth suit out of your church for conference."[84] "How is that?" I asked. "Haven't we paid you your salary? Do we still owe you anything?" "No, you don't owe me anything, but I am going to have the suit, or I'll send you to the dogs." My reply was, "Then to the dogs I go." With the

---

become Clarke University (see brief biography in 1 MACON, 42). He served Atlanta's Western Mission (1867–1868) before being elected a deacon in 1870. He was appointed to Thomaston Mission (1870–1871); elected elder 1871; appointed to Lumpkin Station and School, Stewart County (1872–1873); somewhere in FL (1874–1875); Buena Vista, Marion County, GA (1876); Washington, Wilkes County (1878–1879); Forsyth, Monroe County (1880); and appointed presiding elder of the Augusta District (1881–1883). He was not appointed in 1884 or 1885, but he was appointed to Powersville, Houston County (1886) and other appointments in GA over the next twelve years. (*Minutes of the South Carolina Annual Conference of the African M. E. Church, 1865, 1866, 1867* [Charleston, 1867], 13; 5 GA, 18; 6 GA, 62; Gaines, *African Methodism*, 14, 26, 75).

The GA Annual Conference in January 1898 expelled Harris "from the ministry and connection for rebellion" (*Christian Recorder*, 27 January 1898). He had probably joined the breakaway Independent African Methodist Episcopal Church.

Holloway's low opinion of Harris may have been colored by knowledge of other misdeeds besides Harris's attempt to extort a new suit. Perhaps Holloway knew that Harris, while pastor of Thomaston Mission, Upson County, in 1870, had debauched the nineteen-year-old daughter of Emanuel Speer, one of the church trustees. Although Upson Superior Court found Harris guilty of illicit sexual intercourse with Ory Ann Speer, Harris's crime was either not reported or not noticed by the GA Conference's judiciary committee (charged with examining each preacher's character) at its next annual session. The case of adultery against Harris is in TUA, Upson County Superior Court, Minute Book F (1867–1872), 522, 523, 552–554, 560, 582.

[84] A voluntary present a suit of clothing was a mark of honor or respect; for example, at the 1874 session of the North GA AME Conference, "Conference voted a suit of clothes to Bishop T. M. D. Ward" (1 NGA, 8). In 1900 the "officers and members of St. Mary A.M.E. Church, Thomaston, Ga., presented their pastor, Rev. John Harmon a handsome $40.00 suit of clothes as a new year present" (*Christian Recorder*, 1 February 1900, 2). In contrast with these free-will gifts, Holloway resented Harris' demand for a suit as if it were a shakedown or bribe.

biggest revival the church ever had, still going, I was picked up and sent to Sugar Hill, a little back woods church, eight miles from Barnesville. And strangest part is, I went.

I think I owe my life to an old preacher, whose church was in the country, some miles from Eatonton. He visited me. As soon as he came into the sick room, he began to make fun of me and jibe me. I paid no attention to him at first, but he kept it up till, at length, I began to notice him, and coming to understand one of his wise cracks, I gave an audible "Ha! ha!" From that moment, I began to recuperate.[85]

I went to Sugar Hill, to meet up with the hardest season since the Civil War. At this place, the Rev. Henry O'Neal had a mortgage on funeralizing in the community always taking a collection from the crowds that followed him. During the the spring and summer, he was accustomed to preach the funerals of all the people, old and young, who had died during the rest of the year.[86]

---

[85] John Wesley Holloway, who was teaching school in the rural church, remembered, "[M]y father was stricken down with typhoid. He was given up, and would have died but for the clumsy old pastor of the church where I taught, who came in town to see him one day. On entering the sick room he called out in a loud bantering voice, 'Holloway, what are you lying up there for? Get up from there, sir, and get to your work.' They tried to calm him down, to no purpose. He began to crack jokes and laugh at my father till he began to take notice and finally we heard him softly laugh, 'Ha! Ha!' He had not spoken or made any sign of life for days before, but he immediately began to recuperate and was soon well. This man was named Abrams" (JWH, 55, 57).

William Abrams (b. c. 1829), AME Minister, was married to Charlotte, three years his elder, and lived southwest of Eatonton. Abrams was admitted to the AMEC GA Conference and ordained deacon in 1871 and ordained elder in 1874. He served three consecutive appointments to Log Town Circuit through 1873, one year at LaGrange, four consecutive appointments to Jones County Circuit through 1878, and then was appointed to Putnam County Circuit (1881–1882) and Watkinsville Circuit (1883). He was still serving the North GA Conference as an itinerant elder in 1890 (the last minutes seen by me) (1880 Census, GA, Putnam County, Pop., ED 112, p. 38, dwell. 338; 9 NGC, 49, 60; 18 NGC, 3).

[86] Henry O'Neal (b. c. 1823) was first recorded as an ordained AMEC deacon at the Second Session of the GA Annual Conference at Macon in March 1868. He was elected elder in 1869. His appointments included Sugar Hill (1868, 1869), Crawford County (1871, 1872, 1873), Jones Chapel and Providence Church (1874), Sugar Hill and Barnesville (1875, 1876), and Sugar Hill (1877). Minutes for 1878, 1879 and 1881 were not found. O'Neal lived and farmed with his wife and eleven children in Upson County

[Houston H. Holloway's manuscript resumes]
In the person of Rev Henry Oneail had a morgag, so to speek, on all of that work and a good collection from The Big crowd that followrd him for genrally to him all the spring and sommer to preach the furnals of all the men and woman that had Died in past mounth. The Bishop might [send] who he would but he never got to preach a furnall on that Circut.

Now this yeare 1882 was one of the hardest years. comon Bacon wint upto 18 cts per pound. Corn meail wint to one dollar and a half per Bushell. Now to help myself to live, I oppend up a little Blacksmith shoop on the Colloden vill Road from Barnsvill to Collodcnvill at a whitmans housc by thc namc of W. B. Aadams.[87] he was a premetive Baptist in Religion. Bro H Oneal was my helper while working at this place and preaching in my Humble way at Shugar Hill and At Liberty Chapple, not far from a little Town cald the Rock and at Strouds Cross Roads. one day in the summer of that yeare I was passing along the Road between my little shoop and Broo Oneails house. a Speriet seems to have spoaken to me and The following question was put to me.

"What are you doing heare any way?"
I answered Breathly, "preaching"
question second, "who sent you heare?"
I answerd, "God."
"I did not. God have alredy a number of preachers all redy heare in the person of H O Neail, James fuse[88] of the Baptist Church

in 1880. That year he was appointed to Milner Circuit (Pike County), but his presiding elder had to replace O'Neal for "failing to serve them as a pastor." Perhaps the sixteen-mile trek between his home and Milner was too tiresome. By 1882 or earlier O'Neal had "located"—that is, he chose to serve his home neighborhood as an unsalaried local elder, assisting the work of the appointed itinerant minister.

See *Christian Recorder*, 4 April 1868, 1, and 5 August 1880, 1; 3 GA, 7, 15; Gaines, *African Methodism*, 27; 5 GA, 17; 6 GA, 61; 7 GA, 25; 1 NGA, 24; 2 NGA, 16; 3 NGA, 15; 4 NGA, 23; 1880 Census, GA, Upson County, Pop., ED 140, p. 35, dwell. 302.

[87] William B. Adams (b. c. 1849) was enumerated in the 1880 census as a farmer, age thirty-one, who, with his wife and four sons, lived just four houses away from Henry O'Neal (1880 Census, GA, Upson County, Pop., ED 140, p. 35, dwell. 298).

[88] James Few (b. c. 1823) was a farmer, age fifty-seven, who, with his wife and five children, lived two houses away from Henry O'Neal when enumerated in the 1880 Census (GA, Upson County, Pop., ED 140, p. 35, dwell. 300).

> and Hampbetton of the A. M. E. Church and many outhers. And heare are you with your good wief and children, John Westly, Mary Jaine, Cordilia, And Edwin and Theodo, all heare sufering and thereis no call for it in the world."

Now this question Botherd me all of that after noon no late in Eveing. I wint back home over in monro [County].

After supper I Told my good wief that I wish to take a walk and have her to go with me, and without any perswdeing we wint down into the woods and seting down upon a log I knelt down and offerd pray to the good Lord. Riseing up from prayr I oppend my mind to her In the folloing manner. "My Deare, I Have had a strong thing to come to my mind to day and I must let you know something about it. first we must chaing our way of living and we must do it at once. we have 5 children out heare in the woods and If I am not badely deceaved we are doing no good. If I understand the word Religion and the Church I am not doing any thing. the people do not understand It. they are all mistaken. They have been mis led and they and they are still followig there leaders and I cannot go with them and they will not go with me. And I find that I am only acting as as the cat paw to pull the chestnutts out of the fire for the presiding Elders while they have a district stoward to collect up his money.[89] He still holds me responsable and If do not gat [the money] you and the children must sufer to say nothing about my self. And I have decided to tuff it out heare this yeare and do the best I can untell annother yeare. And then we will go back to Turin And Buy us a home And live more like we aught to live. this life we are living is unbecoming the lief of a minster of the gospell and I cannot stand it any longer." My good wief Asked me, "what is the matter [with] you? I hate for you to leave off preaching." "I am not entending to leave that off my Deare," I said, "my Deare I love the church and the work but it is you and the children that I am studing about now. if one of our Famely should die we are not able to Berry them and if I was to die you are not able to Berry me. Now This will not do for a Free man. we must do better then This. why should we not do as well as any one Els?"

---

[89] At the Forsyth District Conference in April 1882, Presiding Elder Andrew W. Lowe had nominated Holloway for district steward, whose primary duty was to collect the presiding elder's salary from the various churches in his district. Conference members had voted to raise $900 for Lowe's salary (*Christian Recorder*, 29 June 1882, 2).

I was not long befour I had my wief in line with me and I will never for gat the hard yeare of 1881 [he means 1882]. It was that yeare when Every thing wint so high, Corn $ dollar and 50ct per Bushel, Bacon wint to 18 cts per pound. I was living in a little log cabbin[90] at Shugar Hill Church, while I Served Liberty Church and main time I got up a church at Strouds Cross Roads. It was while on this work that Rev. A. W. Lowe[91] My Presiding Elder spoke to me about Taking out The 1.11 [=111 copies of his] confernce minuts on my work and sell them for him. I agreed to do so if I could. I Took them and offord them to the people. I found no Byers. hard times was the only complaint that I could could heare and there was much Truth in what they said. on the first Round holding his quartely confernce he cald for the money for the minutes. I Told him that I Could not Sell them, the times was so hard I could not sell them at all.

I wint on with my work and Took many Into church during that summer and Earley fall I was very successfull at Strouds Cross Roads.[92] I found annother

---

[90] John Wesley Holloway described the family's home as "a double log-cabin" (JWH, 59).

[91] Andrew W. Lowe (1842–1894) and his wife, Sophronia (b. c. 1846), were working on a farm in Warren County, GA, in 1870 when he heard his call to the ministry. Lowe could both read and write, but his wife could do neither. He joined the AMEC GA Conference as a licensed local preacher in 1871 and was elected local deacon at the same session; by 1872 he was itinerant but without appointment. In January 1873 he was elected elder. Appointments included Thomaston (1874), Griffin (1876) and Wood's Chapel in Atlanta (1878), presiding elder of the Atlanta District (1879–1881), then presiding dlder of the Forsyth District (1882–1886), and pastor of Bethel AME Church in Augusta (1888, 1889). The *Christian Recorder* reported that Lowe, presiding elder Albany District GA, "fell dead" on 19 July 1894 "in his district conference" (26 July 1894, 2). John Wesley Holloway elaborated on the story, alleging that Lowe was "an excellent preacher, but a hard drinker," who "fell dead in pulpit, while preaching" (JWH, 374, 376).

See 1870 Census, GA, Warren County, Pop., p. 91, dwell. 576; 1880 Census, GA, Spalding County, Pop., ED 117, p. 13, dwell. 110; 5 GA, 11, 12; 6 GA, 40; 2 MACON, 55; 3 MACON, 29; 4 MACON, 39; *Augusta City Directory 1888*, 288 (Augusta, 1888); *Augusta City Directory 1889*, 265 (Augusta, 1889); *Christian Recorder*, 26 July 1894, 2.

[92] Presiding Elder A. W. Lowe reported at the Macon Annual Conference in February 1883 that "Rev. H. H. Holloway, pastor of Sugarhill Circuit, has built a splendid church at what is known as the Cross Roads, in Monroe county" (1 MACON, 33).

Thing among our people. white people would help us Largely to Build a house of waship in many places in thoese days whare they had large plantations and They subscribed heavey to wards the work at Strouds Cross Roads on account of holding hands on there plantations in that communitty. our last quartely confence came off At liberty [Chapel]. Our presiding Elder A W Low presiding. I had a very good Report. my work had growd considerably speritual[ly] but had not dun much Financlly. Thoes confernce minutes and the money for them was cald for and It was heare That the presideing Elder Hinted that I wouls gat no appointment untill the Eleven dollars for The minuts came up, whether they was sold or not the money had to come wether I sold them or not. From heare I began to gat on to it. So I set down and Roat to Rev James b Hunnicit[93] At Turin and told him that I had decided to leave of the Travling ministrey and move back to Turin and settle my self and famely. He rote back by Return of maiel that they would be ever so glade for me to move back.

The [annual] confence came off.[94] I was left without and appointment. I moved back to Turin and went to work.[95] as a matter of corse I had to, starte

---

[93] James Benjamin Hunnicutt (1836–1905), born in Coweta County, was a white MECS clergyman, prominent in Turin: "the chief man of the village, a preacher, teacher, [dry goods] merchant and farmer" (JWH, 211). His farming success led to his election as professor of agriculture at University of Georgia in Athens, a post he held 1892–1898. He next edited and published an agricultural newspaper, the *Southern Cultivator*, and wrote a book, *Agriculture for the Common Schools* (1903). He spent his last years in Atlanta. (Lucian Lamar Knight, *A Standard History of Georgia and Georgians*, vol. 6 [Chicago: Lewis Publishing Company, 1917] 2813–814; 1880 Census, GA, Coweta County, Pop., ED 39, p. 28, dwell. 265.)

[94] Newly formed out of part of the North GA Conference, the Macon, GA, Conference held its first session at Sandersville, GA, 31 January–5 February 1883.

[95] Holloway's financial problems with his church came to a head at the January 1883 Conference in Macon, GA. The Judiciary Committee read two letters containing separate charges against Holloway. The first letter probably concerned the unsold conference minutes, about which the committee reported, "we recommend that his appointment be withheld until said debts are paid" (1 MACON, 30). The second letter alleged there was "dollar money collected by him and not reported to the Conference" (1 MACON, 30). The committee recommended an investigation into the dollar money. The Committee on Dollar Money recommended presiding elders collect the money from Holloway and two other defaulting members "at all hazards" (1 MACON 38) and Conference minutes reported him "appointment withheld" due to financial debt to the church (1 MACON, 23).

from the ground, chears Bedsteds Stovee and Every thing I needed. It Took myself and famely the Remaing part of the yeare 1882 [actually 1883] to gat stratend out. The confernce conveaind in forsyth. I visitted this session of the confernce.[96]

The yeare 1883 [actually 1884] was close at hand. The fall of this yeare The Macon Confernce conveaind at Millagevill. I Rote The Rev A W Low a Letter after this manner:[97]

> Turin Georgia
>
> Rev A W Lowe,
>
> please find Enclose 11.dollars and 10cts. Now since I find that I was not fit to preace to the people as you had it owing the confernce 11 dollars and 10cts, now I find that I am not fit to preach to the people owing my wief and children severrall Thousand. So Good Bye.

Holloway left the conference in haste without submitting the required annual statistics for his Sugar Hill Circuit. Holloway's son later described his father's exit: "He left the conference before the doxology was sung, stopped at the first hardware store, bought himself a hand hammer & went back to Turin" (1 MACON, Statistical Table following 43; JWH, 61).

[96] Second Session of the Macon, GA, Annual Conference, AMEC, held in Forsyth, 5 November–3 December 1883. The minutes included Holloway's chronology of past church appointments among those of the other conference members (2 MACON, 55).

[97] Holloway may be conflating two letters and two different conferences almost seven years apart. His usually accurate sense of chronology is erratic throughout his telling of the charge brought against him for debt to the conference. The Third Session of the Macon Conference met in Columbus (November 1884), not in Milledgeville.

Holloway tells how he resolved the issue of the unsold conference minutes by paying Rev. Lowe the $11.10, but the matter of the dollar money festered for almost seven years. The church did not clear Holloway's name until the Eighth Session of the Macon Conference meeting in Milledgeville in November 1889 when he sent the conference a letter enclosing fifteen dollars to settle the dollar money account. Minutes recorded that "On motion, the money was received. Bro. Holloway was exonerated from the charge and his character 'passed'" (8 MACON, 15).

I have never acsepted of and appointment from the Bishop from that day untill this.[98] It may be that I acted Rash in that case, And yet you will say that we did ourselves much good while the work was going on.

[98] John W. Holloway remembered, "Bishop Gaines wrote him [Houston H. Holloway] a number of letters a yard long trying to get him back" (JWH, 376).

Chapter Seven

Home and Family

The third yeare I Bought us a home and Built a four Room house.[1] It was from this place My oldes son J W Holloway got of to Fisk university and my oldest Daughter got of To Tuskeega Normall and Industrical Institute. Thease tow children did well Just at the Starte. I was at work all the time day and night, preaching In my Humble way at night and Blacksmithing in the day.[2] And straing to say I Labord much under a misstake in preaching to my people. I found out that they wore not on to it as a rule. I found that they did not Read nor phalasafise. they knew nothing about phalasaphy, And they had a long ways In my Humble Estimation to go to gat there.

It was during of this yeare 1882 [probably 1890 or 1891] I was waitid by tow of the Elders of Mount Sinai Presbiterian Church and they Requested me to preach for them once permounth untill they Could gat a paster. I Thought over the matter and agreed to do so. And It fell to my lot to speek for them every Second Sbbath in the mounth. Durin of the time that [I] served them I collected money and Bilt them a new house of waship and there membership was Dubble and one of the straingest parts of it was I was out of the church and it appeard that that [I] was taking people into It. I did open the doors of the church for the Eders of the church[3] In person of Broo Henry Russell[4] Samyell

---

[1] Holloway bought one square acre of land in Turin, next to the J. B. Hunnicutt home place, from J. B. Hunnicutt for $250 on 23 August 1890. When Holloway mortgaged this land in 1907, it included "one frame dwelling containing four rooms the same being built by me in the year 1891" (Coweta County Deed Book T, 202, and Deed Book 3, 541, Office of the Clerk of Coweta County Superior Court, Newnan, GA).

[2] John W. Holloway wrote, "He with a Mrs. Graham, a devout woman, held neighborhood prayer meetings, weekly, much to the good of all. He was exceedingly helpful to preachers and the poor, furnishing them with food, often heading surprize parties for the former" (JWH, 377).

[3] Holloway ponders the irony that a Methodist elder, outside the Presbyterian Church, was bringing converts into that church. In many evangelical churches the preacher concludes the service with an invitation for people to come forward and join,

Carmicle[5] and Broo Charley North.[6] About this time my good wief, who had Bin down with a stroke of paralisis for about 5 years, Began to gat worse and thease people began to call for more ministerial work. And I was not able on account of my good wief was gating worse and calling for more of my time.[7] and they would have been ever so glade to have goten me to join them and be come a straight out presbiteren. This I Could not do as I faild to understand the

---

which is called "opening the doors of the church" for membership. (For example, Holloway tells us he joined the Methodist church in 1861 when "the Doors of the Church was Throne oppend"—see p. 100.)

[4] Henry Russell (b. c. 1837), Presbyterian elder, was Holloway's near neighbor on Ray Street in Newnan. He was born in VA and was a longtime resident of Coweta County. His first wife was Mariah; after she died he married his second wife, Maria, about 1896. During Reconstruction, he worked as a farm laborer; by 1880 worked his own rented farm; by 1900 he was still farming and paying a mortgage on his own home. In 1910 (the last census in which he appeared), perhaps to work at a pace suitable to his advanced age, he had reverted to working as hired farm labor and was renting a house at 14 Ray Street, Newnan (Holloway lived at 33 Ray Street from 1900 to 1909). He could neither read nor write, but that did not prevent his persistent advocacy for a full-time minister and a school for his church neighborhood.

See 1870 Census, GA, Coweta County, Pop., p. 43; 1880 Census, GA, Coweta County, Pop., ED 40, p. 35, dwell. 310; 1900 Census, GA, Coweta County, Newnan, Pop., ED 18, p. 8, dwell. 157; 1910 Census, GA, Coweta County, Newnan, Pop., ED 32, p. 21, dwell. 462. The 1870–1910 censuses suggest wildly different birth years for Russell: 1837, 1841, February 1830, and 1857.

[5] Samuel Carmichael (b. c. May 1837), Presbyterian elder, was born in SC and lived in Turin District, Coweta County, in 1900. He farmed and rented his farm. He could read and write (1900 Census, GA, Coweta County, Pop., ED 26, p. 16, dwell. 273).

[6] Charles North (b. c. 1825), Presbyterian elder, was born in VA about May 1823 or 1825 or 1832 (depending which census you read) and married Martha in about 1848. He was a longtime resident of Coweta County, a farm laborer, and he boarded with his family in the house of another couple in 1870. By 1880 he was farming for himself; in 1900, still with Martha, he was renting a farm when he was in his seventies. He does not appear in the 1910 census. He could neither read nor write (1870 Census GA, Coweta County, Pop., p. 44, dwell. 304; 1880 Census, GA, Coweta County, ED 40, p. 20, dwell. 179; 1900 Census, GA, Coweta County, Pop., ED 23, p. 4, dwell. 71).

[7] Cordelia fell at her washtub with a stroke from which she never recovered (John Wesley Holloway, "Memoirs of John Wesley Holloway, Thebes Ga., July 3, 1916," 405 [photocopy of unpublished manuscript in author's possession, hereafter cited as JWH]).

Docttrin of Election and Predistination as Taught by the Presbiteriain Church, Though I liked them much.[8]

This Same yeare 1892 [actually 1891] The Presbiterian mishion Bord hearing of this work Through Broo Henry Russel who went anually to meet the presbytery, They sent a man to take charge of the church by the name of Riley[9] who served them a yeare or tow. After he was removed a man was appointed by the name B L Glinn.[10] I never [met][11] him with the church as my good wief grew worse Every day untill the worst and last of this part of our narative comes to the worst for it was on her account I had to drop all the work that took me away from home. In this section of the cuntry we had no particular beneveolent societies to among us, But we was Blest by the help of the good Lord with many Good Frinds such as Mrs Suasan Page,[12] Mrs Narcis Bigby,[13] Mrs Mary

---

[8] The church also tried to recruit Holloway's son, John W. Holloway: "My first time to fill a pulpit was in Coweta county Ga in '91. at a Presbyterian church, some miles west of Turin, known as Mt. Sinai. My father was supplying there. A series of meetings, night sessions, was in progress. On this occasion he could not go and sent me in his place. I do not remember anything I said, but the elders were so highly pleased that they offered to send me to one of their schools, to educate me for their pastor" (JWH, 258).

[9] Manson Riley pastored Mt. Sinai for a year, 1891–1892, when it had about 40 members and 35 Sunday school students (*Home Missions: Twenty-Second Annual Report (The Ninetieth from its Organization) of the Board of Home Missions of the Presbyterian Church in the United States of America. Presented to the General Assembly, at Portland, Oreg., May 19th, 1892* [New York: 1892] 28).

[10] In 1900 B. L. Glenn (1860–1904) and wife Catherine were close neighbors to the Holloway family in Newnan. See pp. 209-211 for a biographical sketch of this interesting couple.

[11] The missing word occurs at the page break between manuscript pages 161 and 162. In his paraphrased transcript, John Wesley Holloway supplied "met" which makes good sense of the context.

[12] Susan Page (c. 1845–before 1900), formerly Susan Arnold, married Richard Page (b. c. 1845 or April 1852) in Coweta County on 22 December 1871. By 1880 the family lived in Senoia, Coweta County, immediately next door to Houston H. and Cordelia Holloway. The census described Susan as a laborer who could neither read nor write, and Rich Page as a farm worker, living with their three children (Florance, Mazura, Columbus) and Rich's mother, Katie. Susan Page's daughter Florance later married Houston Holloway's son, Edwin Stanton Holloway. Susan apparently died before the 1900 when the census found Richard Page boarding in his son-in-law's house. Page was then a blacksmith, perhaps having learned the trade from his former neighbor (1880

Edward,[14] Mrs Mariah Shell,[15] and Mrs Sharlot North,[16] and Mrs Caroline Russell[17] and Mrs Sarah ann Cannon,[18] The last 3 being members of the Baptist

---

Census, GA, Coweta County, Pop., ED 39, p. 28, dwell. 266; 1900 Census, GA, Coweta County, Turin, Pop., ED 26, p. 11A, dwell. 173; Dianne Wood, ed., *1827–1900 Coweta County Georgia Marriages*, available at http://www.georgiagenealogy.org/coweta/dianne%20corner.htm [accesed 4 November 2012]).

[13] Narcis (or Narcissa) Bigby (b. c. 1854), formerly Narcissa Page, married Richard Bigby in Coweta County on 7 November 1872. The 1880 census described her as keeping house with husband Rich, five sons, and one daughter (1880 Census, GA, Coweta County, Senoia, Pop., ED 39, p. 25, dwell. 238; Wood, ed., *1827–1900 Coweta County Georgia Marriages*).

[14] Mary Edwards (b. October 1849), formerly Mary Peak, married Louis (or Lewis) Edwards (b. June 1825) on 16 November 1870 in Coweta County The 1900 census described Mary as a farm laborer who could neither read nor write, while her husband, also a farm laborer, could read but not write. Lewis Edwards was one of the three people who signed and sent Cordelia Holloway's obituary to the *Christian Recorder* (1900 Census, GA, Coweta County, Senoia, Pop., ED 20, p. 15A, dwell. 315; Wood, ed., *1827–1900 Coweta County Georgia Marriages*; *Christian Recorder*, 24 May 1894).

[15] Mariah Shell (b. May 1850), formerly Maria Glass, was born in GA and married Henry Shell (b. March 1838 in SC) in Coweta County on 9 January 1873; the 1880 census had described both as farm workers. The 1900 census found Henry still a farm laborer but left Mariah's occupation blank. Neither could read or write. In 1900 they still lived with three of their children, sons Algie and Robert and daughter, Marietta—two other children had died. In their household were two grandsons named Joseph Holloway (b. February 1895) and William Holloway (b. June 1898) (1880 Census, GA, Coweta County, Pop., ED 39, p. 24, dwell. 231; 1900 Census, GA, Coweta County, Turin, Pop., ED 26, p. 13A, dwell. 209; Wood, ed., *1827–1900 Coweta County Georgia Marriages*).

[16] Charlotte North (b. Apr 1847), native of GA, married to farmer Daniel North (b. December 1846 in GA). In 1900 they lived with their daughter and grandson, next door to Caroline Russell (see note below) (1900 Census, GA, Coweta County, Pop., ED 23, p. 8B, dwell. 159).

[17] Caroline (Callie) Russell (b. May 1841), married Louis Russell (b. October 1839) about 1878 and lived with two sons, a daughter-in-law, three grandchildren, and a boarder when the census enumerator came in 1900 (1900 Census, GA, Coweta County, Pop., ED 23, p. 8B, dwell. 158).

[18] Sarah [Sallie] Ann Cannon (b. January 1835) was a widowed head of household living with a daughter and three grandchildren (1900 Census, GA, Coweta County, Turin, Pop., ED 26, p. 10B, dwell. 160).

Church, And many outhers. December the 25 was the last Chrismas Holliday that my wief ever saw.

It was on the Incoming yeare 1893 that I Bilt The house in which I now live.[19] My Daughter mary was a student of Tuskege. She was also at home sick. Hers was a Lung [illness]. one may Imageen my situation, a wief who was alreday partely Dead and a Daugt[er] In the last stagees of consumtion,[20] Boath at the Same time. It came about so that I had to send to Tuskege for my Daughter to come home and home she came. And After a lingering Illness, for it was the 12 day of July 6 oclock 45 minutes in the After noon that she carmly Departed this Lief. It was up to that time the sadest day of my lief and it was in this presant residence that she spint her last day. Her furnall was attended by Rev A L Shaw[21] in Tranquill meeting [house] while her last Remains was Berried In the Cemetary th[e]re.[22]

Her mother lived on untell the 3rd day of April in the in the yeare 1894 and she past away and of all the pangs of sorror that I was ever cald upon to endure this was the most severe. I realey wanted to Die in her place for I reather have died myself then stood by and lookt upon [her] pass away. Rev A L Shaw, who had served her 4 years as paster, happend to be heare on a visit to his old Flock at Sharps Burro and Requested him on Sunday Eving Befor she died on monday preach her furnall and I Told him that if he would remain over a day or 2 he would have that to do befour he left and so he did. It was the sadest day of

---

[19] Elsewhere Holloway states he built the house in 1891. See p. 169, n.1.

[20] Her brother John Wesley Holloway wrote, "Sister Mary died of intestinal consumption, contracted at Tuskegee under the following circumstances: It was in the log-cabin and umbrella days of the school. A girl was dying of tuberculosis. [Dr. Booker T.] Washington called for volunteers to attend her during the night. Sister Mary volunteered, contracted the disease and died within a year. I never care to see Tuskegee" (JWH, 235).

[21] Elder A. L. Shaw was first appointed to Sharpsburg for the year 1890 at the November 1889 North Georgia Conference and was reappointed for 1891 (17 NGA, 60). He may have been reappointed to the same place, but I did not look at minutes for later sessions (18 NGA, 58).

[22] Tranquil Cemetery is 1.7 miles southeast by road from Turin. Holloway's wife Cordelia, daughter Mary, and other children, are buried there. If the graves were ever marked, those marks are now lost; no Holloway burials were found by Dianne Wood in her July 2007 survey of Tranquil Cemetery, Turin County.

my lief. on Returing back home from [the cemetery][23] I had my supper at 6 oclock and Retired at once to rest and told my People not to Trubble me at all during of the night as I had not had a nights rest in so long. I had my usual prayr service and was soon fast a sleep. the whole night past away like a vision. about half past 4 oclock the next morning I dremd that I heard my wief calling for something. I Jumpt out of bead quick to see what she wanted and behole she was not th[e]re. and then my Trubbles started. I will not undertake to describe my feeling. you can Imagein how I felt when I say That the woman who lay dead before me had been my companion 29 years 9 mounths and some odd days. And we had never had a cross word[24] Our connection had been sweet In the time of sickness and the time of helth to say nothing about the time of the yeare.

I stade on heare at Turin untill the fall of the yeare. about the first of noventer I was Imployed by by Mr W E Dent[25] as foman of his Black Smith shoop on Deport Street Newnan Georgia. as foman of this shoop I remaind foman more then 13 years. While there I put in my service on the Sabbeth in the Sabbath School of Mount Zion A.M.E. Church. At that time Rev N. L. Homes[26] se[r]ving as paster meeting the Sabbath Schol every Sabbath more or less. the paster assignd me to a class composed mostly of Locall preachers, Wm

---

[23] John W. Holloway inserted "the cemetery" for the missing word or words (JWH, 380).

[24] Ibid. Holloway's eldest son testified, "I am a witness to this."

[25] Holloway later identified this employer as "W A Dent," perhaps the same person found in the 1890 Coweta County tax digest as "W A Dent, treasurer of Newnan Buggy Company" (Coweta County Tax Digest, 1890, 646 Georgia Militia District [Fifth Militia District or Town of Newnan] [n.p.]; JWH, 380, names his father's employer as "W. E. Dent Mfg Co., Newnan").

[26] Nathan L. Holmes (born in GA c. December 1856) was licensed in the North Georgia Conference in 1884 and appointed to Lithonia Circuit for three years, 1885–1887; he was elected deacon in 1885 and appointed to New Hope Circuit for 1888, to Thomaston Circuit for 1889 through 1891 (subsequent minutes not seen, but Holloway tells us Holmes served the Newnan church for 1895 and 1896), transferred to the Southwest Conference before 1900, and died before 1916.

See 1900 Census, GA, Early County, Pop., ED 51, p. 3, dwell. 61; 11 NGA, 4; 12 NGA, 3, 37; 13 NGA, 41; 14 NGA, 68; 15 NGA, 60; 16 NGA, 63; 17 NGA, 60; Wright, *Centennial Encyclopaedia*.

Dunson,[27] S S Sleedge,[28] Wm Coleman,[29] Joe Boyed,[30] A Shachaford.[31] I Soon discoverd that my class was not In It for any good, and assoon as they found out that they could not pusell [=puzzle] me with hard questions they began to Drop off In attendance. They all wantted to preach But only for what they hopet to gat out off it In the forme of callections.

As for the men as a rule they knew nothing about the principall of Religion yet they all beleaved tha they had it and he would be glad to shure that he knew as much about the lessen as I. For Instance one Sabbath morning among outher things our lessen containd The of[t] repeted pasage, Be ye as as wise as serpance and as harmless as Doves. Mr Dunson wanted to know how it was that they was to be as wise as serpance and as harmeles as Doves when the dove was the meainest Burd that there was In the woods. I Replied to him that our Lord said that [it] was harmless. he said that it was not. I Referde him to the Lord himself, he made the Dove and he was the the one that said that the Dove was harmless and you are the one that says that it is not. In a very short time I found that the so cald preachers of my class had dropt out, and out they stade, only calling in as prominant men occasonly.

---

[27] Possibly William Dunson (b. c. 1854), a farmer who lived in Troup County in 1880 with his, wife, Fannie (b. c. 1856), farm hand. Not located in 1900 census. A licensed preacher named W. M. Dunson is listed with an appointment in the Atlanta Annual Conference in 1904 (1880 Census, GA, Troup County, Pop., ED 129, p. 8, dwell. 68; 4 ATLANTA, 79).

[28] Shadrack Sledge (b. April 1840) was a farmer, married since about 1887 to Matilda (b. May 1850). Both were members of the Mt. Zion AME Church building committee (1900 Census, GA, Coweta County, Pop., ED 22, p. 14, dwell. 237; cornerstone of Mt. Zion AME Church, Newnan, GA).

[29] William Coleman (b. June 1842), house painter, was married since about 1883 to Jennie (b. c. 1861) (1900 Census, GA, Coweta County, Newnan, Pop., ED 18, p. 8, dwell. 151).

[30] Joseph Boyd (b. May 1839), day laborer, was married since about 1866 to Nicey (b. June 1844), laundress. Both were members of the Mt. Zion AME Church building committee (1900 Census, GA, Coweta County, Newnan, Pop., ED 18, p. 5, dwell. 9; Mt. Zion AME Church cornerstone).

[31] Andrew Shackelford (b. c. 1842), farmer, was married to Fanny (b. c. 1850), washer woman. He was a member of the Mt. Zion AME Church building committee (1880 Census, GA, Coweta County, Pop., ED 48, p. 57, dwell. 491; Mt. Zion AME Church cornerstone).

Rev Homes se[r]ved there the next yeare and as he had not recomeded tow or 3 of the men as suatable persons to be admitten into the travling connection not one of them liket him. they all wanted him removd and a man appointed there who would Endoss them as suatable persons to be admitted into the travling work. this class of men had given me much Trubble in the past and I began to learn heare that they wore yet on hand, Trubbling ourther men just as they had Trubbled me in gorn by years. I worked on at Newnan that yeare under Rev Homes and while he did not do all the way a round as I Thought he should have dun for the Good of the A.M.E. Church, it may be said that he did the best he could under the low state of knowellage that Existed In it.

Broo Homes served that yeare 1895 and the 1896. Rev Toliver[32] served 1897. He was a good man But on account of His quiet way of doing Bisness He did not do much in the way of Bildind up the work. He took good care of it how ever. Rev John Harman[33] succeeded him. he fail also thogh he did more more

---

[32] Rev. John W. Tolliver (Taliaferro) was admitted on trial to the North Georgia Conference in December 1876, elected deacon in 1880, and served various subsequent appointments, including Thomaston in 1891; subsequent career not researched (4 NGA, 14, 24; 7 NGA, 11, 17; 9 NGA, 51, 53).

[33] John Harmon (b. 1861) was born in Smithville, Lee County, Georgia, 1 October 1861. At age fifteen he was elected superintendent of the Sunday school of New Hope A. M. E. Church. He moved to Montgomery, AL, in 1880. Richard Wright (*Centennial Encyclopaedia*) states that, “In 1881 he was baptized and received into the St. John A. M. E. church, Montgomery, Alabama, as a full member, and the same year was elected a steward and trustee, in which positions he served until his call to the ministry, April, 1893. He was superintendent of St. John Sunday school for four years, and a trustee of Payne and Wilberforce universities” (107). In April 1893 he was licensed to preach and was admitted to the conference in Troy, AL, in 1893; appointments in AL included White Hall, Union Springs, Abbeville, Wells, and Eufaula. During his time in AL he was ordained deacon. In January 1898 he was transferred to GA, ordained elder, and assigned to Palmetto Circuit, Newnan, followed by two years at Thomaston. He was presiding elder of Newnan District for 1902, and after four years was appointed presiding elder of Atlanta District. After two years he resigned his presiding eldership and was appointed in turn to the Griffin District, the Douglasville Circuit, and to Turner Tabernacle, Macon, Georgia. Next he was appointed presiding elder of Augusta District, a post he was holding in 1916. He received an honorary D.D. in 1907 from Morris Brown University. Engaged in politics, he “was a delegate to the National Republican Convention in St. Louis, Mo., July, 1896. He canvassed Alabama for both Harrison and McKinley” (107). He edited of a number of newspapers and by 1916 was “regarded as

then any one had dun in sum years to wardes gating up materiall to Bild a good house of waship. Rev A. L. Shaw was appointed in the yeare 1898. I Forgot to say that in the 1895 on the 9th day of november[34] I married my presant wief. She was the Daughter of Rev Tayler Slaughter[35] of Palmetto one of the Best men that I ever saw. Mis Fannie Slaughter[36] serveing as Brides Made.

I will say heare for 18 years I have lived a sweet plesasant lief with this good woman Pollie Ann Slaughter[37] Holloway. we have had 6 children Bornd unto us. one of them Is dead in the per[son] of Henry Turner who was Bornd September the 15th day 1898. Tayler Slaughter was Bornd September the 15th

---

one of the most forceful writers in his church" (107–108). See also W[infield] H[enri] Mixon, *History of the African Methodist Episcopal Church in Alabama, with Biographical Sketches* (Nashville, TN: A. M. E. Church Sunday School Union, 1902) 155–58.

[34] According to Coweta County Marriage Record K (Black) 1892–1901, 36, H. H. Holloway and Polly Slaughter were married on 10 November 1896 by H. D. Gorman, M. G.

[35] Taylor Slaughter (c. 1844–1924), see biography on pp. 208-209.

[36] Fannie Slaughter (b. c. 1877), named for her mother, was a younger sister of Polly Slaughter (1880 Census, GA, Campbell County, Palmetto, Pop., ED 24, p. 41, dwell. 357).

[37] Polly Ann (Slaughter) Holloway (c. 1875–1941), daughter of Taylor Slaughter, was probably born in Palmetto, Campbell County, about April 1875 while Houston H. Holloway and family were neighbors. JWH, age nine at the time, would recall, "I remember the day Polly (Ann) Slaughter was born.... [She and her children] are at this writing, Aug. 1932, in Detroit, and, so far as I know, doing well" (JWH, 242). Sons Taylor Slaughter Holloway and William F. Holloway were the first to move to Detroit, where the 1920 census found them living on Crane Avenue with Uncle Thomas and Aunt Lizzie Slaughter. Polly Ann and the rest of her family followed to Detroit by 1930, where that census found her working as a live-in house servant for the family of Sam Lieberman, wholesale merchant. By 1940 she had moved in with daughter Anna Mae Thornton. She died 5 December 1941 at the Eloise Hospital complex in Wayne County, MI.

See 1880 Census, GA, Campbell County, Palmetto, Pop., ED 24, p. 41, dwell. 357; 1900 Census, GA, Coweta County, Newnan, Pop., ED 18, p. 9, dwell. 179; 1930 Census, MI, Wayne County, Detroit, Ward 10, Pop., ED 82–307, p. 13A, dwell. 3, fam. 29 (boarder "Polly A Holliway [*sic*], widow, married 19 years, negro 54, servant"); JWH 242, 243; 1940 Census, MI, Wayne County, Detroit, Pop., ED 84–951, p. 8A, dwell. 5777, household 135; Detroit Public Library, Wayne County Death Records Index, 1940–1944 ("Annie Hollaway") (viewed online at http://www.detroitpubliclibrary.org/wayne-county-death-record-index [accessed 10 April 2015]).

1896. The furnall Sevice of Henry Turner was Tended by the Rev John Harmon. His last Remaines was lade to Rest in Tranqull Semetarry neare Turin. He was Baptised by Bishop Henry M Turner.[38]

---

[38] Henry McNeal Turner (1834–1915) was born into a family of free people of color at Newberry Court House, SC. He learned to read and write largely by his own efforts and joined the MECS in 1848. He was licensed to preach in 1853. He and his family moved to St. Louis, MO, in 1858 after the 1857 Dred Scott decision had threatened the tenuous liberties and safety of free persons of color in the South more dangerously than before. He transferred his membership to the AMEC and studied at Trinity College (he earned a D.D. from Wilberforce University in 1873). He was ordained deacon in 1860 and elder in 1862. During the Civil War he organized a unit of US Colored Troops in which he served as chaplain.

After the war he served briefly as a Freedmen's Bureau agent in GA, helped organize GA's Republican Party, and was elected to the state's constitutional convention in 1867 and to the Georgia House of Representatives in 1868. Votes of the white majority expelled Turner and others from the state legislature on the excuse that the new constitution did not specifically authorize Negroes to hold elective office.

From 1865 through the 1870s Turner proselytized vigorously throughout Georgia on behalf of the AMEC. Largely as a reward for these efforts, he was elected bishop in the AMEC in 1880. He served as bishop for Georgia for twelve years. In the 1890s he visited Africa four times, establishing the AMEC on that continent, and shaping his advocacy of a back-to-Africa movement. Jim Crow laws and state laws disfranchising black voters dismayed Turner and persuaded him that the US promise of freedom for all was false. In 1900, a Georgia newspaper quoted Turner saying that "this is the white man's country and always will be"—to which the white editor added, "He is right" (Thomaston *Times*, 8 June 1900, 1; similar statement that blacks have "no country here and never will have" quoted in Gregory Mixon, "Henry McNeal Turner versus the Tuskegee Machine: Black Leadership in the Nineteenth Century," *Journal of Negro History* 79/4 [Autumn 1994]: 372). Turner had often told friends he did not want to die in the United States, a nation that denied him civil and political rights. God granted his wish. Enroute to a church conference in Canada, Turner disembarked from the ferry at Windsor, Ontario, collapsed of a massive heart attack on the wharf, and died hours later in a Canadian hospital, 18 May 1915.

Stephen Ward Angell, *Bishop Henry McNeal Turner and African-American Religion in the South* (Knoxville: University of Tennessee Press, 1992); New Georgia Encyclopedia (entry for Henry McNeal Turner) available at http://www.georgiaencyclopedia.org/nge/Article.jsp?id=h-632&sug=y (accessed 22 January 2015); Wright, *Centennial Encyclopaedia*, 231.

Durin of this yeare I enjoyed good helth and I Bought property no 33 Ray Street newnan Georgia.[39] The Anuall Confernce conveaind in Atlanta. Rev C A Wingfeild[40] was appointed to Newnan. Rev A L Shaw was a good man But the work that need[e]d to be dun for the A M E Church he faild to see it. Wing feild being a young man He came took hold of the work to make his marke. The Small membership composed largely of old people but few young people in it. And Wingfeild porposed to the Church that we Bild a Brick Church. this was Considerd by all who heard of it as a matter of Imposabilety. on the night The members was cald out to decide whether tha wanted a good house and if so what kind of a house, The largest portion of them stadc at home, while I with afew and the young men on that side of Town with the paster decided to Bild a Brick House.

A grand Rally was held soon after and to the asstonishment of Every Body we rased one Hundred and some odd Dollars. A Car Lode of Brick was orderd and Differrant men give Thre Teerns [=their turns] and fu[r]nished hands to put the Brick on the ground. The Rock also for the Basement was also forth coming. The time was set to lay the cornner stone. Bishop Turner came down and conducted the services. Some thing over one Hundred dollars was Raised And to Every Bodies astonishement in 3 week the wals was up for a large Brick House and preperation was being made to put on the Rufe. This was soon dun and preperration was being made to entertain the Anuall Confernce witch was to meet there in november. Mount Zion Making such a fast move foward in such a short time put Mount Vernun Baptist Church on a move and

---

[39] I visited 33 Ray Street in May 2012 and found an empty lot. Neighbors said the house had been torn down many years ago.

[40] Charles A. Wingfield (b. 1874) was born in Washington, Wilkes County, 11 June 1874, son of Jack Wingfield (a house carpenter) and Louisa Wingfield (keeping house), both AMEC members. He entered school at age ten. Converted in 1885, he was licensed to preach in September 1892, ordained deacon in 1894, and ordained elder in 1895. Appointments included East Atlanta Mission, 1893–1896; Reynoldstown, 1897–1900; Mt. Zion (Newnan), 1901–1902. When appointed to Mt. Zion he had earned his A.B. degree from Morris Brown; he would eventually earn his D.D. from the same school. His later appointments included Barnesville 1902–1903; superintendent of industries at Morris Brown College, 1903–1904; Eatonton, 1905–1907; Athens, 1907–1909; besides four years at Forsyth; a year and a half at Milledgeville; and as presiding elder over Gainesville District and Milledgeville District (Wright, *Centennial Encyclopaedia*, 253; 1880 Census, GA, Wilkes County, Pop., ED 136, p. 53, dwell. 477).

notwithstanding Rev H R Bennet,[41] who was once a member of the Methodist Church but now serveing the Baptist, succeeded in Bringing about a split in Mount vernon and gating up Zion Hill. Mount vernun Bilding at the same time a Brick House of waship. The Atlanta Confernce meet at Mount Zion dun its work and Adjornd leaveing C A Wingfeild there for annother yeare.[42]

For some Reason Best known to Himself he chused to be Removed from the charge and nother young man was appointed in the person of E. K. Nickels[43]

---

[41] Henry R. Bennett (b. c. 1855), native of Georgia and a past president of the Western Union Baptist Association 1895–1897, was enumerated as a minister in Newnan by the 1910 Census, GA, Coweta County, Newnan, Pop., ED 31, p. 25B, dwell. 496.

[42] The Second Atlanta Annual Conference met at Mount Zion AME Church, 17–23 December 1901. The new Church sanctuary had cost $4,000 (Wright, *Centennial* Encyclopedia, 253). Conference minutes spoke with great pride of the new brick building: "Newnan station is safe for all time. A good brick building with new settees, plastered, with electric lights, with a membership of 128 and all of this work paid for except $765, means very much to African Methodism in this section. For twenty-five years we have done literally nothing at this point. We can but say out of the fullness of our hearts, God be praised and men and women be thanked for what has been done" (2 ATLANTA, 60).

[43] Edward Kingston Nichols (1879–1963) was born in Atlanta, GA. After his two years as pastor of Mt. Zion AME Church, Nichols transferred to Hampton Circuit, followed by other appointments in the Atlanta Conference. In 1914 he was the first African American to earn a B.A. from Yale Divinity School. The next year he worked as an AME minister in NY, but returned to GA to earn a D.D. from Morris Brown in 1918. He married Laura Ella Drake (1894–1987) of Athens, GA, fourteen years his junior, perhaps having met her while he pastored First AME Church in Athens. Nichols returned to Atlanta, worked as an insurance agent, was affluent enough to own his own home and employ a live-in domestic servant to assist his wife and their infant son. Although in June 1920 the census taker found him still in Atlanta, Nichols had already arranged to transfer from the North GA Conference to the New England Conference from which he was appointed to Bethel AME Church at Bloomfield, CT, for two years before being transferred to Bethel Church, New Bedford, MA. In the 1930s the family settled in Philadelphia, PA, where Nichols served at least three local AME churches. He died in 1963.

Exemplifying W. E. B. DuBois's vision of a "Talented Tenth," Nichols, like the Presbyterian minister and educator B. L. Glenn (see Appendix A, pp. 209-211), was part of a new generation of college-educated Southern black clergymen who had not known slavery firsthand. Like Glenn, Nichols partnered with a well educated wife whose skills

who served the Church dirng of the yeare 1899 [actually 1901–1902] with great success. he was a good manger And I will say heare he was a splendid preacher, yess, a good man. He was Reappointed in the yeare 1900 [actually 1902]. Durin the Sumer of that yeare 1900 He held the great tent meeting. During that meeting quiet a number was Added to the Church.

During of theas years I Served as foman of W A Dent Buggy Shoop on Deport Street. I had quiet a plesant time with theas men for more then 13 years.

Rev D R Fobbs succeeded Nickels as paster of this Church. He was a Theologian. also he was a splinded orrator and also above all a christtian and he had no Equils as an alround man. untell this day he serves the Church at Thomaston Upson County with great Acseptability.[44]

In the yeare 1908 Rev O Slade[45] served the Church at Newnan while Rev Langston[46] Seved the Church at Sharpsburro.

I have devoted my time through the week to Bisness of my traid, doing all that I could to learn my oldes son by my last wief, Taylor Slaughter, to learn the Blacksmith trade. And I am glade to say at this day, September the 16th 1913, he has goten to be a good horse shuer and he could be come a good workman

---

were not merely marketable but well-suited to the agenda of racial uplift. Laura Nichols graduated from Fisk University and would later study at University of Pennsylvania School of Social Work, specializing in childcare, eventually joining the faculty as an instructor.

See *Catalog of the Officers and Graduates of Yale University in New Haven, Connecticut, 1701–1915* (New Haven: Yale University, 1916) 443; "Colleges and Their Graduates in 1914," *The Crisis* 8/5 (July 1914): 133, 134 (photograph); New York State Archives (Albany, NY), NY State Census, 1915, State Population Census Schedules, Election District 3, Assembly District 1, Catskill, Greene County, p. 8, line 41 (FamilySearch, "New York State Census, 1915," https://familysearch.org/search/collection/1937454 [accessed 24 February 2015]); *Alumni Directory of Yale University, Graduates and Non-Graduates* (New Haven: Yale University, 1920) 165; Philadelphia *Tribune*, 8 June 2012, obituary "Marjorie Louise Nichols Farmer, educator, minister," available at http://www.phillytrib.com/obituaries/marjorie-louise-nichols-farmer-educator-minister/article_a5c9e44f-f228-5226-bd1b-0b06f82225af.html (accessed 10 April 2015); 1920 Census, GA, Fulton County, Atlanta, Ward 1, Pop., ED 51, p. 33B, dwell. 653.

[44] David R. Fobbs, born in MS, August 1873. Fobbs was pastor of Thomaston Station, Upson County, November 1911–November 1913.

[45] Willis O. Slade, born in GA about 1878.

[46] J. W. Langston.

some day. I hope and pray that he will. I can hardely hope to see thease five children by my good wief Taylor Slaughter Holloway, William Fisher Holloway, Ann May and Floreainna Holloway and Nepton Holloway I named for my Farther and Tayler for my wiefs Farther. I can not hardely hope to see Theas children do what I would like as I am now 66 years old And am In many respects acttive but Theas yease are on and I have striven with all my might to live and upright lief, have failed often, but have not given it out.

I hope that I am mistaken in my oppinion about my people in many respects. That is they might get theire so to speek so much quicker If they could be made to see the necessitee of saveing some think [=something] of what they make. I notice many of them seems to be satisfied with a buggy and a mule. beyound that they to have no desire to go [to] the preachers meeting. They Seems to never Think Be yound to day enjoy themselves for the passing day. I do hope and pray that the day is not far distant when they will began Think on the great and Important subject of morrill and principals. I have noticed The yound Colord men never seems to think That it is his Buisniss to help his farther and mother take care of his sister. And Annother Think [=thing] the young colord man seems never fall out with the young [man] that seduceses his sister. He never losees a frind by Runining a yound girel. offten times conduct of that kind seems Build him up among his people. My obsavation we have never been Taught as a reace virture. many of us has been taught it as Inviguals. untill it is dun we will never succeed on theas lines. Now Inspite of all of that we have many vertuus woman and men and Thousands of Besniss men and when you comes to farming we have Thousands.

In the yeare 1909 I moved back To Turin to my home There And wint to work with quiet a lode on my Sholdus. I can hardely say on paper what fell to my lot that yeare.[47] The Bisness men of Turin wanted me there And to gat me to move from newnan. I had 6 children and myself and wief, cow and calf and many fouls like chichen and Turkeys. It [took] us sum time to settled down. I went to work at once In the Blacksmith shoop in the day and soon had a large Bisniss and on the Sabbath I went to work with the A.M.E. Church and Sunday School. I have put in all the time on the Lords day for many years and Delight in that work yet and will as long as I live I gess.

[47] John W. Holloway wrote, "I do not know of the details, but seems that the oldest boy was guilty of manslaughter" (JWH, 390). I reviewed all issues of the *Newnan Herald and Advertiser* for the year 1909 but found no mention of Holloway or any member of his family.

I have nothing particlular to say about our people In this section of cuntry save this, they do not Read and Enform them selves on no particular Topic. Throug thre [=Through their] prachers they have learnd to say I do not beleeve something or I do be leeave In su somthing while they Know Knothing abouth any way they have learnd to say they Do or do not as the case may be and they are graduates in History as fine as are wanted any wheare.

The yeare 1910

was quiet and Reather a good crope yeare most of our people did well as farmers.[48]

[End of the Manuscript]

[48] This sentence ends at the bottom of a page. The manuscript as now preserved includes an unnumbered page between pages 200 and 201. On this page Holloway had written nine words: "Durin of theas last few years I have but." Originally this sheet may have been the last page of the manuscript, and these words may have been the last, unfinished sentence (Houston Hartsfield Holloway papers, 1894–1932, MSS84205, MMC-3695, Library of Congress Manuscript Division Washington, DC).

Appendix A

Biographies

Phillip (H. H. Holloway's maternal grandfather)

Philip (b. c. 1798) probably lived in the neighborhood of Clouds Creek, Oglethorpe County, Georgia, during the 1820s and 1830s, espoused to Holloway's grandmother, Susan. He almost surely came into Henry Hartsfield's possession at or before Hartsfield's migration to Upson County in 1834.[1] By 1840 Hartsfield had sold Philip, probably to a professional interstate slave trader, who transported and sold him to George Washington Lore in Barbour County, Alabama. All other information yet discovered about Philip comes from one of the longest runaway ads ever printed. The ad appeared on page three of the Columbus *Enquirer*, 11 September 1840:

> TWENTY DOLLARS REWARD!
>
> RAN AWAY from the subscriber living on the middle prong of the Cowiggee Creeks [on modern maps called Middle Fork Cowikee Creek, in north Barbour County, Alabama], adjoining Dr. Battle, and about one mile and a half north of Capt. Jenkins' plantation, on Tuesday evening last, his negro man Philip, about 40 or 45 years of age, rather of a yellow complexion, or bright color, has a down cast look, a sepulchral voice, full six feet high, and athletically made. He is a professor of religion, has a wife at Dr. C. Battle's plantation on the middle Cowiggee creek. He was brought from Upson county, Georgia: this negro has been out most of the present year, and about four weeks since was gotten hold of, and on attempting to correct him for misconduct, he made off again. The above reward will be paid to any person or persons who will deliver him to me at my place of residence, or ten dollars to lodge him in any jail, so that I get

[1] A man named Phill, enslaved to William Winfrey, joined Clouds Creek Baptist Church in 1827 but was expelled in 1830 for "being caught with a woman not his wife at a late hour of the night" and Washington Hartsfield was appointed "to ask Phill to attend" the church trial—however, any connection between this Phill and Philip is speculative (Clouds Creek Baptist Church Minutes 1826–1856, Oglethorpe County, Georgia; microcopy RHS 1300; Georgia Archives, Morrow, Georgia, 73, 75).

him, and all expenses paid.

GEO. W. LORE
Barbour co. Ala. July 16, 1840.

P.S. From circumstances, it is reasonable to believe that Philip has a forged pass, and had one also when he was out before, and that he has endeavored to make his way, if he has not already done it, to Pike or Upson county, Georgia. He formerly belonged to Mr. Hartsfield, of Upson county, who did and I presume does now, own his former wife and children. He said that when he was out before, he went to Pike, or, on the line of Pike and Upson—that he was about Columbus during the races in the spring. When interrogated by a white person who he suspected never would tell it again, how was it that he was enabled to get about so, without being taken up, he said he told such as asked him, that he was sent off by his master to keep out of the way of the Sheriff. This tale with a forged pass, it is reasonable to conclude, that he went, if at all, without being arrested, and it is likely that he has been put up to it again to resort to some like stratagem. From several circumstances, Philip and a fellow by the name of Jordan, who went off about the same time, and from the same neighborhood, started together. Jordan has been caught in Merriwether county, Geo. who states that another fellow came with him untill [*sic*] they had passed Columbus six miles, when they seperated [*sic*], being pursued by men and dogs. Jordan was taken, so he says, but got away with many thumps and bruises. This was about the first week in August. Jordan, it is said, had a forged pass, and no doubt Philip has one also.

The reward shall be increased to justice, for any vigilance used to apprehend Philip, and one hundred dollars will be given for the conviction of any white person or persons, who may have comforted him.

GEORGE W. LORE.[2]

Susan (H. H. Holloway's maternal grandmother)

Susan (c. 1800–1862) is listed by her nickname "Sucky with her infants twins Luisa & Lurendy," valued at $500, in an appraisement of Richard Hartsfield's property in Oglethorpe County, Georgia, on 21 September 1821. If

[2] In an interesting but unrelated development, Lore was lynched in 1842 by his neighbors who believed he had murdered a man named Henry Blake. See Douglas Clare Purcell, "Controversy in Old Barbour County: The Lore-Blake Murder Case" (1986) available at http://www.mhmitchell.org/projects/BrowderMitchell/ControversyinBarbourCty.pdf (accessed 22 January 2015).

these were Susan's first children she was probably then aged between eighteen and twenty-two. Susan was married to Philip. She joined Clouds Creek Baptist Church in Oglethorpe County by professing her experience of God's grace on 11 April 1829. After Richard Hartsfield's death (c. 1830), Susan became property of his son, Henry Hartsfield. When Henry Hartsfield migrated to Upson County five years later, Susan took out a letter of dismission from Clouds Creek Baptist Church on 13 December 1834. In Upson County she joined Bethesda Baptist Church by presenting this letter on 21 February 1835. By 1840, Hartsfield had sold her husband, Philip, who was transported to Barbour County, Alabama, permanently rupturing Susan's marriage.[3]

Susan remarried to Charles (b. August 1793), enslaved to Edward Holloway. When the Hartsfield heirs sold Henry Hartsfield's estate about 1847, Charles prevailed on Holloway to buy Susan. Edward Holloway died in 1850 but left his entire estate to his widow, Nancy Holloway, "during her life and widowhood" and making special provision that "my old negro man Charles and his wife Sucky have the right to choose their homes among my children or among my [wife] and children if my wife be living." Suckey (Susan) was appraised at $350 and Charles at $300 on 14 October 1850. Susan and Charles's marriage and co-residence on the Holloway home place was undisturbed until Susan's death in 1862. The residual provisions of Edward Holloway's will did not affect Susan's surviving kinfolk because Nancy Holloway outlived slavery, dying on 5 May 1866.[4]

Neptune Holloway (H. H. Holloway's father)

Neptune Holloway (c. 1820–1861)[5] is most likely the unnamed slave enumerated as a mulatto man, age forty, belonging to Nancy Holloway in the 1860 Census, Upson Co., Slave Pop., p. 39, right-hand column, line 10.

---

[3] Richard Hartsfield inventory; Clouds Creek Baptist Church Minutes 1826–1856, 60, 126; Bethesda Baptist Church Minute Book 1, 56.

[4] Upson County Will Book A, 109–110 (Edward Holloway's will dated 5 August 1850); Upson County Record of Accounts Book C, 260 (appraisement). No record found of Charles after 1863.

[5] For other local use of "Nepton" as alternate spelling of "Neptune," compare the name of George Powell's slave, Neptune, in TUA, Upson County Court of Ordinary, Record of Accounts Book B, 232, and Upson County Deed Book F, 159, with same man's name, Nepton, in Record of Accounts Book E, 89.

Records found to date do not identify his parents; we do not know his history prior to his enslavement to Edward Holloway or his occupation.

Houston H. Holloway tells us his father was "Reather Bright Complecttion long Black hair about five feet six Inches In hight he always wore a tall Beaver hat and a Brord Cloth Suat." Houston Holloway inherited his father's velvet vest, in which Neptune had married both his first and second wives.

Neptune Holloway probably married Louisa (enslaved to Henry Hartsfield) about 1838 or 1839. They had four sons, including Houston H. Holloway. After Louisa's death in 1846, Neptune married another Holloway bondwoman, Mary, with whom he seems to have had at least four more children (see p. 83,, n.51 and n.52, and p. 102, n.32).

Neptune Holloway was a Methodist, probably a member of the Methodist Church at Thomaston, Georgia, but no antebellum membership lists survive for that church. An older enslaved man, Moses, was Neptune's spiritual adviser. Houston Holloway tells us Neptune could read and write and that "his advice was much Sought for by the Colord people of his naborhood." Neptune Holloway kept a family Bible and a book of Wesley's sermons that would be inherited by his youngest son, Jacob C. Hartsfield.

Edward and Nancy Holloway considered Neptune a "confidential negro" who was authorized to have his own shotgun and ammunition and to buy whiskey on his own word from neighborhood shopkeepers. A bill from Timothy Mullancy's store survives to show one of his whiskey purchases (see p. 83-84 n. 56).

Probably on or about 21 August 1861, Neptune died of blood poisoning or other complication nine months after the master's son, Dr. John O. Holloway, had pulled some troublesome teeth from Neptune's mouth (see p. 84 n. 57).

John Wesley Hartsfield (H. H. Holloway's eldest brother)

John Wesley Hartsfield (b. c. 1840–d. by 1888), Neptune and Louisa's eldest son, was born in Upson County. He was first enslaved to Henry Hartsfield, then to Washington ("Wash") Hartsfield. He learned house carpentry, and Wash Hartsfield hired him out to do construction work. In one business receipt dated 1859, he is called "Wess"—the Thomas G. Rose estate paid Wash Hartsfield $36.50 for "Work done by Mose & Mose & Wess."[6]

[6] Upson County Record of Vouchers Book C, 523.

Later that year at Christmastime, when Houston Holloway came to visit kin at the old homeplace, John Wesley was not among the folks who met him; perhaps he was at a remote work site. When Holloway paid his next visit in 1862, he was pleased to find that "Brother John Westly who was a house Carperter was at home." Months after the end of the Civil War, J. W. Hartsfield was at planter Benjamin Manes's mills in Pleasant Hill District, Talbot County, when he wrote to his brother Houston H. Holloway in August 1865 to share the good news of his emancipation. He identified himself by the Hartsfield surname, rather than the patronym used by Houston Holloway.

John W. Hartsfield soon moved to Fulton County to profit from Atlanta's building boom. He registered to vote there in 1867 and was living in Atlanta's Fourth Ward in 1870, with his wife, Zipporah (b. c. 1837, "an octoroon" according to nephew John Wesley Holloway), and their two-year-old son, John. In the next seven years the couple had two [JWH, 235] more sons, Thomas and Candless. Hartsfield and his family spent summer 1878 in Senoia, living with brother Houston Holloway and his family. After they moved back to Atlanta, tragedy struck. Zipporah was diagnosed with consumption, and twelve months later (May 1879) she was dead.[7]

Hartsfield, a contracting carpenter, built the first sanctuary for Atlanta's Congregational Church and built Stone Hall in 1882 on the Atlanta University campus.[8] Stone Hall was designated a National Historic Landmark in 1974.

Hartsfield's nephew and namesake reported that he was "a sweet singer" and "one of the softest-spoken, cultured gentlemen I ever met" (JWH, 237, 236). Hartsfield first appeared in Atlanta city directories in 1874 and last appeared in the 1883 edition, living at 125 Houston Street. He was dead by 1888.[9] His nephew wrote, "Uncle Wesley died in Atlanta, boarding on Wheat

---

[7] Upson County Record of Vouchers Book C, 523; Georgia, Returns of Qualified Voters, 1867, Fulton County, Election District 1026, precinct 1 (June 27, 1867), p. 15; 1870 Census, GA, Fulton County, Atlanta, Ward 4, Pop., p. 79, dwelling 674; 1880 Census, GA, Fulton County, Schedule 2 (Mortality), family 502; 1880 Census, GA, Fulton County, Atlanta, Pop., ED 98, p. 49, dwell. 534.

[8] JWH, 236.

[9] The Walton family mentioned by JWH was probably the family enumerated in 1880 Census, GA, Fulton County, Atlanta, Pop., ED 99, p. 47, dwell. 139 (Claiborn W. Walton, mulatto, house carpenter; family included niece Susan Hartsfield, mulatto, age nineteen; kinship to John Wesley Hartsfield unknown). Atlanta City Directories list Walton as a head waiter who lived at 139 Houston at the same time (1883) that

St with a family by the name of Walton. They asked him for money. He had none, but got up from his sick bed and walked across town. This was the end of him" (JWH, 417).

Green Holloway (H. H. Holloway's elder brother)

Green Holloway (c. 1842–c. 1884), second son of Neptune and Susan, was born in Georgia, enslaved first to Henry Hartsfield, then to Washington Hartsfield, in Upson County. Wash Hartsfield sold him together with another young man, Cornelius, on 11 December 1858, for $2400, to Travis A. D. Weaver, a planter and merchant, who lived in Thomaston, Upson County. Weaver (a poor speller) listed "Grane" among people on his plantation for whom he bought shoes in 1863.[10]

Green Holloway married Sally Peurifoy, former slave of Charles H. Peurifoy, on 20 October 1866. Sally (b. c. 1843) was already the mother of twin girls, Martha and Catherine, born about 1861; she and Green together had at least 6 children, Louisa (c. 1866), Willie (c. 1869; d. before 1880), John (c. 1872), Chrsanna (?) (c. 1875), Moses (c. 1878), and Ida (March 1880).[11]

When white emigration agents canvassed vigorously in Upson and neighboring counties in 1866 for freedpeople to sign contracts to work on plantations in the Mississippi valley, Green Holloway apparently seriously considered the move, but, like many of his neighbors who had also signed up to emigrate, changed his mind and remained in Upson County.[12] Census

---

Hartsfield lived at 125 Houston; see *Atlanta, Ga. City Directory, 1883*, 318, 444 (ancestry.com, "U.S. City Directories, 1821–1989" collection, http://search.ancestry.com/search/db.aspx?dbid=2469 [accessed 10 April 2015]).

[10] Upson County Deed Book H, 411; Travis A. D. Weaver Account Book (1849–1871), Weaver-Dallas House Collection, Thomaston, GA, 209.

[11] Upson County, Marriage Record to 1876, 11; 1870 Census, GA, Upson County, Pop., p. 79, dwelling 648; 1880 Census, GA, Upson County, Pop., ED 140, p. 21, dwelling 167.

[12] NARA, RG 105.5, Records of the Bureau of Refugees, Freedmen, and Abandoned Lands, Records of the Field Offices for the State of Georgia, M1903, Roll 64, Griffin (Subassistant Commissioner) Register of Contracts, Volume (271), November 1865–July 1868, 139 (frame 954), contract with R. M. Stowers of Lafayette County, MS, dated 20 December 1866; 1870 Census, GA, Upson County, Pop., p. 79, dwelling 648; 1880 Census, GA, Upson County, Pop., ED 140, p. 21, dwelling 167; JWH, 4, 57, 418.

enumerators in 1870 and 1880 found him laboring on a farm with his family in Upson County near the old Hartsfield plantation, not far from Sugar Hill where the AMEC bishop sent Houston H. Holloway in 1882. John W. Holloway (Houston H. Holloway's son) thought that his father accepted the appointment because he would be near his elder brother, Green.[13] John W. Holloway wrote, "Uncle Green was a peculiar sort of man, tall, straight, curly-haired. He died about '84 [in Upson County], from exposure ending, I think, in pneumonia.... John Holloway, his eldest son, lived with us some years, in Turin, learning the [blacksmith] trade from my father."[14]

Jacob C. Hartsfield (H. H. Holloway's younger brother)

Jacob C. Hartsfield (1846–1926), commonly called Jake, was born in Upson County in April or May 1846, six weeks before his mother Louisa died. He inherited his father Neptune's family Bible and book of Wesley's sermons. He was enslaved first to Henry Hartsfield then to Washington Hartsfield. After emancipation his first movements are difficult to trace; his nephew, John Wesley Holloway, wrote that "Jacob Hartsfield...lived to be 80 yrs of age, dying in Palmetto Ga, where for 60 yrs. he had made his home"—which would mean he had moved to Palmetto, Campbell County, in 1866.[15]

When Houston Holloway was appointed to the Palmetto Circuit in 1874, brother Jacob was teaching school there. Holloway's son John Wesley Holloway, about nine years old, attended his school and fondly remembered, "My uncle was one of the best teachers I ever had. I have never forgotten the songs we used to sing in his school, a new one every Monday morning." Jacob Hartsfield wrote these songs himself. According to John Wesley Holloway, "My uncle's [end-of-

[13] 1870 Census, GA, Upson County, Pop., p. 79, dwelling 648; 1880 Census, GA, Upson County, Pop., ED 140, p. 21, dwelling 167; JWH, 57.

[14] JWH, 418.

[15] JWH, 236. I found no evidence for his presence in Palmetto so early. A black man named Jacob Hartsfield registered to vote in Lee County in 1867, and someone of the same name and right age (twenty-three years), a farm laborer, probably the man previously in Lee County, was enumerated in the 1870 census in neighboring Dougherty County—the only black Jacob Hartsfield in Georgia whose recorded age was a good match. Of course, name and age coincidence alone does not prove that this man was Houston Holloway's brother. Perhaps he was, or maybe the 1870 census net did not catch Jacob C. Hartsfield.

term] exhibitions were famous in the community, the whites always attending in large numbers."[16]

In 1880 the census-taker found Jacob Hartsfield unmarried, teaching school, and boarding in Palmetto at the house of elderly Elder Robert Strickland of the AMEC. Jacob Hartsfield probably married his first wife Mandy (b. c. September 1858) shortly thereafter. By 1890 Hartsfield owned town property in Palmetto; decades later at the time of his death he owned his own home, valued at $400. At some point he left teaching and took up house carpentry, the occupation reported to census-takers in 1900 and 1920. (The enumerator missed him in 1910.)[17]

Childless in his first marriage, he remarried after Mandy's death to a woman named Fannie (b. c. 1882) when he was about seventy years old. According to nephew John Wesley Holloway, "He said his family was noted for marrying brown women." He fathered a daughter, Rentha, in about 1916.[18]

Perhaps his advancing age prompted him to take less physically demanding work than carpentry; his death certificate described him as a cotton mill hand. Although his visiting nephew found him "well and strong" at Christmastime 1925, within a few months he may have suffered a stroke that paralyzed his right arm and leg. Jacob Hartsfield died of cerebral hemorrhage on 31 July 1926.[19]

Edmund Lowe (H. H. Holloway's paternal uncle)

Edmund Lowe (c. 1805–1888), identified by H. H. Holloway as his father's brother, was born in South Carolina in the first decade of the nineteenth century. He was a locally licensed preacher sponsored by the MECS, at

---

[16] JWH, 27, 29.

[17] 1880 Census, GA, Campbell County, Pop., ED 24, p. 43, dwelling 374 [misnamed *John* C. Hartsfield, described as mulatto, and age grossly incorrect as twenty-two]; Campbell County Tax Digest, 1890, 652 GMD (Palmetto) (Freedmen section); 1900 Census, GA, Campbell County, Pop., ED 5, p. 2, dwelling 24; 1920 Census, GA, Campbell County, Pop., ED 2, p. 16, dwelling 149.

[18] JWH, 419; 1920 Census, GA, Campbell County, Pop., ED 2, p. 16, dwelling 149; 1930 Census, GA, Campbell County, Palmetto, Pop., ED 21–22, p. 7B, dwelling 147.

[19] JWH, 418; GA State Board of Health, Death Certificate No. 16141, Campbell County, "Jake Hartsfield," 31 July 1926, Georgia Death Certificates, 1919–1927 (http://cdm.georgiaarchives.org:2011/cdm/landingpage/collection/gadeaths [accessed 10 April 2015]).

Thomaston, Upson County, Georgia. Already by 1863 described as an "old man," Edmund Lowe was enslaved to William Lowe whose plantation lay on the northern outskirts of Thomaston. After William Lowe's death, Edmund Lowe was inherited by William Lowe's daughter, Emma R. Lowe, thereby becoming the property of Emma's cousin-husband Benjamin H. Lowe until emancipation in April 1865.[20]

In a 1913 letter to the Thomaston *Times*, Rev. R. W. Rogers remembered Lowe from his antebellum boyhood when he attended slaves' religious services at Thomaston's Methodist Church:

> Special services were held for them at 3 o'clock conducted by the white pastor and in his absence by Edmund Lowe, who was a devout Christian, in whom the white people had confidence. It was the delight of my boyish heart to attend these meetings and hear the negroes sing. When Uncle Edmund preached, he always rubbed the top of his head. He had rubbed all the hair off until his head looked like a peeled onion. Once he said, "all you niggers talk about crossing de mighty River Jordan—ah, but you aint got 'ligion enough to cross Town Branch."

According to Rev. Rogers, "When [Edmund Lowe's] first wife's funeral was preached, it was a big occasion and his second wife was the chief mourner."[21]

Federal censuses are inconsistent about Lowe's literacy. The 1870 enumerator recorded that he could not read or write, but the 1880 enumerator (Sarah A. Jennings, who seems to have been very careful in her work) indicates that he could. Both records agree that his wife, Fannie—who would have been his second wife—could neither read nor write. Both the 1870 and 1880 censuses list Lowe's occupation as "Minister," although I have not determined which branch of Methodism he served after emancipation. He was not ordained by the AMEC, but he may have been ordained in the CMEC, or may have remained a locally licensed preacher in either church.[22]

By 1870 Edmund Lowe and Fannie had settled in Thomaston where Fannie died sometime after 1880. The widowed Edmund Lowe died peacefully

---

[20] Upson County Court of Ordinary, Record of Accounts Book E, 48.

[21] Thomaston *Times*, 4 July 1913.

[22] 1870 Census, GA, Upson County, Pop., p. 183, dwell. 1444; 1880 Census, GA, Upson County, Thomaston, Pop., ED 139, p. 3, dwell. 34.

in his bed at Henry and Lavonia Wesley's house in Thomaston during the night of 6 July 1888 aged about eighty-four years.[23]

Cordelia Thrash (H. H. Holloway's first wife)

Cordelia Thrash (1845–1894), born near Flat Shoals, Meriwether County, on 15 September 1845, was the youngest daughter of Christmas Thrash (b. c. 1797) and Cherry Thrash (c. 1804–1870). She was enslaved to widowed planter Mary Thrash. Cordelia's older brothers and sisters were Mary Jane, Lee, Eli, Pherebe, and Henry.[24]

Cordelia's eldest son, John Wesley Holloway, tells us,

> My mother as a little girl was hired out to a family of very poor white people. She nursed, cooked, washed and ironed their clothes and worked in the field. The washing was done at night, at a spring some distance from the house. They actually propped open her eyes with splinters when she would fall asleep at night while holding the baby. In winter she went scantily clothed—in a single garment.... They used to say to her: "Here, little nigger, you can have the bones, but you can't git the chicken!" She could imitate perfectly their manner of speaking.[25]

While hired to this family Cordelia went barefoot in winter. Son Holloway blamed this childhood abuse for her early death and for peculiarly thick skin on the soles of her feet: "Every [S]aturday night as long as she lived, it was my father's job to take a razor and pare off the dead skin from her feet. It came off in slices unbelievably large."[26]

Cordelia first saw Houston Holloway (then known as Houston Freeman) at a quilting at Jordan Blackburn's house in early 1862. They courted for almost two years, then married on 9 April 1864 on Widow Thrash's front porch.

---

[23] 1870 Census, GA, Upson County, Pop., p. 183, dwell. 1444; 1880 Census, GA, Upson County, Thomaston, Pop., ED 139, p. 3, dwell. 34; loose papers of Upson County Superior Court, Coroner's inquest into the death of Edmond Lowe, 7 July 1888, TUA.

[24] Meriwether County Will Book A (1831–1859), 86 (will of Christopher Thrash); *Christian Recorder*, 24 May 1894, 5 (obituary); JWH, 167. JWH gives Cordelia's birth year as 1845, but her obituary says 1846. If Cordelia was a year younger than her husband, the obituary date was probably based on H. H. Holloway's mistaken belief that his birth was in 1845 rather than in 1844.

[25] JWH, 195, 197.

[26] Ibid., 195.

Cordelia's obituary says, "She joined the M.E. Church, South, in August 1864 and lived a faithful and consistent member of same until 1870, when she joined AME Church and remained a true member until her death of Mount Carmel Church, Sharpsburg."[27] After emancipation Cordelia and Houston Holloway moved almost annually as he pursued his itinerant vocation in the AMEC until 1882 when the family settled in Turin, Coweta County. Cordelia and Houston had seven children together, five of whom survived to adulthood. Besides keeping her own house, Cordelia Holloway cooked for James B. Hunnicutt's large household in Turin, Coweta County. Cordelia Holloway suffered a paralyzing stroke while laboring over the washtub.[28] After seven years as an invalid, increasingly bed-ridden, she died 3 April 1894. Her obituary adds, "Not a harsh word ever passed between husband and wife.... She was always kind, liberal and true to those in trouble or poor circumstances."[29]

Cherry Thrash (Cordelia's mother)

Cherry Thrash (c. 1804–1870) was born enslaved in Elizabethtown, North Carolina, was bought by a speculator and sold in Eatonton, Putnam County, Georgia. Putnam County was home to migrated Virginia farmer and herb doctor Christopher Thrash from about 1817 through sometime in the 1830s, so perhaps he purchased Cherry directly from the speculator. (The 1820 and 1830 censuses enumerate Thrash in Putnam County with a woman slave of the right age to be Cherry.) In Putnam County, Cherry Thrash joined the Primitive Baptist Church about 1830; her 1870 obituary stated she joined "about forty years ago."[30] Christopher Thrash brought her to Meriwether County, Georgia, near Greenville, and finally to Flat Shoals. Her grandson John Wesley Holloway remembered she was "a root doctor trained by the Indians."[31]

Married to Christmas Thrash, she had six children: Mary Jane (b. c. 1833), Lee (b. c. 1834), Eli (b. c. 1838), Pherebe (b. c. 1838), Henry (b. c. 1842), and Cordelia (b. 1845). After emancipation Cherry Thrash lived with her daughter Cordelia and Houston H. Holloway until her death at Flat Shoals on 3

[27] *Christian Recorder*, 24 May 1894, 5.

[28] JWH, 405.

[29] Ibid.

[30] *Christian Recorder*, 5 November 1870, 2.

[31] 1830 Census, GA, Putnam County, p. 192 (Christopher Thrash held seven slaves); 1840 Census, GA, Meriwether County, p. 102 (Christopher Thrash held three slaves).

September 1870, age about sixty-six years. She had joined her son-in-law's African Methodist Episcopal Church at Flat Shoals on 25 July 1870, nine days before she died. Her obituary, submitted to the *Christian Recorder* by H. H. Holloway, noted that "She was a Christian and labored hard for her Church, and did a great deal of good. She was beloved by all who knew her.... Sister Cherry left two sons and three daughters.... She lived to see all her children lively members of the A.M.E. Church." Holloway reminded readers how slavery had sundered families and scattered many human fragments of those families beyond communication with (or knowledge of) their kinfolks: "I hope this, through the columns of the Recorder, will reach the ears of her relation if she has any living."[32]

Christmas and Cherry Thrash apparently separated before Cherry's death, perhaps so that family members could share the cost of their keep. Although Christmas Thrash and son-in-law Houston H. Holloway registered to vote at the same place in Meriwether County and on the same day in June 1867, before Cherry died Christmas had moved in with daughter Jane Thrash and son-in-law Simon Thrash in Pike County. Grandson John Wesley Holloway remembered that Cherry lived in his family but did not mention his grandfather being there. Christmas disappeared from record by 1880.[33]

John Wesley Holloway (H. H. Holloway's eldest son)

John Wesley Holloway (1865–1935), eldest child of Houston H. and Cordelia (Thrash) Holloway, was born 28 July 1865, the first child born into freedom in his Flat Shoals neighborhood. John Wesley's earliest formal schooling was in his father's schools, first at Ringgold in 1871, then at Kingston about 1872–1873. It was his uncle Jacob C. Hartsfield, teaching school near Palmetto, Georgia, from 1873 to 1875, who taught young John Wesley to delight in books. After four short-lived attempts by his father to hire him out as a farm hand to local white families, John Wesley entered his father's shop to train as a blacksmith. When Houston Holloway saw that his eldest son preferred literature to smithing, he resolved to help him attain the best education possible.

---

[32] Meriwether County Will Book A (1831–1859), 86 (Thrash's will); GA, Returns of Qualified Voters and Reconstruction Oath Books, 1867–1869, Meriwether County, Precinct 1213, p. 24; 1870 Census, GA, Pike County, Pop., p. 101, dwell. 717. Birth years of Cherry's children are estimated from census data and from the order in which administrators and executor of estates usually listed enslaved children in their inventories.

[33] 1870 Census, GA, Pike County, Pop., p. 101, dwell. 717.

John Wesley attended Atlanta University for two years, then entered Fisk where he would earn his B.A. (1894) and later his B.D. (1906). He sang with the Fisk Jubilee Singers during their 1889 stateside tour, but he dropped out for health reasons before the troupe embarked for Europe.[34]

Holloway taught school six years in rural Georgia before relocating westward. After disastrous teaching experiences in Texas (he participated in a cheating scandal while principal of a school in Palestine, Texas, in 1897), he migrated briefly to Denver, Colorado, then settled in Guthrie, Oklahoma, where with the sponsorship of the American Missionary Association he was ordained in the Congregational Church in 1900. He served as a Congregational pastor in Guthrie until 1904 and simultaneously served as assistant principal, Lincoln High School, at the same place. He returned to Nashville to study at Fisk Theological Seminary from 1904 until he earned his B.D. in 1906. He served as a pastor of Congregational churches in Newark, New Jersey (1906–1910); Thebes, Georgia (1910–1920); and Anniston, Alabama (1920–1924). At his death he was pastor of Church of the Redeemer, Nashville, Tennessee. He taught French and Spanish at South Highland School in Anniston, Alabama (1927–1928), and was teaching in the public schools of Nashville at his death. He served as moderator of the Congregational Convention of the State of Georgia and was associate editor of *The Georgia Congregationalist*.[35]

Holloway met his first wife, Mary Louise Dismuke (b. August 1876), at Fisk and married her in his father's house at Turin on 6 August 1894 with Rev. J. M. Lee of Senoia officiating. The couple had four children, Guerney Douglass (b. July 1895), Jamie May, Angelus, and Herbert Milo. Mary died of consumption in Guthrie, Oklahoma, between 1900 and 1904. Holloway remarried 24 September 1906 to Henri E. Bransford with whom he seems to have had three children, Lena Mae and two others whose names I could not find.[36]

---

[34] JWH 69–73, 267, 401–403; Frank Lincoln Mather, ed., *Who's Who of the Colored Race: A General Biographical Dictionary of Men and Women of African Descent*, vol. 1, 1915 (Chicago: 1915) 140–41; Thomas Yenser, ed., *Who's Who in Colored America: A Biographical Dictionary of Notable Living Persons of African Descent in America, 1933–1937* (Brooklyn, NY: Thomas Yenser, 1937) 215; *Catalog of the Officers, Students, and Alumni of Fisk University*, 2nd ed. (Nashville, TN: n.p., 1911–1912).

[35] JWH 91–95; Mather, ed., *Who's Who of the Colored Race*, 140–41; Yenser, ed., *Who's Who in Colored America*, 215.

[36] JWH; Coweta County Marriage Record I (Colored, 1889–1896), 349.

Holloway published a well-received book of poetry, *From the Desert* (New York: Neale Publishing Company, 1919), several poems from which have been anthologized. He wrote in August 1925 that a second poetry book, *Last of the Bandanas*, was "in the press," but the book may have been delayed and may be the same book issued about 1928 under the shortened title *Bandanas*.[37]

In his sixties he taught history in the public schools in Nashville, where he and wife, Henri, lived with his beloved son, Guerney D. Holloway. He died of an arteriosclerotic heart at Nashville's Hubbard Hospital, 31 October 1935, age seventy years, and was buried in Greenwood Cemetery. His death certificate listed his occupation as minister and teacher.[38]

Thomas Calvin Trice (Holloway's neighbor, Primitive Baptist, slave-trader)

Thomas Calvin Trice (1808–1866), native of Orange County, North Carolina, converted to Christianity and joined the Baptist church in 1828. He soon began preaching the gospel. In about 1829, he married Miss Sallie H. White and then moved to Jasper County, Georgia, in 1832. In 1839 he moved to Pike County, Georgia, and finally in 1864 to Pike County, Alabama, where he died at home 3 July 1866. In 1860 Trice's family included his wife, two daughters, and a minor ward, living in the service area of the Zebulon post office. Trice owned real estate worth $3,300 and ten slaves.[39] Holloway's narrative tells how Trice bought Aunt Susan and her child Daniel from Isaac Strickland and transported them further South in a drove of people he probably bought from various neighbors for resale. This was unlikely to have been the first time Trice engaged in the slave trade.

As an ordained Primitive Baptist elder, Trice represented Pike County's Shoal Creek Church at the annual conferences of the Towaliga Primitive Baptist

---

[37] JWH, 171; Newman Ivey White and Walter Clinton Jackson, eds., *Anthology of Verse by American Negroes* (Durham, NC: Trinity College Press, 1924) 183–84. The only copy of *Bandanas* I found is listed in the Yale University Library.

[38] 1930 Census, TN, Davidson County, Nashville, Pop., ED 19–25, p. 6A, dwell. 126; TN State Department of Health, Death Certificate No. 21778, Nashville, Davidson County, "J. W. Holloway," 31 October 1935 (available at FamilySearch, "Tennessee Death Records, 1914–1955" collection, https://familysearch.org/search/collection/1417505 [accessed 10 April 2015]).

[39] 1860 Census, GA, Pike County, Free Pop., p. 84, dwell. 602; 1860 Census, GA, Pike County, Slave Pop., p. 36.

Association 1839–1849, then represented Rose Creek Church in 1850 and 1851 before being called to pastor Concord Primitive Baptist Church 1852–1856 and again in 1860 (Towaliga Association minutes for 1857 and 1858 not found). He served as messenger from the Concord church to the Towaliga Association from 1859 through at least 1863. Concord was five miles east of Flat Shoals. Late in life he converted from Primitive Baptist to the Regular (also called Missionary) Baptist church over theological issues including re-baptism.[40]

Trice achieved some statewide fame for a letter he wrote in March 1861 endorsing re-election of Governor Brown in language, which, according to a contemporary journalist, "had a wonderful effect...by voicing the public thought.... Mr. Trice awoke to find himself famous as the unexpected announcer of a universal notion" that Brown was the best man for the job. Trice's letter reputedly triggered an avalanche of similar endorsements that ensured Brown's electoral victory.[41]

J. H. Campbell's short biography (or, rather, hagiography) of Elder Trice in 1874 nowhere hints at Trice's slave trading sideline; indeed, wrote Campbell, Trice's life "exemplified the beauties of our holy religion." Trice illustrates historian Michael Tadman's contention that slave trading carried no social stigma in white Southern society. Extracts from Campbell, below, show how rapidly after the Civil War some Americans erased the slave trade from their public and collective memory:

> For many years he represented his county in the Georgia State Legislature.... In politics, he was an old line Whig and States Rights man, and in the recent struggle for independence, he was uncompromisingly Southern.... As a citizen, he was written down by all as an eminently useful man; as a neighbor, kind and obliging; as a friend, steadfast and trusty; and in the endearing relation of husband and father, none can so well appreciate his superior excellency of character as his heart-broken widow

---

[40] *Minutes of the Towaliga Association of Primitive Baptists*, 1839–1856, 1859–1863 (published as individual annual pamphlets), microfilm reel 1410, Special Collections, Jack Tarver Library at Mercer University, Macon, GA; J[esse] H[arrison] Campbell, *Georgia Baptists: Historical and Biographical* (Macon, GA.: J. W. Burke & Company, 1874) 366–68.

[41] I[saac] W[heeler] Avery, *The History of the State of Georgia from 1850 to 1881, Embracing Three Important Epochs: The Decade before the War of 1861–1865; the War; the Period of Reconstruction, with Portraits of the Leading Public Men of this Era* (New York: Brown & Derby, 1881) 192–94.

> and sorrow-stricken children.... As a consistent and well beloved member of the regular Baptist church, and faithful preacher of the cross of Christ, he closed his mortal career. Much bodily pain and suffering (the consequence of protracted labor as a minister of Jesus) he was called upon to endure by the Master in his last days.[42]

Claiborne Bush—Claiborne Neal ("a preacher of great power")

Claiborne Bush (b. c. 1807) was most likely known as Claiborne Neal in slavery. The name Claiborne and its variant spellings is so rare as a first name, and what else we know of Claiborne Neal and Claiborne Bush is so similar, that I believe they were the same person.[43] He was probably the "negro man by the name of Claiborn" deeded by James Neal as a gift to his daughter Amanda Freeman (James C. Freeman's wife) on 10 June 1845.[44] When Freeman's blacksmith, Richmond, lay on his deathbed in 1864, he gave Freeman a fifty dollar bill (in Holloway's words) "to sind to the plantation down in Pike County Alabamma for Uncle Claibon" to preach his funeral. It is unclear why Claiborne Neal was in Alabama in 1864, but Freeman or James Neal may have had a farm there. Certainly Richmond understood that Freeman had authority to summon Claiborne Neal to preach his funeral, which bolsters his likely identity with the man named in the 1845 deed.

Holloway described Claiborne Neal's preaching at Richmond's funeral as eloquent and moving: "I say I heare no such preaching in this our day as that Truly Logicall and Eloquent sermon was that day.... He spok in such away as to move the people white as well as the colord not all that Hell or sin can say shall tempt me for gat that day." Likewise he described his co-worker Claiborne Bush, after emancipation, as "a preacher of great power in that day."

Claiborne Bush, who earned his living at farming when he was not preaching, may have been born in Alabama. He came to Pike County, Georgia,

---

[42] Campbell, *Georgia Baptists*, 366–68; Michael Tadman, *Speculators and Slaves: Masters, Traders, and Slaves in the Old South* (Madison: University of Wisconsin Press, 1989) 192–200.

[43] Searching the 1870 Georgia census with the search engine at https://familysearch.org, I found only 118 males with names spelled variously Claiborn, Claiborne, Clayborn, Clayborne, Clayburn, and Claybron in a population of 578,955 males. Federal censuses suggest a birth year for Claiborne Bush about 1807, which is consistent with Claiborne being a grown man in the James Neal's 1845 deed of gift.

[44] Pike County Deed Book G, 1843–1850, 464.

about 1841.[45] He was a locally licensed MECS preacher for an unknown number of years. After emancipation, the LaGrange District of the MECS Georgia Conference renewed his preaching license in 1866. The Annual Georgia Conference (convening at Americus in November 1866) elected him deacon, making him one of the first ordained black MECS ministers in the state. At the same time the newly formed North Georgia Conference, MECS, appointed him to Newnan and Flat Shoals Mission (LaGrange District) for 1867, then appointed him for 1868 to Pike and Flat Shoals (Barnesville District) in the "Conference for the Colored People" set up by the conference that year. The bishop gave him no appointment for 1869.[46]

In January 1870 Bush left the MECS and joined the AMEC Georgia Conference. He was enrolled as a local deacon. He remained "local" until the AMEC Georgia Conference divided in 1874, when he enrolled as an itinerant deacon at the First Session, North Georgia Conference—but still had no appointment, perhaps because of his advanced age. In January 1875 the bishop appointed "Clayborn Bush and Son" to the Greenville Circuit—apparently a reference to Henderson D. Bush, who was also a licensed AMEC preacher in the same conference (2 NGA, 16). The Fourth Session, North Georgia Conference in December 1876 reported that Claiborne Bush had "withdrawn from the connection," meaning he had resigned. (His son, H. D. Bush, continued to itinerate for the AMEC for many years.)[47]

The 1870 census enumerator for Pike County recorded that then-sixty-three-year-old Claiborne Bush was a minister of the gospel, owned $225 worth of real estate and $150 worth of personal property, and could read but could not write. His large household included wife Mary Bush (age forty-five, unable to read or write, occupation keeping house) and nine others. In 1880 Claiborne

---

[45] GA Return of Qualified Voters, Pike County, Williamsville, Precinct 505, 10 August 1867, p. 44, no. 20; 1870 Census, GA, Pike County, Pop., p. 102, dwell. 719; 1880 Census, GA, Meriwether County, Greenville, Pop., ED 87, p. 5, dwell. 36. Bush's birthplace is variously reported. The 1867 GA Return of Qualified Voters says he was born in NC; 1870 census says GA; 1880 census says AL; son Henderson Bush (next door in 1880) may have confirmed that his father was born in AL.

[46] Harold Lawrence, *Methodist Preachers in Georgia, 1783–1900* (Tignall, GA: Boyd Publishing County Ltd, 1984) 79; MECS 1866, 29; MECS 1867, 122.

[47] Wesley J. Gaines, *African Methodism in the South; or Twenty-Five Years of Freedom* (Atlanta: 1890) 27; 5 GA, 5; 6 GA, 40; 7 GA, 4; 1 NGA, 3; 2 NGA, 1, 16; 3 NGA, 1; 4 NGA, 15 (called "Clayton Bush").

Bush, Mary Bush, and their children were living in Greenville, Meriwether County, where he still gave his occupation as Methodist minister. This suggests that Bush did not quit preaching when he left the NGC; he was either a local AMEC preacher or possibly had joined a different branch of Methodism.[48]

William Fincher ("a great politician")

William Fincher (b. c. 1822) was a native of North Carolina, who, as an infant in about 1824, arrived in the neighborhood of Zebulon, Pike County, Georgia, probably enslaved to Joseph T. Fincher, also an emigrant from North Carolina. Fincher lived near Zebulon for thirty-six years until he began to itinerate as an ordained Methodist minister in 1870. While enslaved, his work as a farmer and mechanic earned him a reputation for industry in the local white community. He was a locally licensed Methodist preacher in the MECS and influential in the black community among fellow slaves who heard his preaching. A white Methodist minister, Rev. R. W. Rogers, recalled, "Some negroes were licensed as local preachers, and did much good among their own people, some of whom the writer remembers well… [including] Wm. Fincher of Pike County."[49] According to both the 1870 and 1880 census enumerators, he could read but not write.[50]

After emancipation, Fincher, with wife Almeda and their children, remained in their Pike County neighborhood. He continued preaching, but his political activities raised the ire of some local Democrats. Fincher accepted the office of vice-president of the Equal Rights Association in Pike County, a Republican political organization. When a panel of Pike County grand jurors in July 1866 charged Fincher with vagrancy—alleging that he "did wander and stroll about then and there, leading an immoral and profligate life"[51]—some observers suspected that the accusation was retaliation for Fincher's political

[48] 1870 Census, GA, Pike County, Pop., p. 102, dwell. 719; 1880 Census, GA, Meriwether County, Greenville, Pop., ED 87, p. 5, dwell. 36.

[49] R. W. Rogers, *History of Pike County from 1822 to 1922* (Zebulon, GA: n.p., n.d.) 61–62.

[50] 1870 Census, GA, Pike County, Pop., p. 167, dwell. 1203; 1880 Census, GA, Pike County, Pop., ED 104, p. 7, family 64; GA Return of Qualified Voters, Pike County, Zebulon precinct 580, 8 August 1867, p. 27;

[51] House of Representatives, 39th Congress, 2d Session, Ex. Doc. No. 72, in *Executive Documents Printed by Order of the House of Representatives, During the Second Session of the Thirty-Ninth Congress, 1866-'67* (Washington: GPO, 1867) 67.

speeches to the Equal Rights Association. A Pike County jury (including Houston H. Holloway's one-time-owner, Isaac Strickland, a Democrat) found Fincher guilty. On appeal to Pike County Superior Court in October 1866, the court dismissed Fincher's appeal and remanded him into custody of the sheriff to work on the public roads for twelve months.[52]

The U.S. District Attorney referred Fincher's conviction to President Andrew Johnson as an example of malicious prosecution, a violation of Congress's recent Civil Rights Act, and designed "to destroy [Fincher's] influence of action in the community, as a colored preacher, zealously attached to some society or organization which is offensive to [white] public sentiment." Federal authorities let the conviction stand.[53] If many Pike County whites found the Equal Rights Association an "offensive" society, Fincher would later offend them further by affiliating with the northern branch of the Methodist Episcopal Church.

The Methodist Episcopal Church (MEC) was commonly called by Southerners the Methodist Episcopal Church, North, after the schism of 1844 split the MEC into Northern and Southern branches over the issue of whether bishops could own slaves. After the Civil War, MEC missionaries aggressively proselytized in the South in open competition with the native MECS. The MEC, Georgia Conference, admitted Fincher as a preacher on trial in October 1869, elected him to full connection as deacon in October 1871, and to elder in 1876. The conference appointed Fincher pastor to the Barnesville circuit for 1870–1872, then to the Zebulon station for 1873–1875, to Flat Shoals for 1876, and to the Pike & Upson circuit for 1877–1879. Fincher's wife, Almeda, died during his years of itinerancy, and in 1879 he married Grace Owen.[54]

The MEC's transparent sympathy with Republican politics, aggressive pursuit of schools for the freedpeople, and advocacy of political and civil rights, led to initial success in Georgia's rural upcountry counties; for example, the Barnesville Circuit had one local preacher (presumably Fincher) who had

---

[52] Ibid., 67–71.

[53] Henry Stanbery to Andrew Johnson, 21 January 1867, available online at "The Walt Whitman Archive," http://whitmanarchive.org/manuscripts/scribal/tei/nar.00189.html (accessed 22 January 2015); Robert J. Kaczorowski, *The Politics of Judicial Interpretation: The Federal Courts, Department of Justice, and Civil Rights, 1866–1876* (Dobbs Ferry, NY: Oceana Publications, 1985) 34–35, discusses the Fincher case.

[54] MEC 1869, 276, 278; MEC 1870, 286, 288; MEC 1871, 277, 279; MEC (Fall Conference) 1878, 85; Pike County Marriage Book (1872–1883), 295.

gathered 108 members by October 1868; a year later membership had tripled to 310 members. Then began a slow decline in 1870 to 300 members, and by October 1871 Fincher had to report his flock numbered only 275. The early surge of MEC membership in this part of Georgia reversed during the MEC's first decade in the region, probably due to aggressive proselytizing by the AMEC, which enjoyed encouragement from local white MECS Methodists who resented the MEC. By 1879, Fincher's last year as pastor, the Pike and Upson circuit had dwindled to ten members. Meantime most local Methodist freedpeople had joined the AMEC or, after 1870, the Colored Methodist Episcopal Church (an offshoot of the MECS). Faced with a dwindling congregation, Fincher "located" (meaning he quit the travelling ministry) at his own request in 1880 and resumed farming at his home in Pike County. The census enumerator in 1880 reported his occupation as "Farmer & Minister."[55]

Robert Alexander ("I had never seen such a man befour")

Robert Alexander (b. c. 1840), born in North Carolina and described in censuses as a mulatto, was able to read and write. His similarly complected Georgia-born wife, Matilda, could also read. He was a small man, weighing only 101 pounds. In 1866 Henry M. Turner, surveying recently emancipated Georgia for fertile ground in which to plant the AMEC, found and licensed Alexander in Atlanta, then introduced him at the second session, South Carolina Conference, held in Savannah, May 1866. Responding to the urgent need for preachers to fill posts in the rapidly expanding church, the conference advanced Alexander with lightning speed, admitting him as a preacher on trial and later the same day electing and ordaining him deacon. Bishop Payne appointed him to Auburn, Alabama.[56]

At midnight 14 June 1866, after a Thursday night church service in Opelika, four white men broke into Alexander's room "and beat and stabbed him till he appeared…like a lump of curdled blood…. The miscreants told him that no d----d negro schools should be taught there, nor should any negro

---

[55] MEC 1868, 278; MEC 1870, 286, 288; MEC (Fall Conference) 1880, 302; 1880 Census, GA, Pike County, Pop., ED 104, p. 7, family 64.

[56] 1870 Census, GA, Houston County, Fort Valley, Pop., p. 163, dwell. 1376; *Minutes of the South Carolina Conference of the African M. E. Church, 1865, 1866, 1867* (Charleston, 1867) 8, 11; *Christian Recorder*, 9 June 1866 (appointment to Auburn); *Christian Recorder*, 23 June 1866.

preacher remain there." Turner took Alexander to Columbus, Georgia, for medical attention. Alexander recovered from the attack.[57]

At the third session of the South Carolina Conference, April 1867, he received an appointment to Fort Gaines, Clay County, Georgia, near the Alabama border. In May, at the formation of the Georgia Conference, Bishop Wayman reiterated Alexander's posting to Fort Gaines. He was appointed the following year to Sandersville (1868), then to Lumpkin Circuit (1869). Elected elder in 1870, he was appointed to Sugar Hill (1871).[58]

At the sixth session of the Georgia Conference in January 1872, the Committee on Charges and Complaints heard a charge of bigamy against Robert Alexander. At first the committee accepted the validity of the charge and wanted to recommend punishment, but the bishop sent their recommendation back for more thorough investigation, after which the committee reported that the whole thing was the "offspring of wickedness, to strive to ruin the character of this good and useful brother."[59] Alexander was acquitted and received an appointment to Stilesboro for 1872. Perhaps unpleasant residue from this experience with his Georgia brethren prompted him to resign from the Georgia Conference in 1872; in the words of the next session, he had "withdrawn from the Connection."[60] Robert and Matilda Alexander moved to Steubenville, Ohio, where he followed his calling as a preacher, but in what denomination I was unable to discover.[61]

Francis J. Peck (a "leading light" [see p. 155] in the AMEC North Georgia Conference)

Francis J. Peck (1834–1898) was freeborn in Baltimore, Maryland, in 1834. His father, Nathaniel Peck, was a white-washer by trade and a powerful local elder in Baltimore's Bethel African Methodist Episcopal Church. At age

[57] *Christian Recorder*, 23 June 1866 (H. M. Turner reports attack on Alexander).

[58] *Minutes of the South Carolina Conference of the African M. E. Church, 1865, 1866, 1867* (Charleston, 1867) 20; *Christian Recorder*, 9 June 1866 (appointment to Auburn); *Christian Recorder*, 23 June 1866 (H. M. Turner letter reporting attack on Alexander); *Christian Recorder*, 15 June 1867, 2; *Christian Recorder*, 4 April 1868, 1; 3 GA, 13, 19; 5 GA, 17.

[59] 6 GA, 66.

[60] 7 GA, 12.

[61] 6 GA, 46, 63, 66; 7 GA, 12; 1880 Census, OH, Jefferson County, Steubenville, Ward 2, ED 111, p. 3, dwell. 17.

eight, young Francis Peck attended Sabbath school at Bethel church to learn basic reading skills; he quickly advanced to the Bible class taught by Elder (future bishop) Daniel A. Payne. Peck experienced conversion and joined Bethel Church at age seventeen and taught Sabbath school for two years, then preached. In a letter to (future bishop) Benjamin Tucker Tanner, Peck wrote, "I have long been impressed that African Methodism was essential, and that a Church governed by colored men, untrammelled by white association, was the only means by which we could prove our manhood and elevate our people."[62]

About 1860 he married Esther A. Peck (1841–1909). He attended classes at Wilberforce College in Ohio for "a few months" to improve his theological knowledge. Fresh from Wilberforce, Peck joined the New York Conference, AMEC, and served for three years. In May 1867 he transferred to the New England Conference, where he was appointed to Providence, Rhode Island. He probably transferred to the Georgia Conference at its fourth session in January 1870 (though I found no copy of those minutes) and was appointed to the most prestigious AMEC pastorate in Georgia: Atlanta's Bethel Church. The 1870 census found him and family living in Atlanta's Fourth Ward. Rev. Peck was renowned for "his learned talks, and many flocked to hear him." His church hosted the Fifth Session of the Georgia Conference in January 1871 and he was re-appointed to Bethel Church for 1871 and 1872. Subsequent appointments in Georgia included Americus (1873) and Macon, Bibb County (1874, 1875); then back to Bethel in Atlanta (1876). Despite being, in Holloway's words, "a leading light" of the North Georgia Conference, Peck fell afoul of his church's voracious appetite for "dollar money" in 1875 when Bishop Ward called him and others to account for deficient collections.[63] By 1879 he had transferred back to Maryland where his last pastoral appointment was to Union Bethel AMEC, Petersville. Francis J. Peck died 8 March 1898.[64]

---

[62] Daniel Alexander Payne, *History of the African Methodist Episcopal Church* (Nashville: Publishing House of the A. M. E. Sunday School Union, 1891) 232; 1850 Census, MD, Baltimore County, Baltimore City, Ward 11, Free Pop., p. 335(handwritten) /168 (stamped), dwell. 638; Benj[amin] T[ucker] Tanner, *An Apology for African Methodism* (Baltimore: 1867) 331–33.

[63] 2 NGA, 3.

[64] Tanner, *Apology*, 331–33; 1860 Census, MD, Baltimore County, Baltimore City, Ward 11, Free Pop., p. 125, dwell. 800; 1870 Census, GA, Fulton County, Atlanta, Ward 4, Pop., p. 118, dwell. 1029; E[dward] R. Carter, *The Black Side: A Partial History of the Business, Religious and Educational Side of the Negro in Atlanta, Ga.* (Atlanta: 1894)

Scipio H. Robertson (a "leading light" [see p. 155] in the AMEC North Georgia Conference)

Scipio H. Robertson (1840–1896) was born in Alabama, grew up enslaved in Mississippi, and wrote (in the third person) of his earliest education, "He attended college away down on an old plantation in Mississippi and graduated in three weeks. He was taught by his master's little son; but when the overseer found it out his course was brought to a sudden close."[65] (See p. 21 for Robertson's story of learning to write a pass.) After emancipation he migrated to Macon, Georgia, where he registered to vote on 25 June 1867. He was ordained deacon in the AMEC at the Georgia Conference in February 1869 and was elected elder in 1871. Robertson's early appointments included Bibb County Circuit (1869) and Athens (1871). The 1872 session of the Georgia conference elected him conference reporter for the *Christian Recorder* and writer to the *Missionary Record*.[66]

Highly unusual for a junior elder, Bishop Brown appointed Robinson to presiding elder of Americus District for 1872 and 1873. He was transferred to the recently formed North Georgia Conference in 1875 and appointed to Atlanta's prestigious Bethel AME Church (1875). In 1876 he transferred to the South Georgia Conference where he served as presiding elder of the Columbus District, and later presiding elder of Cuthbert District. When the Macon Conference was organized in 1883 Robertson was presiding elder of Augusta District (1883–1886). In November 1886 he transferred back to the Georgia Conference as pastor of St. Philips Church in Savannah, but soon transferred again to the North Georgia Conference where he served as presiding elder of the Atlanta District beginning in 1888. In 1889 Robertson became general superintendent and treasurer of Morris Brown College in Atlanta. Robertson's first wife, Elizabeth (b. 1834), died in 1889. On 17 November 1890 he married

---

221; 5 GA, 3, 4, 17; 6 GA, 63; 7 GA, 23; 1 NGA, 23; 2 NGA, 16; 3 NGA, 15; 4 NGA, 23; 1880 Census, MD, Baltimore County, Baltimore City, Precinct 4, Ward 15, ED 135, pp. 5–6, dwell. 39.

[65] Gaines, *African Methodism*, 137.

[66] Ibid., 74, 137, 178, 208, 215; GA Return of Qualified Voters, Bibb County, 95, oath no. 231; 1870 Census, GA, Bibb County, Macon, Pop., p. 246, dwell. 1734; 3 GA, 9, 15; 5 GA, 15, 17. Alexander W. Wayman (*Cyclopaedia of African Methodism* [Baltimore: Methodist Episcopal Book Depository, 1882] 139) gives his full name as Scipio Africanus Hamilton Robinson [sic], and calls him "one of the strong ment" of the Georgia Conference.

Amanda Lane of Columbus, Georgia.[67] Rev. Scipio H. Robinson died at his home in Atlanta in 1896.[68]

Taylor Slaughter (Holloway's father-in-law, local elder in Campbell County)

Holloway probably met Taylor Slaughter as a neighbor in Palmetto in 1874. Slaughter was born in Jones County, Georgia, probably 24 July 1844. During slavery he was acquired by Major Willis P. Menefee (1814–1855), whose plantation lay near the town of Palmetto, Campbell County. After emancipation in 1865, Slaughter remained and farmed prosperously in Campbell County for the rest of his life except for two years as an itinerant deacon in the AMEC. In 1870 he was a hired hand, but by 1880 he owned an eighty-acre farm. After his first wife, Fannie, died of consumption in February 1880, he married Lucy Jones of Fulton County on 30 May 1880. He also outlived Lucy, who died 14 March 1919. Census records suggest he had twelve children, six by each wife.[69]

The Georgia Conference, AMEC, at its sixth session in January 1872, enrolled Slaughter an unordained "Local Member," and appointed him to Campbell County for the following year. The next session of the conference did not formally appoint local preachers to their localities but listed Slaughter among its unordained local members. The North Georgia Conference (NGC), organized in January 1874, did not list unordained, non-itinerating members in

---

[67] 6 GA, 63; 7 GA, 23; 2 NGA, 15; 3 NGA, 15; 1 MACON, 24; 2 MACON, 31; 3 MACON, 29; 4 MACON, 38; *Directory of the City of Savannah, 1888* (Savannah, 1888) 319; H. G. Saunders, comp., *Atlanta City Directory for 1890* (Atlanta: Constitution Publishing Company, 1890) 1000; Carter, *The Black Side,* 48.

[68] *Grayson, Admr.* v *Robertson, Admr.*, 122 Ala. (1899), 334.

[69] Robert Timmons, "Aged Ex-Slaves Gather at Home of Old Master" (69–73) in C. E. Dowman et al., *The Possibilities of the Negro in Symposium: A Solution of the Negro Problem Psychologically Considered. The Negro Not "A Beast"* (Atlanta: n.p., c. 1904) 70; 1870 Census, GA, Campbell County, Pop., p. 199, dwell. 1633; 1880 Census, GA, Campbell County, Palmetto, Pop., ED 24, p. 41, dwell. 357; 1880 Census, GA, Campbell County, Schedule 5 (Mortality), Fannie Slaughter; 1880 Census, GA, Campbell County, Palmetto, Town Dist, Schedule 2 (Agriculture), ED 24, p. 23, line 3; 1900 Census, GA, Campbell County, Pop., ED 5, p. 1, dwell. 23; Death Certificates, Vital Records, Public Health, RG 26–5-95, Georgia Archives, Campbell County, Cert. No. 2103, 14 March 1919 (Lucy Slaughter).

its minutes, so Slaughter does not appear in the conference rolls for two years. On the third day of NGC's third session, in Cartersville, December 1875, after Elder Houston H. Holloway led the conference in devotional services, Taylor Slaughter was elected deacon but not an itinerant. He received no appointment. Rev. Slaughter was listed as itinerant the next year, but without appointment for 1877. (I could not find conference minutes for the 5th & 6th sessions, 1878–1879.)[70]

Taylor Slaughter may have preferred managing his large, successful farm at home to risking financial loss by neglect if he had (like Holloway) itinerated year-to-year all over west central Georgia; he only itinerated two years. He was listed as local for 1880–1883, then was appointed to Brooks' Station (Fayette County) for 1884; then to Flat Rock (Henry County) for 1885. He was without appointment for 1886; listed supernumerary for 1887–1889; elected elder in 1889; "located" (meaning officially removed from the roll of itinerants) in 1890.[71] Taylor Slaughter died 17 January 1924 of chronic nephritis.[72]

Benjamin L. Glenn and Catherine E. Glenn (Holloway's neighbors, Presbyterian home missionaries and educators)

Benjamin L. Glenn (1860–1904) was born in South Carolina in August 1860 and graduated from the Presbyterian Church's Biddle University in Charlotte, North Carolina, in 1888. His wife, Catherine E. Chappelle (1865–?), was born in Fairfield County, South Carolina, in September 1865, one of eleven children of former slaves Henry and Patsy Chappelle. One of Catherine's older brothers, William David Chappelle, became a bishop in the AMEC. Catherine graduated from Biddle's Presbyterian counterpart for women, Scotia Seminary in Concord, North Carolina. Benjamin and Catherine married in 1888 or 1889. With funding support from the Board of Home Missions of the Presbyterian Church (an organization entirely managed by churchwomen) the Glenns moved to Liberty County, Georgia, to take charge of the Presbyterian church and

---

[70] 6 GA, 40, 43, 63; 7 GA [pages not numbered]; 3 NGA, 4–5; 4 NGC, 4.

[71] 7 NGC, 4; 9 NGC, 3; 10 NGC, 4; 11 NGC, 48; 12 NGC, 37; 13 NGC, 4; 14 NGC, 2; 15 NGC, 3; 16 NGC, 4; 17 NGC, 4; 18 NGC, 5.

[72] Death Certificates, Vital Records, Public Health, RG 26–5-95, Georgia Archives, Campbell County Cert. No. 398, 17 January 1924 (Taylor Slaughter). Slaughter's death certificate gives his birthdate as 24 July 1844, but the 1900 census gives July 1843; the 1870 and 1880 censuses suggest wildly disparate birth years, 1837 and 1845 respectively.

school at Riceboro. The Glenns labored as a team, he as pastor and school principal, she as educator in the same schools.[73]

Under Rev. Glenn's intelligent leadership, the seventy-eight-member Riceboro church in Liberty County remained unmoved by hysteria incited in 1889 by a white man named Dupont Bell. Bell claimed to be the reincarnated Jesus Christ and for a few months disrupted many local black Baptist and Methodist congregations.[74]

For health reasons the Glenns transferred from swampy Riceboro to upcountry Newnan, Coweta County, in about 1892. Rev. Glenn immediately announced plans for a new church building and opened a second pastoral charge, Newnan Mission, with eight members, besides the existing forty-member Mt. Sinai Presbyterian Church (the church for which Houston Holloway had preached in the absence of an appointed pastor). The church-sponsored school Mrs. Glenn found at Newnan was an old hut with five scholars, but the Glenns procured a three-room building and opened McClelland Academy with forty-five students. By 1904 Mt. Sinai membership had shrunk to ten, while the new Newnan church had grown to fifty-four. McClelland Academy enrollment had expanded to 156 scholars with four teachers.[75]

---

[73] Liberty County Tax Digest, 1892, 15th GMD, 5; *Home Missions. Nineteenth Annual Report (The Eighty-seventh from Its Organization) of the Board of Home Missions of the Presbyterian Church in the United States of America. Presented to the General Assembly, at New York, N.Y., May 16th, 1889* (New York: 1889) 36; Wright, *Centennial Encyclopaedia*, 64; John Henry Adams, "Rough Sketches," *The Voice* 4 (July 1907): 241.

[74] James Stacy, *A History of the Presbyterian Church in Georgia* (n.p., n.d.) 269-75; George A. Rogers and R. Frank Saunders, Jr., *Swamp Water and Wiregrass: Historical Sketches of Coastal Georgia* (Macon, GA: Mercer University Press, 1984) includes a chapter on "The Liberty County Christ Craze of 1889" (191–204).

[75] 1900 Census, GA, Coweta County, Newnan, Pop., ED 18, p. 9, dwell. 176; *Home Missions. Twenty-third Annual Report (The Ninety-first Year from the Organization of the Work) of the Board of Home Missions of the Presbyterian Church in the United States of America. Presented to the General Assembly, in Washington, DC, May 18th, 1893* (New York: 1893) 28; *Home Missions. Ninety-sixth Annual Report of the Board of Home Missions of the Presbyterian Church in the United States of America. Presented to the General Assembly, at Winona, Ind., May 19th, 1898* (New York: 1898) 4; *Home Missions: One Hundred and Third Annual Report of the Board of Home Missions of the Presbyterian Church in the United States of America, Presented to the General Assembly, at Winona Lake, Indiana, May 8th, 1905* (New York: 1905) 24, 161–62.

Catherine Glenn's work as an educator was featured in the Presbyterian Church's *Home Mission Monthly*, April 1903, including her portrait and a photo of the McClelland Academy with students and staff posed in front of the neatly appointed building.[76]

On 27 September 1904 Rev. B. L. Glenn "suddenly and unexpectedly without a moment's warning" died of heart failure. Catherine Glenn, widowed with six children, taught a few more years at McClelland Academy under the man sent to replace her husband, but in 1910 she married a building contractor and took up hairdressing.[77]

---

[76] "Prominent Examples of Colored Women As Christian Workers," *Home Mission Monthly* 17 (April 1903): 135.

[77] "A Distinct Loss," *Assembly Herald* 10/11 (November 1904) 711–12; Coweta County Marriage Record Book M, Colored, 1899–1913, 444; 1920 Census, GA, Coweta County, Newnan, Pop., ED 33, p. 16, dwell. 345.

Appendix B

Chronology of H. H. Holloway's Church Career

Conference	*Convening Date*	*Event or Appointment*
---------------	11 Aug. 1861	Joined the MECS
*	14 April 1866	Authorized to exercise spiritual gifts
*	July 1866	Licensed to exhort
**	April 1868	Licensed to preach
**		Appointed to Flat Shoals Circuit
————	Nov. 1869	Left the MECS, joined the AMEC
4th Georgia	20 Jan. 1870	Admitted to GA Conference Ordained Deacon Appointed to Flat Shoals, Meriwether Co.
5th Georgia	14 Jan. 1871	Appointed to Ringgold, Catoosa Co.
6th Georgia	4 Jan. 1872	Appointed to Kingston and Adairsville, Bartow Co.
7th Georgia	11 Jan. 1873	Ordained Elder Appointed to Kingston Circuit, Bartow Co.
1st North Ga.	8 Jan. 1874	Appointed to Palmetto Circuit, Campbell Co.
2nd North Ga.	7 Jan. 1875	Appointed to Cave Springs Circuit, Floyd Co., but refused to go.
---------------	1875	Built Campbell County Mission.
----------------	abt. May 1876	Appointed to Newnan, Coweta Co.
4th North Ga.	1 Dec. 1876	Re-appointed to Newnan, Coweta Co.
5th North Ga.	5 Dec. 1877	Appointed to Sharpsburg, Coweta Co.
6th North Ga.	8 Jan. 1879	Appointed to New Hope and Harralson, Coweta Co.
7th North Ga.	7 Jan. 1880	Appointed to Coweta Circuit, Coweta Co.
8th North Ga.	5 Jan. 1881	Appointed to Eatonton, Putnam Co.
9th North Ga.	11 Jan. 1882	Appointed to Sugar Hill Circuit, Upson Co.
1st Macon Ga.	31 Jan. 1883	Appointed withheld due to charges of debt
---------------	about 1883	Holloway declined any further appointment

* Quarterly Conference, Greenville Circuit, GA Conference, MECS

** Quarterly Conference, Greenville Circuit, N. GA Conference, MECS

Appendix C

H. H. Holloway's Children

Children with Cordelia (Thrash) Holloway

John Wesley Holloway, 28 July 1865–31 October 1935[1]

Mary Jane Holloway, 31 September 1867–12 July 1891[2]; "died of consumption of the bowels" contracted at Tuskegee Institute

Cordelia Achsah Holloway, 23 August 1870–unknown, after 1894; "married a roust-about and died of neglect"

Edwin Stanton Holloway, 23 June 1872–?, perhaps 1903–1909; "a black smith, a preacher, and a sweet singer"; married next-door neighbor Florence Page; "died of exposure and alcoholism"

Houston H. Holloway, Jr., 5 September 1876–23 June 1878

Theodore H. Holloway, 18 September 1880–25 September 1915; "He fell dead on the back porch of the old home place" at Turin

Eunice Irene Holloway, born and died in the 1880s; "died at two years of age from having been allowed to eat green apples"

Children with Polly Ann (Slaughter) Holloway

Taylor Slaughter Holloway, 15 September 1896–22 September 1959[3]

Henry Turner Holloway, 15 September 1898–c. 1899

William Fisher Holloway, c. 1901–?

Ann (Anna or Annie) May Holloway, c. 1903–?[4]

---

[1] John W. Holloway's death date from death certificate. Siblings' exact birth and death dates come from a partial list in JWH, 167, or from Houston H. Holloway's autobiography. Approximate dates are estimated from censuses and from JWH's narrative of events. Quoted commentary on causes of death is from JWH, 2.

[2] JWH, 167, dates her death to 1891, but H. H. Holloway states that his eldest daughter died the year he built his house in Turin, which was probably 1891, (see p. 169, n. 1), or possibly 1893 (see p. 173).

[3] Death date derived from NARA RG 92, US Headstone Applications for Military Veterans, 1925–1963 (DA Form 1815), Taylor S. Holloway (available online at ancestry.com as part fo the "Headstone Applications for Military Veterans, 1925–1963" database).

Florina Holloway, c. 1905–?[5]
Neptune Hartsfield Holloway, 29 September 1908–27 July 1995[6]

[4] 1910 and 1920 censuses of Turin, Coweta County, give her name as "Annie May." The 1940 Census, MI, Wayne County, Detroit, Pop., ED 84–951, p. 8A, dwell. 5777, household 135, gives her married name as "Anna Mae Thornton." Her mother Annie Holloway and brother Neptune H. Holloway were living with her.

[5] JWH, 387, spelled her name "Florina." The 1910 and 1920 censuses of Coweta County spelled it "Florine." Her father spelled her name "Floreainna"—see p. 182.

[6] H. H. Holloway's autobiography gives his first name as Nepton. JWH spells it Neptune. The 1910 census calls him "Hartsfield Holloway." The 1940 census for Detroit (see note 4) adds a middle initial: Neptune H. Holloway, from which I construct his name as Neptune Hartsfield Holloway. The 1930 and 1940 censuses list his occupation as music teacher. Birthdate and death date from the United States Social Security Master Death Index (searchable at https://familysearch.org/search/collection/1202535 [first name: Neptune H; last name: Holloway] [accessed 22 February 2015]).

Appendix D

Autobiographical Letter

"Thirteen Years Ago."[1]
By Rev. H. H. Holloway

MR. EDITOR.—This the 5th day of June brings to our mind the 5th day of June 1865 at the Flat Shoals in Meriwether County, Geo, at 1 o'clock P.M., when my old master called all his people or slaves together and read to them the proclamation of emancipation; visiting two other plantations in the morning and doing the same thing. After having read and [*sic*] document, he went on to tell all about what caused it; and among other things he said we had served his race as slaves long enough, and had he lived in other parts of the Union he would have set us free four years ago; but as he could not then, he was doing what he was perfectly willing to do, as he was a strong Union man and was opposed to the bloody struggle between the North and South. "As for you, you are now all free. I wish now to give you this advice: go to work, you will always have much to do if you do it." Your humble correspondent was one of the number from whose wrists that day fell the shackles of slavery. Then being a member of the M.E. Church South, in that Church he and thousands of his race remained several years afterward. In the year 1867, he went up to Griffin and went out to see a man by the name of Alexander, an old friend. On going out he found a man by that name, but not the man he wished to see. It proved to be the Rev. Robt. Alexander pastor in charge of the A.M.E. Church, whose mission at that time I did not understand from the fact I had never heard of such a body. That same year he attempted to teach the first school that had ever been taught in that surrounding country. Incompetent as he was, as you may suppose, the amount of good done can be estimated from the following facts: three young boys who learned their alphabet, are now holding important charges in the A.M.E. Church. The year 1868 being a high political excitement year, little was done in the religious line. Having been previously licensed to exhort, it was

---

[1] *Christian Recorder*, 4 July 1878, 2.

April 14th, he was licensed to preach in the A.M.E. [*sic*—should be M.E.] Church South, and appointed to Flat Shoals Circuit, including Flat Shoals, Ebenezer and Mt. Carmel. In the fall he got acquainted with the A.M.E. Church. Calling upon the Rev. A. McGhee, then at Griffin, that year, January 1869, he was ordained a deacon by Rev. J.M. Brown D.D., at Americus Ga., and returned back to the Flat Shoals, serving a year with remarkable success. Reported at Conference in Atlanta, and was sent to Ringgold, staid one year and had a slight difficulty with a Democrat Negro; reported at Conference at Savannah, was sent to Kingston—there he staid two years. Reaped a gospel harvest, reported at Conference at Augusta, Ga. Was sent by Bishop T.M.D. Ward in 1873 to Palmetto; took into church over two hundred souls; 1874 was sent to the Campbell County Mission; found seven in society; reported at Conference at Cartersville sixty-five in society. At this Conference 1876 he got a respite for five months and was then appointed to fill out the unexpired term of the Rev. Burl Mitchell on the Nenman [*sic*] Circuit. Reaped in much gospel fruit in 1876 and '77. Reported at Annual Conference at Eatonton in 1877. The Rev. J. P. Campbell, D.D., LL.D., appointed him to the Sharpsburg Circuit. So having served in the Conference from 1869 to 1878 without ever being marked, he craves an interest in the prayers of all, that he ever more may succeed in the time to come, as he has in time past, only more so. You will see from the foregoing that the larger portion of my life or time, since the emancipation has been devoted to the ministry. The Sharpsburg circuit is very large, and is said to be one of the best circuits in the North Georgia Conference. One thing we know, the harvest here is very great and the laborers are few, yet we will not despair. We are blowing our gospel trumpet, and from present indication much fruit is to be gathered.

Senoia, Ga., June 5, 1878.

Bibliography

Primary Sources

Manuscript Collections

Houston Hartsfield Holloway Papers. 1894–1932. Library of Congress MSS84205. Library of Congress Manuscript Division, Washington, D.C.

Holloway, John Wesley. "Memoirs of John Wesley Holloway, Thebes Ga., July 3, 1916." Photocopy of manuscript in private possession; location of original unknown.

US Government Documents

Biographical Directory of the United States Congress 1774–Present. http://bioguide.congress.gov.

Headstone Applications for Military Veterans, 1925–1963. RG 92. National Archives and Records Administration, Washington, DC. Available online at ancestry.com as part of the "Headstone Applications for Military Veterans, 1925–1963" database.

Internal Revenue Assessment Lists for Georgia, 1865–1866. RG 58. NARA Microfilm Publication 762. National Archives and Records Administration, Washington, DC. Available online at https://familysearch.org/search/collection/2075263.

Records of the Bureau of Refugees, Freedmen, and Abandoned Lands, Records of the Field Offices for the State of Georgia. RG 105.5. Microfilm Publication M1903. National Archives and Records Administration, Washington, DC.

Records of the Bureau of the Census, Census Schedules, 1820–1940. RG 29.8. National Archives and Records Administration, Washington, DC.

Records of United States Army Continental Commands, 1821–1920. RG 393. National Archives and Records Administration, Washington, DC.

Register of Officers and Agents, Civil, Military, and Naval, in the Service of the United States, on the Thirtieth of September, 1873. Washington, DC: Government Printing Office, 1874.

Registers of Signatures of Depositors in Branches of the Freedmen's Savings and Trust Company, 1865–1874. RG 101. Microfilm Publication M816. National Archives and Records Administration, Washington, DC.

Southern Claims Commission, Disallowed Claims. RG 233. Microfilm Publication M1407. *Barred and Disallowed Case Files of the Southern Claims Commission, 1871–1880.* National Archives and Records Administration, Washington, DC.

US Department of the Interior. *Statistics of the United States, (Including Mortality, Property, &c.,) in 1860; Compiled from the Original returns and Being the Final Exhibit of the Eighth Census, under the Direction of the Secretary of the Interior.* Washington: Government Printing Office, 1866.

US House of Representatives. *Executive Documents Printed by Order of the House of Representatives, During the Second Session of the Thirty-Ninth Congress, 1866–'67.* Washington: Government Printing Office, 1867.

United States Social Security Master Death Index. Available at https://familysearch.org/search/collection/1202535.

Veterans Administration Pension files. RG 15.7.3. National Archives and Records Administration, Washington, DC.

Georgia State and County Records

Acts of the General Assembly of the State of Georgia, Passed in Milledgeville, at an Annual Session in December 1865, and January, February, and March, 1866. Milledgeville: Boughton, Nisbet, Barnes & Moore, 1866.

Catoosa County, Georgia, Tax Digest, 1872–1877. Revenue-Property Tax Unit, County Property Tax Digests. RG 34-06-001. Georgia State Archives, Morrow, Georgia. Searchable at http://search.ancestry.com/search/db.aspx?dbid=1729.

Georgia Death Certificates, 1919–1927. [Georgia State Archives, Morrow, Georgia]. Searchable at http://cdm.georgiaarchives.org:2011/cdm/landingpage/collection/gadeath.

Georgia, Office of the Governor. Reconstruction registration oath books, 1867. RG 1-1-107. Georgia State Archives, Morrow, Georgia. Searchable at http://search.ancestry.com/search/db.aspx?dbid=1857.

Georgia, Office of the Governor. Returns of qualified voters under the Reconstruction Act, 1867. RG 1-1-108. Georgia State Archives, Morrow, Georgia. Searchable at http://search.ancestry.com/search/db.aspx?dbid =1857.

Liberty County, Georgia, Tax Digest, 1892. Revenue-Property Tax Unit, County Property Tax Digests. RG 34-06-001. Georgia State Archives, Morrow, Georgia. Searchable at http://search.ancestry.com/search/db.aspx?dbid=1729.

Meriwether County, Georgia, Court of Ordinary, Estate Book F. 1856–1859. Meriwether County Courthouse, Office of Probate Judge, Greenville, GA. Accessed at "Georgia Probate Records, 1742–1990." Searchable at https://familysearch.org/search/collection/1999178.

Meriwether County, Georgia, Tax Digest, 1863. Revenue-Property Tax Unit, County Property Tax Digests. RG 34-06-001. Georgia State Archives, Morrow, Georgia. Searchable at http://search.ancestry.com/search/db.aspx?dbid=1729.

Meriwether County, Georgia, Will Book A. 1831–1859. Meriwether County Courthouse, Office of Probate Judge, Greenville, GA. Accessed at "Georgia Probate Records, 1742–1990." Searchable at https://familysearch.org/search/collection/1999178.

Oglethorpe County, Georgia, Unbound Estate Records. 1790–1962. Drawer 307, Box 7. Georgia Archives, Morrow, GA. Original at Office of Probate Judge, Lexington, GA.

Pike County, Georgia, Deed Books E, F, G, L. Office of Clerk of Superior Court, Pike County Courthouse, Zebulon, GA.

Pike County, Georgia, Marriage Book. 1872–1883. Office of Probate Judge, Pike County Courthouse, Zebulon, GA. Accessed at "Georgia Probate Records, 1742–1990." Searchable at https://familysearch.org/search/collection/1999178.

Upson County, Georgia, Court of Ordinary. Loose estate records. Thomaston-Upson Archives, Thomaston, GA.

Upson County, Georgia, Court of Ordinary. Record of Accounts Book C. Thomaston-Upson Archives, Thomaston, GA.

Upson County, Georgia, Court of Ordinary. Record of Vouchers Books A, B, C, D. Thomaston-Upson Archives, Thomaston, GA.

Upson County, Georgia, Deed Book H. Thomaston-Upson Archives, Thomaston, GA.

Upson County, Georgia, Tax Digests. 1846–1848, 1859, 1869, 1871. Thomaston-Upson Archives, Thomaston, GA.

Upson County, Georgia. Loose records of Inferior and Superior Courts. "Court Records by Defendant/Court Records by Plaintiff." Thomaston-Upson Archives, Thomaston, GA.

Upson County, Georgia, Marriage Record to 1876. Upson County Probate Court, Thomaston, GA.

Miscellaneous Government Records

City of Griffin, GA. "Samuel Bailey Building." Available at http://www.cityofgriffin.com/visitors/PlacesofInterest/SamBaileyBuilding.aspx. Accessed 17 February 2015.

New York State Census, State Population Census Schedules. 1915. Accessed at FamilySearch.org, "New York State Census, 1915." Available at https://familysearch.org/search/collection/1937454. Accessed 17 February 2015.

Wayne County, Michigan, Death Records Index, 1940–1944. Available at http://www.detroitpubliclibrary.org/wayne-county-death-record-index. Accessed 24 February 2015.

Newspapers

Atlanta *Constitution*, 1899
Atlanta *Georgian and News*, 1911
Christian Recorder, 1867–1900
Columbus *Enquirer*, 1840
[Cartersville GA] *Courant-American*, 1896
[Atlanta] *Daily Constitution*, 1879
[Richmond, VA] *Daily Dispatch*, 1865
Georgia Journal and Messenger, 1848–1858
[Newnan, GA] *Herald & Advertiser*, 1899–1909
Meriwether Vindicator, 1895–1899
Newnan *Herald*, 1917
Philadelphia *Tribune* [online edition] 2012
Pike County Journal, 1890
Southern Christian Advocate, 1868
[Milledgeville] *Southern Recorder*, 1865
Thomaston *Times*, 1899–1913
[Milledgeville] *Union Recorder*, 1899
Wesleyan Christian Advocate, 1898–1899

City Directories

Directories are accessible at ancestry.com, "U.S. City Directories, 1821–1989" collection available at http://search.ancestry.com/search/db.aspx?dbid=2469.

Savannah, GA, 1888.
Augusta, GA, 1888, 1889.
Atlanta, GA, 1874–1883, 1890

Minutes of Churches, Church Conferences and Missionary Organizations

African Methodist Episcopal Church, Atlanta Conference

Minutes of the Second Session of the Atlanta (Georgia) Annual Conference of the African Methodist Episcopal Church, held in Mount Zion A. M. E. Church Newnan, Georgia, Dec. 17–23, 1901. Atlanta: The Franklin Printing and Publishing Co., 1902.

Minutes of the Fourth Session Atlanta (Georgia) Annual Conference of the African Methodist Episcopal Church held in Big Bethel A. M. E. Church, Atlanta, Ga. November 11–17, 1903. Atlanta: The Franklin Printing and Publishing Co., 1904.

African Methodist Episcopal Church, Georgia Conference

Minutes of the Third Session of the Georgia Annual Conference, of the A. M. E. Church: held at Columbus, Georgia, February 6th, 1869. Macon, GA: American Union Office, 1869.

Minutes of the Georgia Annual Conference! [*sic*] *of the African Methodist Episcopal Church, Fifth Session—For 1870, Held with Bethel Church, Atlanta, Ga., From Jan. 14th, to 24th, 1871: and Sixth Session—For 1871, Held with Saint Philip's Church, Savannah, Georgia, From Jan. 5th, to 14th, 1872.* Savannah: Thomas Robinson's Book and Job Shop, 1872.

Minutes of the Georgia Annual Conference of the African Methodist Episcopal Church, Seventh Session, Held in the First A. M. E. Church, at Macon, from January 11th to the 20th, 1873. Atlanta: Economical Book and Job Printing House, 1873.

African Methodist Episcopal Church, Macon Conference

Minutes of the First Session of the Macon, Ga., Annual Conference of the African Methodist Episcopal Church, held at Sandersville, Georgia. January 31st–February 5th, 1883. Atlanta: Jas. P. Harrison & Co., 1883.

Minutes of the Second Session of the Macon Annual Conference of the African Methodist Episcopal Church, held at Forsyth, Ga., from Nov. 5 to Dec. 3, 1883. Atlanta: Jas. P. Harrison & Co., 1884.

Minutes of the Third Session of the Macon Annual Conference of the African Methodist Episcopal Church, held at St. James Church, Columbus, Georgia, from Nov. 19 to Nov. 25, 1884. Atlanta: Jas. P. Harrison & Co., 1884.

Minutes of the Fourth Session of the Macon, Georgia, Annual Conference of the African Methodist Episcopal Church. Held at St. John's Church, Eatonton, Georgia, November 18, 1885–November 23, 1885. Atlanta: Jas. P. Harrison & Co., 1885.

Minutes of the Eighth Session of the Macon, Ga., Annual Conference of the African Methodist Episcopal Church. Held in Wesley Chapel, Milledgeville, Ga., Wednesday, November 13, 1889–Sunday, November 17, 1889. Atlanta: Jas. P. Harrison & Co., 1890.

African Methodist Episcopal Church, North Georgia Conference

Minutes for 1874, (in Two Books) of the North Georgia Annual Conference of the African M. E. Church, First Session, Held in Bethel Church, Augusta, From Jan. 8 to 13, and the South Georgia Annual Conference of the African M. E. Church, First Session, Held in the City Hall, Thomasville, from Jan. 22 to 26. Atlanta: Franklin Steam Printing House, 1874.

[*Minutes of the Second Session of the Annual North Georgia Conference of the A. M. E. Church, from January 7 to January 12, 1875.*] [p.p., p., and p.d. unk.; title page missing in copy viewed.]

Minutes of the [Third Session] North Georgia Annual Conference of the A. M. E. Church, held in St. Luke's Chapel, Cartersville, Ga., from Dec. 16th to 20th, 1875. Atlanta: Jas. P. Harrison & Co., 1876.

Minutes of the Fourth Session of the North Georgia Annual Conference of the African M. E. Church, held in A. M. Church, Griffin, Ga., from Dec. 1st to 8th, 1876. Atlanta: James P. Harrison & Co., 1877.

Minutes of the Seventh Session of the North Georgia Annual Conference of the African Methodist Episcopal Church, held in the Cotton Avenue A. M. E. Church, Macon Ga. from January 7 to 14, 1880. Macon, GA: A. E. Seibert's Book and Job Printing House, 1880.

Minutes of the Ninth Session of the North Georgia Annual Conference of the African Methodist Episcopal Church, held in Bethel Church, Augusta, Georgia, from 11th to 18th January 1882. Atlanta: Jas. P. Harrison & Co., 1882.

Minutes of the Tenth Session of the North Georgia Annual Conference of the African Methodist Episcopal Church, held in Jackson Chapel, Washington, Ga., from 10th to 16th of January 1883. Atlanta: Jas. P. Harrison & Co., 1883.

Minutes of the Eleventh Session of the North Georgia Annual Conference of the African Methodist Episcopal Church, held in Turner Chapel, Marietta, Ga., from the 9th to 15th of January, 1884. Atlanta: Jas. P. Harrison & Co., 1884.

Minutes of the Twelfth Session of the North Georgia Annual Conference of the African Methodist Episcopal Church, held in Pierce Chapel, Athens, Georgia, from the 3d to 8th of December, 1884. Atlanta: Jas. P. Harrison & Co., 1885.

Minutes of the Thirteenth Session of the North Georgia Annual Conference of the African Methodist Episcopal Church, held in St. Philip's Chapel, Griffin, Ga., from the 2d to 6th of December, 1885. Atlanta: Jas. P. Harrison & Co., 1886.

Minutes of the Fourteenth Session of the North Georgia Annual Conference of the African Methodist Episcopal Church, held in Allen Temple, Atlanta, Ga., from the First to the Eighth of December, 1886. Atlanta: Jas. P. Harrison & Co., 1887.

Minutes of the Fifteenth Session of the North Georgia Annual Conference of the African M. E. Church, held in the A. M. E. Church, Rome, Ga., from the 9th to the 15th of November, 1887. Atlanta: Jas. P. Harrison & Co., 1888.

Minutes of the Sixteenth Session of the North Georgia Annual Conference of the A. M. E. Church, held in Dalton, Ga., November 7–12, 1888. Atlanta: Jas. P. Harrison & Co., 1889.

Minutes of the Seventeenth Session of the North Georgia Annual Conference, of the A. M. E. Church, held in Washington, Ga., November 6–12, 1889. Atlanta: Jas. P. Harrison & Co., 1889.

Minutes of the Eighteenth Annual Session of the North Georgia Conference of the A. M. E. Church held in Cartersville, Ga., Nov. 5th to 10th, 1890. Atlanta: Jas. P. Harrison & Co., 1890.

African Methodist Episcopal Church, South Carolina Conference

Minutes of the South Carolina Annual Conference of the African M. E. Church, 1865, 1866, 1867. Published by Order of Said Conference, By T. G. Steward and H. M. Turner. Charleston, SC: Record Printing House, 1867.

Baptist Churches and Associations

Bethesda Baptist Church Minute Book 1, Upson Co., Georgia. First Baptist Church, Thomaston, GA (also accessible at Special Collections, Mercer University Library, Macon, GA, microfilm reel 95).

Clouds Creek Baptist Church Minutes 1826–1856, Oglethorpe Co., Georgia. Georgia Archives, Morrow, GA, microfilm RHS 1300 (drawer 307, box 7).

Minutes of the Echoconna Association, 1860. Special Collections, Mercer University Library, Macon, GA, microfilm reel 1069.

Minutes of the Rehoboth Baptist Association, 1860. Special Collections, Mercer University Library, Macon, GA, microfilm reel 1201.

Minutes of the Towaliga Primitive Baptist Association, 1838, 1839, 1841-1856, 1859-1863. Special Collections, Mercer University Library, Macon, GA, microfilm reel 1410.

Methodist Episcopal Church

Minutes of the Annual Conferences of the Methodist Episcopal Church for the Year 1868. New York: Carlton & Lanahan, n.d.

Minutes of the Annual Conferences of the Methodist Episcopal Church for the Year 1869. New York: Carlton & Lanahan, n.d.

Minutes of the Annual Conferences of the Methodist Episcopal Church for the Year 1870. New York: Carlton & Lanahan, n.d.

Minutes of the Annual Conferences of the Methodist Episcopal Church for the Year 1871. New York: Carlton & Lanahan, n.d.

Minutes of the Annual Conferences of the Methodist Episcopal Church. Fall Conferences of 1878. New York: Nelson & Phillips, n.d.

Minutes of the Annual Conferences of the Methodist Episcopal Church. Fall Conferences of 1880. New York: Phillips & Hunt, 1880.

Methodist Episcopal Church, South

"List of Male Members 1857," Greenville Methodist Church, Meriwether County, GA. Greenville United Methodist Church, Greenville, GA.

Minutes of the Georgia Annual Conference of the Methodist Episcopal Church, South, Held in Columbus, Ga., Nov. 25–Dec. 3, 1863. Macon, GA: Burke, Boykin & Co., 1864. Available at http://american-south.org/export/html/geu/

confederateimprints/amso_geu_confederateimprints_8hxs8.html (accessed 15 December 2013).
Minutes of the Georgia Annual Conference of the Methodist Episcopal Church, South, Held in Macon, Georgia, Nov. 15th 1865 [p.p., p., and p.d. unk.; title page missing in copies viewed].
Minutes of the Annual Conferences of the Methodist Episcopal Church, South, for the Year 1858. Nashville, TN: Southern Methodist Publishing House, 1870.
Minutes of the Annual Conferences of the Methodist Episcopal Church, South, for the Year 1859. Nashville, TN: Southern Methodist Publishing House, 1870.
Minutes of the Annual Conferences of the Methodist Episcopal Church, South, for the Year 1860. Nashville, TN: Southern Methodist Publishing House, 1870.
Minutes of the Annual Conferences of the Methodist Episcopal Church, South, for the Year 1861. Nashville, TN: Southern Methodist Publishing House, 1870.
Minutes of the Annual Conferences of the Methodist Episcopal Church, South, for the Year 1862. Nashville, TN: Southern Methodist Publishing House, 1870.
Minutes of the Annual Conferences of the Methodist Episcopal Church, South, for the Year 1863. Nashville, TN: Southern Methodist Publishing House, 1870.
Minutes of the Annual Conferences of the Methodist Episcopal Church, South, for the Year 1864. Nashville, TN: Southern Methodist Publishing House, 1870.
Minutes of the Annual Conferences of the Methodist Episcopal Church, South, for the Year 1865. Nashville, TN: Southern Methodist Publishing House, 1870.
Minutes of the Annual Conferences of the Methodist Episcopal Church, South, for the Year 1866. Nashville, TN: Southern Methodist Publishing House, 1870.
Minutes of the Annual Conferences of the Methodist Episcopal Church, South, for the Year 1867. Nashville, TN: Southern Methodist Publishing House, 1870.
Minutes of the Annual Conferences of the Methodist Episcopal Church, South, for the Year 1868. Nashville, TN: Southern Methodist Publishing House, 1870.
Minutes of the Annual Conferences of the Methodist Episcopal Church, South, for the Year 1869. Nashville, TN: Southern Methodist Publishing House, 1870.
Minutes of the Annual Conferences of the Methodist Episcopal Church, South, for the Year 1870. Nashville, TN: Southern Methodist Publishing House, 1871.
Minutes of the Annual Conferences of the Methodist Episcopal Church, South, for the Year 1871. Nashville, TN: Southern Methodist Publishing House, 1872.
Minutes of the Annual Conferences of the Methodist Episcopal Church, South, for the Year 1872. Nashville, TN: Southern Methodist Publishing House, 1876.

Presbyterian

Home Missions. Nineteenth Annual Report (The eighty-seventh from its Organization) of the Board of Home Missions of the Presbyterian Church in the United States of America. Presented to the General Assembly, at New York, N. Y., May 16th, 1889. New York: [n.p.] 1889.

Home Missions. Twenty-Second Annual Report (The Ninetieth from its Organization) of the Board of Home Missions of the Presbyterian Church in the United States of America. Presented to the General Assembly, at Portland, Oreg., May 19th, 1892. New York: [n.p.] 1892.

Home Missions. Twenty-Third Annual Report (The Ninety-first Year from the Organization of the Work) of the Board of Home Missions of the Presbyterian Church in the United States of America. Presented to the General Assembly, in Washington, D.C., May 18th, 1893. New York: [n.p.] 1893.

Home Missions. Ninety-sixth Annual Report of the Board of Home Missions of the Presbyterian Church in the United States of America. Presented to the General Assembly, at Winona, Ind., May 19th, 1898. New York: [n.p.] 1898.

Home Missions. One Hundred and Third Annual report of the Board of Home Missions of the Presbyterian Church in the United States of America. Presented to the General Assembly, at Winona Lake, Indiana, May 18th, 1905. New York: [n.p.] 1905.

Secondary Sources

"A Distinct Loss." *The Assembly Herald* 10 (November 1904): 711–12.

Adams, John Henry. "Rough Sketches." *The Voice* 4 (July 1907): 238–41.

Alumni Directory of Yale University, Graduates and Non-Graduates. New Haven: Yale University, 1920.

Angell, Stephen Ward. *Bishop Henry McNeal Turner and African-American Religion in the South.* Knoxville: University of Tennessee Press, 1992.

Angell, Stephen W[ard]. "Henry McNeal Turner (1834–1915)." New Georgia Encyclopedia. 28 August 2013. http://www.georgiaencyclopedia.org/articles/history-archaeology/henry-mcneal-turner-1834–1915 (accessed 20 December 2013).

Arnold, Edwin T. *What Virtue There Is in Fire: Cultural Memory and the Lynching of Sam Hose.* Athens, GA: University of Georgia Press, 2009.

Avery, I[saac] W[heeler]. *The History of the State of Georgia from 1850 to 1881, Embracing Three Important Epochs: The Decade before the War of 1861–1865; the War; the Period of Reconstruction, with Portraits of the Leading Public Men of this Era.* New York: Brown & Derby, 1881.

Barnes, William Horatio. *Biographies of Members of the House Representative of The Forty-Third Congress.* Volume 2 of The American Government. New York: Nelson & Phillips, 1874.

Bennett, J. C. "The Medical Fraternity of Jackson County." Originally printed in *The Jackson Herald*, 14 December 1905; republished at http://www.victorianmaysville.com/history/jchistory/jcdoctors.htm (accessed 4 February 2015).

Biehle, Reba Strickland. "Edward Oxford, Pioneer Farmer of Middle Georgia." *Georgia Historical Quarterly* 52 (June 1968): 187–98.

Blight, David W. *A Slave No More: Two Men Who Escaped to Freedom including Their Own Narratives of Emancipation.* Orlando, FL: Harcourt, Inc., 2007.

Boles, John B. "Introduction." In *Masters and Slaves in the House of the Lord: Race and Religion in the American South, 1740–1870*, ed. John B. Boles. Lexington: University of Kentucky Press, 1988. 1–18.

Bowers, Fredson. "Transcription of Manuscripts: The Record of Variants." *Studies in Bibliography* 29 (1976): 212–64.

Burch, Jarrett. *Adiel Sherwood: Baptist Antebellum Pioneer in Georgia.* Macon, GA: Mercer University Press, 2003.

[Burke, John William]. *Autobiography: Chapters from the Life of a Preacher.* Macon, GA: J. W. Burke & Co., 1884.

Camp, Stephanie M. H. *Closer to Freedom: Enslaved Women & Everyday Resistance in the Plantation South.* Chapel Hill: University of North Carolina Press, 2004.

Campbell, J[esse] H[arrison]. *Georgia Baptists: Historical and Biographical.* Macon, GA: J. W. Burke & Company, 1874.

Capers, William. *Catechism for the Use of the Methodist Missions. First Part.* Charleston, SC: John Early, 1853. http://docsouth.unc.edu/church/capers/capers.html (accessed 4 February 2015).

Catalog of the Officers and Graduates of Yale University in New Haven, Connecticut, 1701–1915. New Haven: Yale University, 1916.

Catalog of the Officers and Students of Fisk University, Nashville, Tennessee, for 1897–1898. [and subsequent catalogs through 1908–1909]. Nashville, TN: Marshall & Bruce Co., 1898 [through 1909].

Catalog of the Officers, Students, and Alumni of Fisk University, 2nd ed. Nashville, TN: 1911–1912.

Carter, E[dward] R. *The Black Side: A Partial History of the Business, Religious and Educational Side of the Negro in Atlanta, Ga.* Atlanta: 1894.

Cliburn, Edwin L. *In Unbroken Line: A History of the First Baptist Church of Thomaston, Georgia, From its Beginnings at Bethesda to its One Hundred Fiftieth Anniversary (1825–1975).* Tallahassee, FL: 1978.

Cobb, Thomas R. R. *A Digest of the Statute Laws of the State of Georgia in Force Prior to the General Assembly of 1851, with Explanatory Notes and References.* Athens, GA: Christy, Kelsea & Burke, 1851. Available at https://archive.org/details/digestofstatute102stat.

Coleman, Phares. *Reports of Cases Argued and Determined in the Supreme Court of Alabama during the November Term, 1898.* Volume 122. Montgomery, AL: Brown Printing Co., 1900.

"Colleges and Their Graduates in 1914." *The Crisis* 8 (July 1914): 129–40.

Cornelius, Janet Duitsman. *Slave Missions and the Black Church in the Antebellum South.* Columbia: University of South Carolina Press, 1999.

Cornelius, Janet Duitsman. *When I Can Read My Title Clear: Literacy, Slavery, and Religion in the Antebellum South.* Columbia: University of South Carolina Press, 1991.

Cornell, Nancy, ed. *Strickland Scene.* Riverdale, GA: Strickland Research, Inc., 1980–1983.

"Culpepper Connections! The Culpepper Family History Site." Henry Hartsfield page. http://gen.culpepper.com/ss/p45961.htm (accessed 4 February 2015).

Dobbs, Linda, Anne Threadgill, Lelia Freeman, Sally Neal, Mary Anne Harman, and Sallie Mabon, eds. *The Heritage of Meriwether County Georgia 1827–2004.* Meriwether Historical Society: 2004.

Dossey, William, comp., ed. *The Choice, in Two Parts; Part I, Containing Psalms and Hymns; Part II, Containing Spiritual Songs, Designed for Public and Private Worship.* Philadelphia: Charles De Silver & Sons, 1836.

DuBois, W[illiam] E[dward] B[urghardt]. *Black Reconstruction.* Philadelphia: Albert Saifer, [1935?].

Douglass, Frederick. *Narrative of the Life of Frederick Douglass, an American Slave. Written by Himself.* London: H. G. Collins, 1851.

Epstein, Dena J. "Slave Music in the United States Before 1860: A Survey of Sources (Part 2)." *Music Library Association Notes* 20 (Summer 1963): 377–90.

Eskew, Glenn T. "Paternalism among Augusta's Methodists: Black, White, and Colored." In *Paternalism in a Southern City: Race, Religion, and Gender in Augusta, Georgia.* Ed. Edward J. Cashin, Glenn T. Eskew. Athens: University of Georgia Press, 2001. 85–109.

Foner, Eric. *Reconstruction: America's Unfinished Revolution, 1863–1877*. New York: Harper & Row, 1988.

Fountain, Daniel L. *Slavery, Civil War, and Salvation: African American Slaves and Christianity, 1830–1870*. Baton Rouge: Louisiana State University Press, 2010.

Frey, Sylvia R. and Betty Wood. *Come Shouting to Zion: African American Protestantism in the American South and British Caribbean to 1830*. Chapel Hill: University of North Carolina Press, 1998.

Gaines, Wesley J. *African Methodism in the South; or Twenty-Five Years of Freedom*. Atlanta: 1890.

Gardner, Robert G., Charles O. Walker, J. R. Huddlestun, and Waldo P. Harris III. *A History of the Georgia Baptist Association*. 2nd ed. Atlanta: Georgia Baptist Historical Society, 1996.

Genovese, Eugene D. *Roll, Jordon, Roll: The World the Slaves Made*. New York: Vintage Books, 1976.

Joyner, Charles. *Down by the Riverside: A South Carolina Slave Community*. Urbana: University of Illinois Press, 1984.

Hadden, Sally E. *Slave Patrols: Law and Violence in Virginia and the Carolinas*. Cambridge, MA: Harvard University Press, 2001.

Hahn, Steven, Steven F. Miller, Susan E. O'Donovan, John C. Rodrigue, and Leslie S. Rowland, eds. *Freedom: A Documentary History of Emancipation, 1861–1867: Selected from the Holdings of the National Archives of the United States*. Chapel Hill: University of North Carolina Press, 2008.

Heard, William H. *From Slavery to the Bishopric in the A.M.E. Church: An Autobiography*. Philadelphia: A.M.E. Book Concern, 1928. Electronic edition at "Documenting the American South." http://docsouth.unc.edu/neh/heard/heard.html#ill8 (accessed 4 February 2015).

Higginson, Thomas Wentworth. "Negro Spirituals." *The Atlantic Monthly* (June 1867). http://www.theatlantic.com/past/docs/issues/1867jun/spirit.htm (accessed 4 February 2015).

Hildebrand, Reginald F. *The Times Were Strange and Stirring: Methodist Preachers and the Crisis of Emancipation*. Durham: Duke University Press, 1995.

Holsey, L[ucius] H. *Autobiography, Sermons, Addresses, and Essays of Bishop L. H. Holsey, D. D.* Atlanta: Franklin Printing and Publishing Co., 1898.

Jones, Jaqueline. *Soldiers of Light and Love: Northern Teachers and Georgia Blacks, 1865–1873*. Chapel Hill: University of North Carolina Press, 1980.

Journal of the Proceedings of the Constitutional Convention of the People of Georgia, Held in the City of Atlanta in the Months of December, 1867, and January, February and March, 1868. Augusta, GA: 1868.

Kaczorowski, Robert J. *The Politics of Judicial Interpretation: The Federal Courts, Department of Justice, and Civil Rights, 1866–1876.* Dobbs Ferry, NY: Oceana Publications, 1985.

Knight, Lucian Lamar. *A Standard History of Georgia and Georgians.* Volume 6. Chicago: Lewis Publishing Company, 1917.

Lakey, Othal Hawthorne. *The History of the CME Church (Revised).* Memphis, TN: CME Publishing House, 1996.

Lawrence, Harold. *Methodist Preachers in Georgia, 1783–1900.* Tignall, GA: Boyd Publishing Co. Ltd, 1984.

Lockwood, Lewis C. *Mary S. Peake, The Colored Teacher at Fortress Monroe.* Boston: American Tract Society, n.d.

Litwack, Leon F. *Been in the Storm So Long: The Aftermath of Slavery.* New York: Vintage Books, 1980.

Malone, Jaqui. *Steppin' on the Blues: The Visible Rhythms of African American Dance.* Urbana: University of Chicago Press, 1996.

Martin, B. Y. *Reports of Cases in Law and Equity Argued and Determined in the Supreme Court of Georgia, Containing the Decisions at Macon, January Term, 1859; and Part of the Decisions at Atlanta, March Term, 1859.* Volume 27. Columbus, GA: 1860.

Mather, Frank Lincoln, ed. *Who's Who of the Colored Race: A General Biographical Dictionary of Men and woman of African Descent.* Volume 1. Chicago: 1915.

Maynor, Natalie. "Written Records of Spoken Language: How Reliable Are They?" In *Methods in Dialectology*, Alan R. Thomas, ed. Clevendon: Multilingual Matters Ltd, 1988. 111–15.

McCurry, Stephanie. "Women Numerous and Armed: Gender and the Politics of Subsistence in the Civil War South." In *Wars Within a War: Controversy and Conflict over the American Civil War*, ed. Joan Waugh and Gary W. Gallagher. Chapel Hill: University of North Carolina Press, 2009. 1–26.

McGehee, John Boykin. *Autobiography of Rev. J .B. McGehee, of South Georgia Conference.* Buena Vista, GA: 1915.

McPherson, James M. *Battle Cry of Freedom: The Civil War Era.* New York: Oxford University Press, 1988.

Memoirs of Georgia, Containing Historical Accounts of the State's Civil, Military, Industrial and Professional Interests, and Personal Sketches of Many of its People. Volume 2. Atlanta: The Southern Historical Association, 1895.

Mixon, Gregory. "Henry McNeal Turner versus the Tuskegee Machine: Black Leadership in the Nineteenth Century." *Journal of Negro History* 79/4 (Autumn 1994): 363–80.

Mixon, W[infield] H[enri]. *History of the African Methodist Episcopal Church in Alabama, with Biographical Sketches.* Nashville, TN: A.M.E. Church Sunday School Union, 1902.

Mohr, Clarence L. "Slaves and White Churches in Confederate Georgia." In *Masters and Slaves in the House of the Lord: Race and Religion in the American South, 1740–1870*, ed. John B. Boles. Lexington: University of Kentucky Press, 1988. 153–72.

Moore, George W. "Southern Field Notes." *The American Missionary* 48/10 (October 1894): 357–59.

O'Donovan, Susan Eva. *Becoming Free in the Cotton South.* Cambridge, MA: Harvard University Press, 2007.

———. "William Webb's World," New York *Times* (18 February 2011) http://opinionator.blogs.nytimes.com/2011/02/18/william-webbs-world/?_r=0 (accessed 9 January 2015).

Odum, Howard W. "Religious Folk-Songs of the Southern Negroes." *The American Journal of Religious Psychology and Education* 8/3 (July 1909): 265–365.

Olney, James. "'I Was Born': Slave Narratives, Their Status as Autobiography and as Literature." In *The Slave's Narrative*, ed. Davis, Charles Twitchell, and Henry Louis Gates, Jr. Oxford: Oxford University Press, 1985. 148–74.

Owen, Christopher H. *The Sacred Flame of Love: Methodism and Society in Nineteenth-Century.* Athens: University of Georgia Press, 1998.

Payne, Daniel Alexander. *History of the African Methodist Episcopal Church.* Nashville, TN: Publishing House of the A.M.E. Sunday School Union, 1891.

Penningroth, Dylan C. *The Claims of Kinfolk: African American Property and Community in the Nineteenth-Century South.* Chapel Hill: University of North Carolina Press, 1993.

Philadelphia Museum of Art. "Dox Thrash: Revealed: a Companion Site to the Philadelphia Museum of Art exhibit: 'Dox Thrash: An African American Master Printmaker Rediscovered,' 1893–1907." http://www.philamuseum.org/doc_downloads/education/ex_resources/dox Thrash.pdf. (Accessed 17 February 2015.)

Pinkston, Regina P., comp. *Historical Account of Meriwether County 1827–1974.* Greenville, GA: Gresham Printing Company, 1974.

Porter, Grace Cleveland. *Negro Folk Singing-Games and Folk Games of the Habitants. Traditional Melodies and Text Transcribed by Grace Cleveland Potter, Accompaniments by Harvey Worthington Loomis.* London: J. Curwen & Sons, 1914.

Prindle, Cyrus, comp. *A Collection of Hymns, for the Use of the Wesleyan Methodist Connection of America.* New York: O. Scott, 1846.

"Prominent Examples of Colored Women As Christian Workers." *Home Mission Monthly* 17 (April 1903): 131–35.

Raboteau, Albert J. *Slave Religion: The "Invisible Institution" in the Antebellum South.* Updated ed. New York: Oxford University Press, 2004.

Rawick, George P., ed. *Georgia Narratives.* Volume 13 in series 2 of *The American Slave: A Composite Autobiography.* Westport, CT: Greenwood Publishing Company, 1972.

Rogers, George A. and R. Frank Saunders, Jr. *Swamp Water and Wiregrass: Historical Sketches of Coastal Georgia.* Macon, GA: Mercer University Press, 1984.

Rogers, R. W. *History of Pike County from 1822 to 1922.* Zebulon, GA: n.d.

Schwartz, Marie Jenkins. *Birthing a Slave: Motherhood and Medicine in the Antebellum South.* Cambridge: Cambridge University Press, 2006.

Smith, Charles Spencer. *A History of the African Methodist Episcopal Church: Being a Volume Supplemental to A History of the African Methodist Episcopal Church, by Daniel Alexander Payne, D.D., LL.D., Late One of Its Bishops: Chronicling the Principal Events in the Advance of the African Methodist Episcopal Church from 1856 to 1922.* Philadelphia: Book Concern of the A. M. E. Church, 1922.

Smith, George G. *The History of Georgia Methodism from 1786 to 1866.* Atlanta: A. B. Caldwell, 1913.

Smith, Mrs. Herschel W., comp. *Historical Collections of the Georgia Chapters, Daughters of the American Revolution, Volume V: Marriage Records of Greene County, Georgia (1787–1875), and Oglethorpe County, Georgia (1795–1852).* Atlanta: John T. Hancock, 1949, repr. 2001, Baltimore, MD: Genealogical Publishing Co., 2001.

Stacy, James. *A History of the Presbyterian Church in Georgia.* n.p.: n.p., n.d.

Steward, T[heophilus] [G]ould. *Fifty Years in the Gospel Ministry from 1864 to 1914. Twenty-seven Years in the Pastorate; Sixteen Years' Active Service as Chaplain in the U.S. Army; Seven Years Professor in Wilberforce University;*

Two Trips to Europe; A Trip in Mexico. Philadelphia: A.M.E. Book Concern, [1921]. http://docsouth.unc.edu/church/steward/steward.html (accessed 4 February 2015).

Stowell, Daniel W. *Rebuilding Zion: The Religious Reconstruction of the South, 1863–1877*. New York: Oxford University Press, 1998.

Tadman, Michael. *Speculators and Slaves: Masters, Traders, and Slaves in the Old South*. Madison: University of Wisconsin Press, 1989.

Tanner, Benj[amin] T[ucker]. *An Apology for African Methodism*. Baltimore: 1867.

Timmons, Robert. "Aged Ex-Slaves Gather at Home of Old Master." In *The Possibilities of the Negro in Symposium: A Solution of the Negro Problem Psychologically Considered. The Negro Not "A Beast."* Ed. C. E. Dowman, John Temple Graves, Henry W. Grady, et al. Atlanta: c. 1904: 69–73.

Twain, Mark. *The Adventures of Tom Sawyer*. Hartford, CT: The American Publishing Company, 1884.

Wayman, Alex[ander] W[alker]. *Manual, or Guide Book, for the Administration of the Discipline of the African M. E. Church*. Baltimore: Hoffman & Co., n.d.

Weiner, Marli F. *Mistresses and Slaves: Plantation Women in South Carolina, 1830–80*. Urbana: University of Illinois Press, 1998.

White, Newman Ivey and Walter Clinton Jackson, eds. *Anthology of Verse by American Negroes*. Durham, NC: Trinity College Press, 1924.

Williams, Heather Andrea. *Help Me to Find My People: The African American Search for Family Lost in Slavery*. Chapel Hill: University of North Carolina Press, 2012.

_________. *Self-Taught: African American Education in Slavery and Freedom*. Chapel Hill: University of North Carolina Press, 2005.

Wood, Dianne, ed. *1827–1900 Coweta County Georgia Marriages*. http://www.georgiagenealogy.org/coweta/dianne%20corner.htm. Accessed 4 February 2015.

Wright, Richard R. *A Brief Historical Sketch of Negro Education in Georgia*. Savannah: 1894.

———. *Centennial Encyclopaedia of the African Methodist Episcopal Church. Containing Principally the Biographies of the Men and Women, both Ministers and Laymen, Whose Labors During a Hundred Years, Helped Make the A. M. E. Church What It Is; Also Short Historical Sketches of Annual Conferences, Educational Institutions, General Departments, Missionary Societies of the A. M. E. Church, and General Information about African Methodism and the Christian Church in General; Being a Literary Contribution to the Celebration of the One Hundredth Anniversary of the Formation of the African Methodist Episcopal Church Denomination by Richard Allen and Others, at Philadelphia, Penna., in 1816*. Philadelphia: [Book Concern of the A.M.E. Church], 1916. http://docsouth.unc.edu/church/wright/menu.html. Accessed 4 February 2015.

Yenser, Thomas, ed. *Who's Who in Colored America: A Biographical Dictionary of Notable Living Persons of African Descent in America, 1933–1937*. Brooklyn, NY: Thomas Yenser, 1937.

Index